MINERAL RESOURCES

Environmental Resource Management Series

Consulting Editor

Donald R. Coates
State University of New York, Binghamton

In the same series:

Soils and the Environment
G. W. Olson

Field Guide to Soils and the Environment
G. W. Olson

MINERAL RESOURCES
A WORLD REVIEW

John A. Wolfe

A Dowden & Culver book

Chapman and Hall
New York   London

553
W 855

First published 1984 by
Chapman and Hall
733 Third Avenue, New York NY 10017

Published in Great Britain by
Chapman and Hall Ltd
11 New Fetter Lane Landon EC4P 4EE

© 1984 Dowden & Culver, Inc.

Printed in the United States of America

ISBN 0 412 25180 9 (cased edition)
ISBN 0 412 25190 6 (paperback edition)

Library of Congress Cataloging in Publication Data

Wolfe, John A., 1920–
  Mineral resources

  Bibliography: p.
  Includes index.
  1. Mines and mineral resources. 2. Mineral industries.
I. Title.
TN145.W65 1984   553   83-27275
ISBN 0-412-25180-9
ISBN 0-412-25190-6 (pbk.)

This book is dedicated to the memory of Francis and A. Stanley Elmore, metallurgists and discoverers of the flotation process for concentrating sulphide minerals. Born in England, they patented the process in London in 1898. This was one of the key inventions of civilization. The name Elmore should be ranked with heroes of the past century.

ACKNOWLEDGMENTS

This presentation has been greatly improved by suggestions made by several readers. These include an unnamed reader suggested by the publisher, Mr. Paul Graf, and Asa Wolfe. Special sections on sulphur and diamonds were improved by Mr. Stewart H. Folk and Dr. Peter Nixon, respectively. Data on aluminum were provided by the Aluminum Corporation of America and photographs by American Metals Climax (AMAX) and Dresser Industries. I am particularly indebted to Dr. C. K. Burton, who made a special effort to assist me in improving the book. Any errors or misinterpretations of data are my own.

CONTENTS

LIST OF TABLES

This volume discusses the mineral resources upon which modern civilization is built. Take away these minerals and humanity will rapidly return to the stone age, with its greatest concern the depletion of flint (also a mineral). It would, of course, result in about a 99% reduction in population. In other words, approximately 99% of the worlds' population is dependent on minerals for its existence.

That is a pretty strong statement, but how many have even seen a travois? Without minerals, pack animals, rafts, rowboats, sail boats, sledges, and the backs of man would be the only forms of transport. Sufficient food could not be transported, nor could it be grown on our tired soils without tractors and fertilizer. Even in the more fertile tropics where nearly half of the population is now suffering from malnutrition, crops are dependent on "miracle" grains that require mechanization and mineral fertilizers. Modern buildings cannot operate without electricity and, without mineral fuels, few people in the northern latitudes would survive the first winter. Buildings are either entirely made of mineral products, or, in case of wood, shaped, transported, and erected through the use of mineral products. If buildings of any kind could not be erected, this would leave caves and shelters of branches and grass for habitation. As a rough approximation, for every building constructed anywhere, a hole the same size has to be dug somewhere else. Clay for brick and tile, limestone and shale for cement, aggregate for concrete, silica for glass, and various ores for steel, copper, lead, zinc, aluminum, etc., go into the construction of a building.

Food, clothing, shelter, and energy are almost totally dependent on mineral commodities; they are the foundation of civilization. The author hopes that this book will be useful as a quick reference on the mineral industries and that it may help dispel some of the misconceptions about mining and the environment. Mining *creates* the environment of civilization. It must do a good job of housekeeping, but to restrict or eliminate mining is to impede or destroy civilization.

Since the author's bias will be readily apparent, it will be admitted at the outset. Thirty-five years of professional experience in mining throughout the world, plus information culled from reading thousands of books and periodicals have been distilled to present what it is hoped will be a useful summary. It is designed for the person interested in the mineral resources and economy but with training in another field. Jargon has been avoided, but where understanding a technical word is important to the subject it is italicized when first used and defined in a short glossary.

The book is divided into two parts. Part I consists of a few short essays on important aspects of the mineral industries. These are not all "conventional wisdom." For example, I believe there are few critical shortages of minerals; apparent shortages are the result of misguided policies that have prevented development of resources or of alternative substances. Petroleum extraction is a mature industry and from this time on there will be a gradual decline in production. Coal is in adequate supply but development is handicapped by rigid, strict controls. Likewise uranium and thorium are in abundant supply, but restrictions on the development of breeder reactors make these fuels only available in the future.

Part II is a condensed review of the most important mineral commodities. Importance is judged by tonnage produced, the most convenient method of measurement available. This summary includes metals and nonmetals, but does not include the fuels other than uranium, which is a metal. Except for a short chapter on energy, fuels are too complex to try to cover in this space.

This book is not a comprehensive study of the mineral industry, but merely a capsule of its major features. The Bibliography lists a few volumes which the reader can consult if he wishes to obtain information in depth on some aspect of the subject. Beyond these references there is a whole library on earth sciences, fuels, mining, and metallurgy. There are literally thousands of professional specializations in the minerals field, and for the imaginative, intelligent, ambitious individual, there are many career opportunities.

PART I

CHAPTER 1

MINERALS IN HISTORY

The history of man is divided into ages named for the minerals he had mastered. In many respects it was the capability to use a metal that caused a burst of cultural advance. Gold was the first metal recognized, and because of its beauty it was used for ornamental purposes. Because of its scarcity, gold found few practical uses. On the other hand, copper was more plentiful so it moved from jewelry into weapons, then to vessels and household usage. Bronze was discovered accidentally, but it proved so superior to copper that an effort was made to solve the mystery of its origin. The evolutionary pattern from art form to military applications to civilian uses was again followed. Bronze armor provided better protection than copper, and the bronze sword could be longer since it was tougher and more durable; therefore bronze-equipped armies were invincible, until the enemy, too, developed bronze. Even uranium has followed the sequence of intensive development for military purposes, then adaptation to the civilian economy.

Figure 1 illustrates the correlation of the ages of man, the minerals and metals which developed and approximate dates which bracket the ages. The steps to an advance to a new age are:

1) Some conceptual genius developed an idea—that there is energy in uranium, or that tin melted with copper resulted in an alloy far superior to anything available before.

2) An engineer developed an application of the concept.

3) A military authority pre-empted the idea and demanded production regardless of cost, e.g., a Manhattan atomic bomb project, or a new sword factory.

4) An entrepreneur saw a way to utilize the material in the civilian economy, e.g., a nuclear power plant.

5) Price reduction through mass production resulted in a burst of usage, changing world economics.

This pattern has been repeated many times, but some of the inventions were so overwhelmingly important that they are the milestones of progress. In a book on mineral resources these major events need to be discussed.

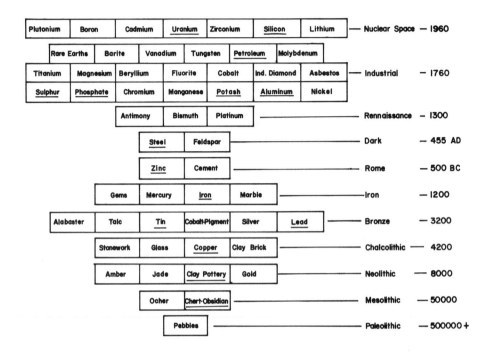

Plutonium	Boron	Cadmium	Uranium	Zirconium	Silicon	Lithium	Nuclear Space	— 1960
Rare Earths	Barite	Vanadium	Tungsten	Petroleum	Molybdenum			
Titanium	Magnesium	Beryllium	Fluorite	Cobalt	Ind. Diamond	Asbestos	Industrial	— 1760
Sulphur	Phosphate	Chromium	Manganese	Potash	Aluminum	Nickel		
Antimony	Bismuth	Platinum					Rennaissance	— 1300
Steel	Feldspar						Dark	— 455 AD
Zinc	Cement						Rome	— 500 BC
Gems	Mercury	Iron	Marble				Iron	— 1200
Alabaster	Talc	Tin	Cobalt-Pigment	Silver	Lead		Bronze	— 3200
Stonework	Glass	Copper	Clay Brick				Chalcolithic	— 4200
Amber	Jade	Clay Pottery	Gold				Neolithic	— 8000
Ocher	Chert-Obsidian						Mesolithic	— 50000
Pebbles							Paleolithic	— 500000 +

Figure 1 The chart shows which additional minerals were important to man during the various geologic and historic ages.

PALEOLITHIC AGE

The term *Paleolithic* is derived from words meaning "ancient" and "stone." It is sometimes called the Old Stone Age. It represents paleo- or dawn-man, the first humanoid to reason that he could lay an oyster on one rock and crack it open with another. It was a grim time of struggling for survival. The first use of a stone as a tool may go back three million years, into the *Pliocene epoch* of geologic time, predating the Pleistocene or *Ice Age*. By the time the first big ice sheets piled up in Europe and North America paleo-man had learned to use stones for defense and probably for hunting. By 500,000 B.P. (before present), stones were crudely chipped to present a sharp edge that made them more formidable as weapons and at the same time produced flakes or chips of stones for use in cutting open animal carcasses. For 98% of humanoid history there was no tool much more sophisticated than a stone for throwing or pounding. Only the strong, healthy, and bright survived. Natural selection effectively weeded out the weaklings and the less intelligent. Average intelligence (I.Q. = 100) gradually increased on some kind of an hypothetical absolute scale of ability.

MESOLITHIC AGE

Some Anthropologists do not recognize a "middle" stone age, and there are no sharp dividing lines between the old, middle, and new stone ages. A few tribes of pure hunters and gatherers have survived to the present. An example is the Tasaday tribe of cave dwellers on Mindanao Island in the southern Philippines, first contacted by modern man in 1971. At that time they had no knowledge of metal. While a dominant group makes an advance and provides the basis for further development, isolated segments of the species may be left far behind.

There seems to be a basis for a new age about 50,000 years ago, during a glacial interstadial time (the last *interglacial* age). A new race of man spread across Europe and the Middle East. He has been named *Homo neanderthalensis*, or Neanderthal man, after the valley east of Düsseldorf, Germany, where his remains were first identified. He dominated the European continent and had bi-facial tools (sharpened on both sides). He had learned that certain stones provided superior workability and sharper cutting edges, and he sought these out. Examples were *chert* or *flint* (silica formed in limestone beds or around hot springs), and *quartzite* (also silica that was originally sandstone, but by heat and pressure has been metamorphosed into a very hard stone). Another suitable material was found around old volcanoes, a natural volcanic glass called *obsidian.* All of these stones had the property of flaking when struck, and when a method of controlled flaking was learned, increasingly sophisticated knives, scrapers, and axes could be made.

Subsequently, as the last ice sheet spread over Europe another race of man appeared and took over the hunting grounds. He has been named Cro Magnon man after the site near Les Eyzies, France, where his remains were first discovered. This species is *Homo sapiens*, and his direct descendants are present-day Europeans. He had tribal organization, a more sophisticated social structure. He was hairless, taller, and probably more intelligent than the race that had previously inhabited Europe, who were heavy-jawed with a strong brow ridge and were probably hairy.

During the maximum extent of the last *Ice Age*, when much water had been withdrawn from the sea and heaped on the land as ice, sea level was lowered by possibly 150 m (500 feet). This exposed areas formerly under shallow seas. For the first time man crossed on the exposed "land bridge" from Asia to North America. These were Mesolithic tribes, following migrating animal herds. *Radiocarbon dates* on charcoal from their camp fires show that they were in Alaska by 14,000 B.P. They never returned to Asia. They wandered southward in the new world along the front of the ice sheet and found a hunter's paradise. The continent was populated with vast herds of animals that had never been hunted by man. When some of these people spread into Central and South America they settled, developed agriculture and cities, and made cultural progress parallel with that in Europe.

Climatic changes occurred in the ninth and tenth millennia B.C. and the great ice sheets began to melt. The resulting water caused sea level to rise, generally quite slowly, but sometimes in spurts of 10's of meters during short time periods. Since most communities existing at that time were probably located within 10 meters of sea level, this was a time of enforced migration to higher ground. It was also a time of many cultural changes, and stone tools became more sophisticated.

NEOLITHIC AGE

Nearly all of the ice sheets had melted by 8000 B.C. This marked the beginning of what geologists call the Holocene Age, or the Neolithic Age of the archeologist. New uses of mineral commodities developed. People learned how to make vessels out of clay, which, when fired, became quite durable. Storage jars and cooking pots were made. By trial and error the best kinds of clay were identified. With the beginning of agriculture a new concept, storage of food, developed to preserve grain after the harvest. The Neolithic was distinguished by shaped and crafted stone tools, some of them beautiful in their workmanship. The artistic skills of Neolithic man were also expressed in his learning to paint the walls of his cave with mineral pigments, suggesting that a sense of artistic appreciation had developed.

Agriculture required development of tools to break and turn the sod. The axe or adze could be bound to a crooked limb and swung over head to cut the grass. A polished tool would cut roots and brush more easily, and tools with smooth, ground edges became the distinctive mark of the Neolithic. The same materials (*chert, flint, obsidian* and *quartzite*) were used but other hard rocks were also utilized. Metamorphosed volcanic rock and nephrite (one of the forms of jade) were added to the list. One only has to watch a line of men swinging metal adzes in a paddy in tropical Asia today to see how a nephrite blade could be used for the same purpose.

Jade sometimes occurs in beautiful colors, particularly shades of green. When one of these pieces turned up in the quarry, Neolithic man worked it into a string of beads. Gold, too, was collected and made into ornaments. He learned it could be beaten into thin leaf and impressed with designs. *Amber* was developed as a form of jewelry, and trade in these three substances was established over areas stretching thousands of kilometers. Rudiments of a medium of exchange developed to supplement barter.

Some quite efficient flint mines were opened in England and on the continent. The soft limestone or *chalk* could be excavated by digging a *shaft* to reach the bed in which flint nodules occurred. By the end of the Neolithic, at about 4200 B.C., 99.83% of human history had passed, and few if any metal tools had been used.

CHALCOLITHIC AGE

"Chalco" is derived from Latin and French words for copper. Some authorities regard this time (4200–3200 B.C.) as part of the Bronze Age. The free metal (native copper) was hammered into shapes for weapons and utensils. Often associated with native copper are the attractive blue-green and deep blue carbonates of copper, malachite and azurite. Someone deduced that they also contained copper and *pyrometallurgy* commenced. Later when malachite and azurite were observed with a heavy black mineral (chalcocite, copper sulphide) it was concluded this, too, must contain copper and metallurgy advanced another step.

This was the time of the beginning of technology and ideas began to be translated into structures. Clay had been used for pots, but early man also realized that clay blocks could be shaped and burned and used to construct buildings and city walls. With metal tools made of copper it was easier to quarry stone, and subsequently city walls were built of blocks of stone.

There was more technological ferment in the Chalcolithic period than ever before. This period cannot truly be separated from its successor.

THE BRONZE AGE

The first *bronze* was probably developed by accident. It was probably an antimonial or arsenical bronze, because tin and copper rarely occur together. The resulting "copper" had some superior properties, such as a lower melting point (which made it easier to smelt), and greater hardness and durability. Presumably, about 3000 B.C., this led to research to find ways to duplicate the properties, resulting in the copper-tin alloy that was so superior to any metal previously known that it dominated weaponry for 3000 years. It was even superior to the early iron implements.

The experimentation with minerals resulted in expanded usage of lead, which had been used as solder in a minor way a thousand years earlier. Silver in the native form had been used probably as long as gold, but in the Bronze

Age it was separated from lead. Talc, the softest mineral, was introduced to the ladies as a face powder, and alabaster was carved into figurines.

Using nothing but bronze tools, the Egyptians built some of the most outstanding structures in history. These included the giant pyramids, the collossi, and the carving of the Sphinx from a natural outcrop. The most important of these structures were built in the third millennium (3000–2000) B.C.

A clay of a quality unsuitable for bricks or pottery melted into a sticky slag when it was fired. Someone may have experimented with it, and developed a green glass. As early as 2600 B.C. glass was being produced in Babylonia and by 2500 B.C. was known in Egypt. Pressed glass made with molds was developed in Alexandria about 320 B.C. Glass blowing was probably invented in Syria about 100 B.C. and quickly spread to Rome, where it was highly developed.

THE IRON AGE

What a drab world this would be without iron. Its structural strength and utilitarian aspects are very important, but virtually all soil and rock colors are caused by forms of iron. In the ferric or three-valence state colors range from maroon to red to red-brown, to dark brown and the ocher shades from seal brown through yellow. In the ferrous or two-valence state it is found in various shades of green and blue. No other substance causes as much color in the earth.

Meteoric iron was a curiosity, and in the Stone Age was considered to have mystical powers, having fallen from the heavens. An iron meteor 30 cm in diameter, found in antiquity in western Arabia, was worshipped by the inhabitants on the western side of the peninsula. After the time of Mohammed, as the Islamic religion swept the area, this meteorite was given an honored place in Mecca, in the most sacred place, the Ka'aba. Iron was first produced accidentally as "sponge" around camp fires, probably on a winter night when a roaring blaze was maintained. The metal had an inauspicious beginning, being soft and easily corroded, but it was found to be common and thus cheaper than bronze. Trying to date the beginning of the Iron Age is a little difficult, but by 1200 B.C. use of the metal was becoming widespread. Weapons made from iron were inferior, so bronze maintained its supremacy through the fall of Rome, but iron had utilitarian applications. At first only *sponge iron* was used because no vessel that could contain molten iron had been invented. In China, however, early in the first millennium B.C., ceramics had improved to the point that crucibles could be made, charcoal burned, and bellows used to reach the necessary temperatures to "cast" iron.

During this same period, carving and polishing of marble for decorative and esthetic purposes was well developed. The Greeks created some of the most beautiful structures of all time. The fluted columns and ionic, doric and corinthian capitals of their temples and public buildings are classics that are still being copied. The marble was quarried and carved with bronze or iron tools.

Gems were cut and polished to delight the ladies. The fabulous Valley of Gems on the Island of Ceylon was one of the major sources of sapphires and rubies, while diamonds and other stones came from India. Commerce was quite well developed throughout Eurasia and North Africa. Mercury was discovered and found to be a solvent for gold, so it was used in refining this metal. Undoubtedly there were many cases of mercury poisoning, but since the victims were only slaves, it did not cause great concern.

Iron was the last metal to develop to such an extent that an Age of Man is named for it. By the middle of the first millennium B.C. only copper, tin, and iron were in common use, with gold, silver, and mercury utilized for esthetic purposes. At this point 99.99% of man's history had passed. Subsequently political institutions dominated the planet. Another two millennia were to elapse before a great burst of ideas, called the Industrial Revolution, changed the face of the planet.

THE AGE OF ROME

About 500 B.C. what was to become a mighty Empire began to emerge in Italy. By the time of the birth of Jesus of Nazareth the Empire included most of the known world. Decay set in and Rome was finally sacked by Gaiseric and the Vandals in A.D. 455.

Organizational genius made Rome great but philosophic, artistic, and scientific progress were limited. Zinc was discovered and *brass* alloys (copper plus zinc) were developed. Cement of quite good quality was made, probably first by accident. Lime for mortar was developed by burning limestone, but "poor grade" limestone was found to produce a product of much greater strength. The temperatures reached in a shaft kiln were adequate to form dicalcium and tricalcium silicates, the important compounds in portland cement. Some of the *volcanic ash* in the vicinity of Pozzuoli was mixed with the ground cement powder, accidentally solving what would otherwise have been a serious problem, excessive "free" lime.

Roman cements have endured for 2000 years and in many respects, are equal to the best of today. They even seemed to have properties like the air-entrained cements developed only recently. Henry Kennedy, a student of cement, has hypothesized that they may have bled slaves into the cement mixers, hemoglobin being an excellent air-entraining agent.

In its ascendance, Rome was in conflict with a strong nation across the Mediterranean, Carthage. The collision occurred in Spain. Carthage operated the great lead and silver deposits near Cartagena, and possessing silver, was able to finance its war. Hannibal, the Carthaginian military genius, used elephants as "tanks" and invaded northern Rome by crossing the Alps. Because of poor communications the attack was a complete surprise to the Romans, but for the same reason he was unable to coordinate the other arm of his pincers which was supposed to come north through Sicily, and was finally defeated. Rome captured the Carthaginian silver mines and with them financed its own conquests.

Lead from Spain was such a convenient and easy metal to use that it was formed into water pipes and even cooking vessels, but only for the elite. One hypothesis suggests that the final decadence of Rome was caused by massive lead poisoning of the ruling class.

THE DARK AGE

Following the sack of Rome, civilization collapsed in Europe. From A.D. 455 to about A.D. 1300, religious institutions suppressed knowledge and forbade new ideas. The so-called Holy Inquisition was especially zealous in trying to suppress new concepts. The Bible was upheld as the unquestionable authority that the earth was flat, that day and night were created before the sun, and that there was a firmament in the sky above which there were waters. One of the most famous examples of censorship of science took place well past the end of the period. Galileo constructed a telescope, and on studying the planet Jupiter, discovered that it had moons that travelled around it. The Church forced him to recant and deny the Copernican doctrine on 21 June 1633.

During this period of anti-intellectualism in Europe scientific progress was unfettered in the East. In China during the T'ang dynasty (A.D. 618–906) feldspar was added to ceramics, creating porcelain, and by about A.D. 1200 cobalt was imported and used to make a blue glaze. During this period a very important Arabian concept was clandestinely imported to Europe, without which there could be little science or mathematics. The Church considered it a device of the devil, but by A.D. 1000 the Pope admitted zero into enumeration. Before that, only Roman numerals, which did not include a null symbol, were used.

Another important discovery was made, first in China and then in Damascus, doing for iron what the admixture of tin had done for copper. Iron was alloyed with carbon and tempered to *steel*, and the Damascus sword blade carried the armies of Islam into southern Europe both in the east and in the west, earning for the Arabs the reputation of being invincible.

Europeans tried to use iron in swords, but after one blow they would bend or curl up. Of course the secret could not be kept indefinitely, and steel making soon spread through Europe.

THE RENAISSANCE

The rebirth of learning was under way by A.D. 1300 and three metals, antimony, bismuth, and platinum were added to the six already in use. The printing press was invented, making dissemination of ideas much more rapid, and contributing to the Reformation which pitted Martin Luther and John Calvin against the Church of Rome. The Catholic Church was generally much more open-minded toward scientific discoveries than many of the protestant sects which were soon to become the strongholds of anti-intellectualism.

THE INDUSTRIAL REVOLUTION

Once the bonds of repression were burst, knowledge expanded in a geometric progression. Alloying metals for steel developed, utilizing manganese, nickel, chromium, cobalt, tungsten, vanadium, and molybdenum. Cutting tools using industrial diamonds were produced. Use of coal as a fuel grew rapidly, and coke was developed for steel making. The discovery of the vast East Texas oil field reduced the price of petroleum and opened new concepts in transportation. As diseases were controlled populations, too, increased geometrically, increasing the need for agricultural products. While there were great advances in plant pathology and genetics, the minerals economy was affected by demand for fertilizer to replenish soils that had been depleted by intensive cultivation. Big sulphur deposits were opened to produce the acid to make phosphatic fertilizer from rock phosphate. Potash mines were opened in Europe, then in North America to supply another ingredient of fertilizer. Asbestos became an important industrial mineral. Light metals were produced: aluminum, magnesium, titanium, and beryllium. Fluorite was developed to supply the chemical industry and to produce the flux needed in the refining of aluminum. Barite became important in making drilling mud for oil wells. The period from 1760 to 1960 was far more dynamic than any previous time in the history of man and minerals.

This dynamic growth was not universally accepted. Displaced workers banded together, adopted the name *Luddites*, and in 1811 set out to destroy other machines, particularly textile looms.

THE NUCLEAR-SPACE AGE

World War II saw the development of a fantastic new weapon that one hopes has ended major wars as a human institution: The nuclear bomb. Civilian uses for nuclear power were developed just in time to replace petroleum. That fuel peaked in production in the U.S. in 1970 and probably in the world in the 1980s and faces inevitable decline before the end of the century. Nuclear power has brought into being a new generation of Luddites. They are determined to destroy the economies of Western nations by preventing use of nuclear power in these countries. In part this is the psychological problem called "future shock" by Alvin Toffler. There are genuine concerns about the safety of nuclear power plants; indeed, proper safety may be too expensive for commercial operation. Fission of uranium resulted in the production of plutonium that is becoming an abundant fuel, and which poses a deadly threat in the proliferation of nuclear weapons. Fission required the development of zirconium metal, which is the best element for cladding the fuel, in what is called the zirconium-uranium sandwich, or fuel element. The nuclear reaction must also be moderated. Cadmium, which has high "cross section" (see Part II, Uranium) is an important metal for control rods. Boron is useful in absorbing neutrons, so it is used in shielding reactors. Boron filaments, combined with other substances, are lighter, stronger, and stiffer than an equal volume of steel, so it also has promise in structural applications.

Fission pointed the way to fusion, the ultimate process, which is on the threshhold of being mastered in the laboratory but is decades away from becoming commercially viable. Lithium will be one of the fuels in the fusion reaction.

As nuclear physics developed electronics also made changes in science that can only be described as fantastic. The proliferation of computers has been maintained at an exponential rate, coupled by a thousand-fold reduction in their price. While computers have made conquest of space possible, the full consequences of this development are fundamental and, at this time unfathomable. The progress was made possible through the use of silicon in electronics. This element is now also used in alloying steel.

With the discovery of methods of altering plant and animal genes, another unlimited field, bioengineering, began to develop by 1980, promising advances in food production, disease control, and improvement of species.

CONCLUSION

This brief review of the use of minerals is designed to introduce the subject in a different perspective. There are many who think of metals in terms of refrigerators, furnaces, and automobiles, never considering their sources, taking the metals used in their fabrication for granted. To build a two-ton automobile in Detroit about 15 tons of mineral ores have to be taken out of the ground and about four tons of fuel are produced and burned. This results in about 15 tons of mineral waste and 15 tons of carbon dioxide being dumped into the atmosphere. One-half ton of sulphuric acid is used in part, with a substantial portion vented into the atmosphere. It is to the benefit of society to demand that these excavations do minimum damage to the environment, as long as the addition to the cost of the product is recognized and accepted. To demand that production of minerals and fuels be halted or locked up in preserves is a demand for the impoverishment of civilization. Some people like to see dynamic, growing cities but they must realize that for every building that reaches for the sky, a hole the same size must be dug somewhere else, in someone else's environment. There are others who regard cities as a disease, a cancer, the ultimate in environmental pollution. Yet others regard them as reservations in which to coop up all of the non-productive people to make it easier to fill and control their consumer demands. But whatever their *raison d'être*, the demand of the cities for minerals seems insatiable.

Only a small percentage of the population is involved in the production of the world's mineral wealth, but everyone lives off of the "value added" by these minerals. Thus basic information about the minerals industries should be of interest to everyone.

CHAPTER 2

NATIONAL MINERAL POLICY

A *mineral policy* is the sum total of laws, regulations, agreements, and customs that affect the production, utilization, conservation of, and commerce in mineral commodities. Each government must formulate a mineral policy that may be in conflict in some degree with the policy of several other nations. In other words, each country tries to look after its own interests.

In socialistic countries the mineral policy is quite simple on the surface. The government owns all minerals, produces what it needs, and tries to get what it does not have from abroad. Internally, where there are no economic standards of measurement, a mineral policy can become quite involved with welfare, military requirements, etc.

JAPAN'S POLICY

Japan is highly industrialized, but has to import nearly all of its energy and other major minerals. It has to buy its raw materials as cheaply as possible and manufacture enough products both to satisfy the domestic market and to export sufficient goods to pay for all raw materials imported. Diversified sources of supply are developed so that political risks are hedged. Maintaining this balance is a matter of utmost urgency. All external mineral purchases are coordinated through the Ministry of International Trade and Industry (M.I.T.I.), by which every contract has to be approved. Even Japanese foreign aid programs are structured to assist developing nations with their mineral surveys, with a view to developing additional sources of supply. Japan plans to keep vital materials in surplus around the world so that prices will remain low. This might be called a value-added mineral policy, or essential self interest, since the economy of the nation would be on its knees in a matter of weeks if cut off from external supplies. Securing minerals through military power was not a permanent solution, so the country now relies on financial power. It is a precarious condition, but Japan has no alternative. The pressure from developing nations to keep the processing of raw materials at home, to advance their own economies, will place Japan in a difficult position.

Japan has a very farsighted program on mineral policy. The Institute for International Mineral Resources Development in Shizuoka admits only highly qualified mineral specialists. Students are given a year of very intensive training in mineral economics, geology, political science, and languages, and are sent out as the "front line troops" of Japan's mineral policy.

In spite of Japan's dependence on external resources it has been rather slow to invest in resource research. Since manganese nodules contain resources of manganese, nickel, copper, cobalt, and molybdenum on the ocean floor not subject to political whimsy, it is surprising that Japan has not been one of the leaders in the field. Only in 1975 was a company formed by 23 (now 48) Japanese firms to participate in Ocean Resources Development Co., a multi-national deep-sea mining research company. In contrast, Japanese fuel research has resulted in economy of operation of internal combustion engines to the point where American- or European-made automobiles cannot compete. Imports have taken over one-fourth of the U.S. market. Japan can buy iron ore in Australia and coking coal in Canada, transport them to Japan, produce steel, and ship it to the United States for less than it can be made in Pittsburgh from domestic materials.

Other nations similarly dependent on foreign raw materials are Korea, Taiwan, France, and Germany. None of these countries has a minerals policy as closely integrated as does Japan, however.

OPEC POLICY

At the opposite extreme to Japan is the developing nation with a single resource in abundant supply, a mineral product that must be exported to derive foreign exchange for all imports. Several nations in a similar position tend to form a *cartel* or an agreement to restrict production and set prices not directly related to costs. The classic example is the organization of Petroleum Exporting Countries (OPEC), the most arrogant and, until late 1982, most successful cartel ever established. The expressed objective of several OPEC nations was to charge all of the customers the highest price that the rich nations could pay. The poor nations were left to fend for themselves. This amounted to a huge *severance tax*, as high as 20,000%. In some cases this tax on the customers yielded so much revenue that the oil producing nation concerned literally did not know what to do with all of the money. In some countries citizens paid no paxes whatsoever. As a side effect, there were lots of "sticky fingers" in the money pot. Never has such vast wealth been concentrated in so few hands. Some of this may be used to finance wars or subversion, but there have probably been more new billionaires made by the energy crisis than ever before in history. With a combination of conservation and recession, demand for petroleum dropped sharply, disrupting the cartel. The so-called "oil glut" will be temporary, however; the real oil crisis will probably appear in the late 1980s.

This situation is so new, dating only from 1974, that extrapolation is difficult. Ordinarily any system that results in concentrating wealth has beneficial results for society. Someone will have access to the funds and put them to work. In this instance, however, the exorbitant tax is a burden on all nations that are not self sufficient. A conceivable catena is progressive economic collapse, commencing with the least developed countries (LDCs), extending to the least efficient industrial nations. The major economies will finally be drawn into the maelstrom. This is the first time in history that aggression of the grossest sort has not been met by force. It is also the first time that gnats have attacked without at least getting slapped.

C.I.P.E.C. POLICY

There are also cartels that do not work, for example C.I.P.E.C. The initials represent the name in French that translates as Intergovernmental Council of Copper Exporting Countries. There are many reasons for its failure. (1) The U.S., the largest producer and consumer, is fairly close to self sufficiency in copper production, so a "gouge Uncle Sam" policy will not succeed. (2) There is no cohesion among producers. Several nations would be delighted to set up a "beggar thy neighbor" policy, but some refuse to join and others want every nation to agree to reduce production so they themselves can produce at full capacity. (3) If agreement were reached among several of the producers to establish a price of $5 per pound, new production would rapidly develop in other nations outside of the cartel and break the price. So the attempt to form a copper cartel has been a wining, dining, and talking club, and its history to date has been exactly the opposite of OPEC's. The producing nations tax their own people to subsidize their customers. Japan and the E.E.C. are much happier with C.I.P.E.C. than OPEC.

TIN CARTEL POLICY

The International Tin Council (I.T.C.) was initiated on July 1, 1956 and was designed to stabilize tin prices. It is composed of tin producing and consuming nations. Tin is a minor metal, world production amounting to about 260,000 tons per year. To four countries (Malaysia, Indonesia, Thailand, and Bolivia) it is a major component of their exports. Since these countries produce some 80% of the free market nations' supply, by associating they can control the price. Regardless of the price there is not likely to be a major geographical shift in production, since the occurrence of tin is very restricted.

The stabilization policy of the I.T.C. sets a floor price at which the manager must buy (if he has funds) and a ceiling price at which he must sell (if he has metal). There is supposed to be considerable room between the two for market forces to interact. The "wild card" in tin stabilization is the stockpile program of the U.S. government, which built up to about 350,000 tons in 1962, reduced by successive stages to the level of 200,000 tons. The stockpile hanging over the market and theoretically available in part for disposal has moderated price increases, but the price has risen from the level of about $1.30 per pound when the I.T.C. was established to about $8.00 in 1980. This price at a time of recession reduced consumption and a modest surplus resulted in a sharp drop in the price to $5.80 in June 1981. Meanwhile producers had rapidly adjusted their expenditures to the maximum price. Consumers switched from tin to substitutes in some cases. Part of the market is probably lost forever.

There has been a great deal of friction in I.T.C. Producers want the control price levels raised, and the consumers, not wanting a high floor, hope that the price might drop. Consumers have suggested that the best way to make opening new mines profitable would be to lower the extremely high taxes levied on tin production. The producers' reaction was to accuse consumers of meddling in their internal affairs. Their objective is a higher price.

With world production above consumption, the tin reserve of I.T.C. is being re-established and the price has dropped below the ceiling level.

THE U.N. MINERAL POLICY

The United Nations Organization operates on a special interest basis, where power blocks trade off support for their pet projects. In regard to mineral development, the "developing nations" stick together. They do not even criticize the OPEC nations for virtually destroying several economies by their action.

In 1974 the General Assembly adopted the "Charter of Economic Rights and Duties of States," in which most of the economic rights are the prerogative of the developing nations and the duties are the responsibility of the industrial nations. One significant but unsought result has been to focus new exploration and development even more strongly toward the industrialized mining nations, such as the United States, Canada, Australia, and South Africa because the *duty* of an investor is to protect his capital and see that it earns a reasonable return. The U.N. charter gave little weight to this duty.

Without having an official mineral policy, the U.N.O. supports the interests of the developing nations because they have the weight of numbers in the General Assembly. Examples of this are the Revolving Fund, used to explore for mineral deposits in these nations and the Law of the Sea, which is strongly biased in their favor. The essence of this is that nations that produce raw materials are entitled to a share of the value added by manufacturing, not just a "cheap" raw material price. Resource-starved nations are sure to suffer.

There are minerals on the ocean floor of two types, which may eventually become commercial. These are manganese nodules which contain varying amounts of manganese, nickel, cobalt, copper, and molybdenum, and massive sulphide deposits containing base and precious metals. These minerals are found outside of recognized national territories. A series of conferences have been held to try to draft a treaty called "Law of the Sea." Representatives of the U.S. government under the Carter administration participated in the drafting. With the advent of the Reagan administration, the proposed treaty was reviewed and thought to be inimicable to the interests of the United States. Time for study was requested and in 1982, Ambassador James Malone reported to the conference that the United States would not sign the treaty. The U.S. government objected to provisions for an international venture called the Enterprise would itself engage in mining and it would be managed by the same socialistic group that made the rules for everyone else. It would essentially be under the control of the "Group 77" with a large enough vote to change the rules as they see fit, with no veto power by industrial nations, as in the Security Council of the United Nations. The Treaty has no relation to the economic needs or industrial capacity of the nations. It does not establish objective standards on licenses. It sets up a "system of privileges" which discriminates strongly against private enterprise. It would require "technology transfer" by the U.S. and other industrial nations in the form of the extensive research, exploration, and development paid for by private parties, amounting to confiscation of hundreds of millions of dollars worth of proprietary information. It would *commit* the Enterprise to fund movements of national liberation, such as the Palestine Liberation Organization (*Science*, 1982 (215): p. 1480). That would amount to American industry being taxed to underwrite world terrorism. The U.S., United Kingdom, West Germany, and Russia were among the few nations that refused to sign.

THE U.S. MINERAL POLICY

There has been more talk about mineral policy in the United States than in all other nations combined, more commissions, more hearings, and more committees; yet it is fair to ask if the United States does have a mineral policy. Some Europeans feel the OPEC program is the minerals policy of the U.S. Europeans would have been unlikely to tolerate this situation without pressure from the United States. The U.S. benefitted from OPEC action in two ways. First, dollars and gold had been accumulating in Europe at a rapid rate. Europe was becoming a financial collosus with Eurodollars being in a position to destroy the U.S. economy. In very few years those Eurodollars have been converted into Petrodollars. They are now owned by weak nations not capable of competing with the U.S. in industrial products, and Europe's position has been greatly weakened. Second, the U.S. oil companies, five of the famous Seven Sisters, have profited enormously from increased oil prices.

Some say the United Stated is "positively irrational" when it comes to minerals. It practically gave away half of its gold and 90% of its silver. (See Part I, Chapter 4, and Part II, Gold and Silver). It established stockpiling programs, then dumped the minerals on the market, then decided to buy them back at far higher prices (for examples, see Part II, Titanium and Vanadium). It tolerates and seems to encourage legalistic harassment of all programs that would alleviate the energy shortage. It establishes "environmental protection" programs so severe that mineral commodities must be imported rather than produced, thus hurting the economic position of the nation and exporting environmental damage to the fragile environments of the developing nations. (A good example of the pyramiding of governmental controls is detailed in Part II, Phosphate.) It has effectively locked up the resources in one-sixth of the nation by creating huge wilderness reservations not open to mineral exploitation, an area larger than all but 12 other nations of the world. These "frozen assets" occur in the region that is potentially the richest in the country.

Envrionmental problems are discussed in another chapter, but it should be emphasized that while everyone should be concerned about damage to the environment, we should be just as knowledgeable and concerned about damage to the economy. In the recent past the cost of environmental protection for producing copper in the United States has been about 10 cents per pound, or 10%–15% of the sale price. Some mines were forced to close, resulting in exploration funds and capital being exported to secure foreign sources where government policies emphasize economic importance. Of course this means purchases must be made from abroad as well. If anyone doubts this, all he has to do is look at the roster of mining companies in

Australia. Few of the big names of the U.S. are missing. Yet there are about 30 large porphyry copper deposits in the United States awaiting a favorable economic climate for development.

The United States foolishly and unnecessarily exported its energy sources. To regain self-sufficiency will cost hundreds of billions of dollars, plus the hundreds of billions of tax paid to OPEC members and other oil exporting nation. The economic damage far exceeds the environmental damages that might have resulted from a few additional coal mines and nuclear power plants.

POLICY SUMMARY

The trends in mineral policy are toward grouping together of nations with similar interests to increase their bargaining power. The industrial nations are to a major degree dependent on developing nations for their raw materials. The United States is the least dependent, but because of preservationist pressure, more and more of its resources are being locked up, so its economic position is deteriorating and it is becoming vulnerable to outside producers' demands.

OPEC is the model of producers' cartels, and many developing nations are trying to manuever themselves into a position to become members of a similar organization. They are understandably not content with producing the raw material and seeing the value added in processing, 10–20 times the price of the raw material, accrue to the industrial nation. The U.N.O. has become the pulpit of the developing nations for trying to enforce this change in world economic structure.

If the industrial nations want to avoid "averaging down" of their economic systems, they urgently need to undertake research on alternate energy sources. They must prepare for an accelerated program to develop marine mineral resources, open to participation by all nations. The United States needs to outgrow its self-flagellation complex and establish national priorities. Are snail darters (a small fish living within a reservoir site in Tennessee), grizzly bears, and inaccessible wilderness areas more important than electricity, automobiles, machinery, and homes? If so, electricity and automobiles should be outlawed. If not, resources should be given the higher priority they need for development.

PRICE CONTROLS

When governmental economic policies result in failure to maintain balance, violent swings of inflation and deflation, boom and bust, result. In the long run, price is always determined by supply and demand. If through spending beyond its income, government pumps up the money supply, demand for goods may exceed supply of commodities, and prices rise accordingly. Under these conditions a favorite crutch of govenment is to impose *price controls*. The need for this action is a confession of failure of policy. Some contend that in wartime, this is necessary to mobilize the national effort. War is the ultimate failure of government, however, and if the planet ever becomes truly civilized, war and machines of war will be unknown. We should look for an example to what happened to the economies of Japan and Germany in the period from 1950 to 1975, when they were forbidden to have war machines. By 1982 Germany and Japan were rearming at an accelerating rate and the Reagan administration was demanding that the U.S. spend itself into insolvency for armaments. Simultaneously with the waste of resources for military purposes, the worst recession of the post-war period developed. The danger of sinking into a serious world-wide depression is very real.

Inflation is theft by government from the weakest portion of its citizens. Price controls merely compound the felony, making the producers of commodities temporarily bear the burden of the theft for many others.

The controlled price of gold, fixed at $35 per ounce from 1934 to 1972, was first a subsidy, which later inverted to a price ceilng. It prevented production of gold in most of the mining districts of the United States after 1945. During the post-war period, the U.S. endeavored to impose a world price control on gold, selling to any foreign government all it wished to buy for about one-tenth the price the U.S. government would have had to pay to buy the equivalent amount. This foolish policy was finally halted, the price shot up, and mines with a substantial gold co-product were able to open or maintain operation.

The case of silver is quite similar. A buy-and-sell price control was set, which initially operated as a subsidy. The U.S. Treasury bought huge amounts and then issued silver certificates (paper money backed by the silver), so there was no "cost" to the government. In fact there was a handsome profit, because the buying price was 90 cents per ounce and the value attributed to it in the dollar was $1.29 per ounce. The selling price of 92 cents an ounce for the metal aroused no interest for years, until production fell behind consumption. The Treasury, with two billion ounces, was glad to dispose of its accumulated stock until a flood of buying at this bargain price, again well below cost of production of new mines, depleted the supply. Next the dollar coin price became a ceiling ($1.29 per ounce), and the run on silver dollars rapidly exhausted the supply. The next step was the subsidiary coinage (dimes, quarters, and halfs). By the time this supply was gone, consumption far outstripped production, and since there is a 5–10 year lag in bringing new mines into production, the price shot up.

The 20,000% severance or export tax on petroleum by OPEC nations is an example of the unsettling effect of controlled price, by a cartel of governments. Price controls are artificial and ultimately unsettling. When lifted, or in the case of the cartel, when imposed, a sudden price surge results.

CHAPTER 3

ENVIRONMENT

The thesis of this chapter is there are two kinds of environments and both are very important to man's well being. At times the requirements of one are in conflict with those of the other; compromises must be made because society cannot be healthy unless both environments are healthy. The first is the physical environment, and second is the economic environment.

Emphasis is placed on the economic environment in this book only because so many environmentalists seem to have little knowledge or concern about the economy. They seem to have no sense of proportion or perspective. For example, why should a surface coal mine in Wyoming be required to replant sage brush to the restored surface after coal has been mined, when the Department of Agriculture is subsidizing a sage brush eradication program?

In attacking the mineral industries, the preservationists ignore the trade-offs. Without mining, there can be no civilization as we know it, and the earth cannot support a population of seven to eight billion people. By piling regulation after regulation and tax after tax on one side of the balance, there has to be something stacked on the other side to keep things even. This something is price increase, or inflation. In North America in 1960, every man thought an automobile was a "right." In the future it will become a "privilege." A plethora of regulators and regulation constitute a major source of damage to the economic environment.

The United States is the largest copper producing nation in the world and copper is essential to a high standard of living. Yet the 32 copper mines in the country need less than 1000 km² (400 square miles) of land surface. In the next 50 years new mines may need another 650 km² (250 square miles). These new mines will be essential because people want electricity, automobiles, sanitary water, and motors to do their work for them. Copper is absolutely essential to a healthy physical environment.

If a man wants to build a school, church, or supermarket, he can look around and study hundreds of sites before decidng where to place it. There is a great deal of flexibility in siting. The United States needs 30 new copper mines in the next 50 years. The problem, and the point environmentalists cannot seem to understand, is there is *no* flexibility in siting those 30 copper mines. It is impossible for a planner to point a finger and say, "O.K., put your old copper mine there." A plume of hydrothermal solutions rose at a particular point in the earth's crust and permeated a specific volume of rock with about 10 pounds of copper per ton. Each site is relatively small, but it is one of the most concentrated accumulations of essential resources on earth. There can be no compromise. With only few possible exceptions, the production of mineral resources is of higher priority in any specific site and it must pre-empt the site. The only conflicting uses that should be considered are if a substantial pre-existing community, an energy development (hydro-electric dam and reservoir), or a National Park already occupies the site. Figure 2 is a diagram of the hierarchy of priority of land use which is essential for a healthy economic environment. This ranking demonstrates the relative importance of the competing users of land. In such a ranking, if a use higher on the chart needs lands held by a lower usage, it should "bump" the lesser usage. Unfortunately the three bottom uses have had the most vociferous advocates and have grabbed about one-fourth of the nation's land. This is economically acceptable only if the right to "bump" is established. Otherwise it means the standard of living of the nation must be lowered to accommodate the least important uses.

Conflicts have arisen because the same natural forces that form the relatively minute mineral deposits are often the forces that form the majestic mountain ranges which themselves are resources for recreation, silviculture, grazing, and enjoyment. This conflict is one of principle to the paid professional of the Sierra Club or Wilderness Society, so he opposes the mine vociferously, determined to make it costly or uneconomic by strangling it if his goal of prevention cannot be obtained by legal force.

Unfortunately, by preventing a needed mine from opening in the United States, the economic environment of the country is seriously damaged. It cranks up the inflation another notch, because citizens are unwilling to give up electricity and automobiles to compensate for less copper. The copper has to be purchased abroad. The international mining companies carry their concern for the environment abroad with them, but many foreign companies are unhampered by uneconomic environmental restrictions and do not concern themselves with practices that reduce profit. We are all in the same spaceship. Preventing a mine from opening where good practice will prevail may result in a net deterioration of the earth's physical environment.

Table 4 (see p. 93) shows that copper is about 10% by weight of the non-ferrous metals. Only two more of these metals are mined in significant tonnage in the U.S. (in excess of 100,000 tons). All of the non-ferrous metal mines in the country occupy about 1500 km² (580 mi²), or only

Hierarchy of Land Use

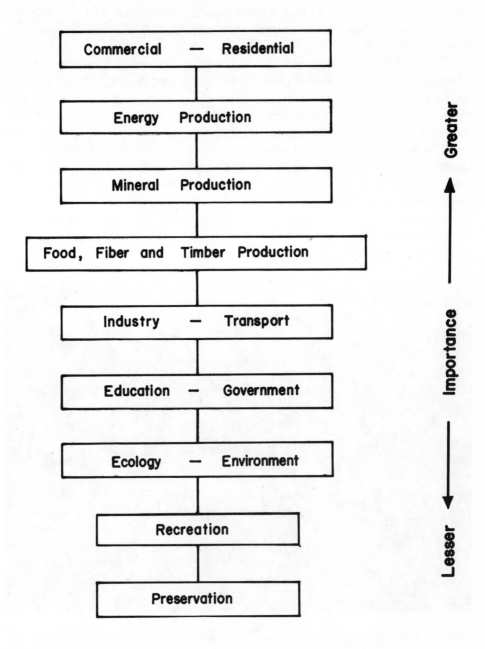

Figure 2 A hierarchy of priorities for land use is proposed here.

0.02% of the land surface of the nation. Surely not more than a like amount will be required in the next 50 years, hardly a significant area. Yet a very large percentage of the value added to the economy will come from that area. Possibly 0.0015% of the nation's surface will need to be withdrawn from the vast preserves or reservations now closed or severely restricted from mining.

Coal mining, which is not covered in this volume, will require a much larger area of the plains of Wyoming, Montana, and North Dakota, but this land will be reclaimed and restored as soon as mining has progressed out of the way. Western coal mines rent the land for only a short time; the method used there is almost like harvesting a crop.

If one flies across the mining districts of the western United States at 40,000 feet elevation and looks steadily out of a window, he can spot every city and town with no trouble. He can see the superhighways slashing through the forest, but it is doubtful if he will recognize a single mine. They are too small and scattered; yet the cities and highways could not exist without them. Golf courses in the U.S. alone occupy far more land than metal mines (see Figure 3).

Figure 3 The surface facilities of the Henderson molybdenum mine of AMAX near Jones Pass, Colorado. With minimum impact on the environment, a vital resource is produced to make high quality steel. (Courtesy Climax Molybdenum Co.)

There was a time when the United States as a young nation had so much land it did not know what to do with it. Much of it was classed as "waste land." Some extractive industries during this period used land, abandoned it, and moved on to new sites. No effort was made to restore it for another use. These practices would not be tolerated today. Most of the evidence of "bad" mining practices that one can find if he looks hard enough date from more than 50 years ago. Society was not then prepared to tax itself, to pay the cost, to restore the land.

Some "new" problems have arisen unexpectedly and when they are understood, efforts to correct them must be made. Radioactive waste from uranium mining operations is a case in point. The dangers from this exposure were inconceivable 35 years ago. For example, Madame Curie, who discovered radium and worked with it extensively, did not understand the physiological damage caused by radiation; she died of leukemia, caused by excessive exposure. Until it is understood that a problem exists, no effort can be made to cope with it.

Today it is possible to insist on proper precautions in disposal of waste from uranium mines. The cost of these precautions is added to the price of the product and paid for in the electric bill. Where the cost was not included in the price 30 years ago, and it becomes necessary to go back and undo the damage, society must pay the cost. This was properly a charge against the defense budget, as all uranium then went to the military.

ENERGY AND ENVIRONMENT

Energy has become so disproportionately immense in both the physical and economic environment that some special consideration must be given to it. About 28% of all investment in the United States is now going into energy, which will continue to pre-empt investment funds as long as it is the most profitable place to put them. This situation alone is adversely affecting the economic environment, increasing interest rates by companies bidding for available funds, and thus contributing to inflation. The housing industry is one that cannot get funds at a cost that home owners can afford to pay, so houses are not being constructed rapidly enough to meet needs.

President Carter urged Americans to burn wood. It will be difficult to measure the environmental damage of that executive urging. Many gallons of gasoline were used in going to the store to buy a chain saw, then to a governmental agency to buy a wood-cutting permit, and then travel to a wooded area to find trees that could be cut.

Forest is the natural vegetation covering areas of heavy to moderate rainfall, prairie or grass land for those with fairly light to light rainfall, and barren desert for areas of low rainfall. Man has been steadily pushing the woodlands back to make way for agriculture, and on the other margin, desert has been encroaching on agricultural lands as the result of poor farming practice. By cutting down forests and raising goats that nibble every blade of grass, denudation followed by rapid soil erosion has been steadily expanding deserts for centuries. When the president of the United States urges citizens to burn more wood, that call does not stop at the borders of the U.S. While it is fashionable for politicians around the world to kick Uncle Sam in the shins to show how big they are, the U.S. and its actions are very widely copied. In the fragile environments of the Third World, the words of United States presidents may echo hollowly.

The highly industrialized nations (Japan, western European nations, and the United States) want to build with wood that they do not have. There is a ban on cutting redwoods in California, so to line a den with a pretty, red wood, Philippine mahogany is used. Thus the tree line in the tropical jungle is pushed further back into the mountains. Even though the logging company may try to reforest the area, impoverished, uneducated farmers move in with their families of six or eight children, clear the brush and young trees, and plant a few hills of corn. With a tropical storm that may bring 12 inches of rain in as many hours, sheet-wash strips off the soil. With no trees to hold the rainfall, the mountain streams become torrents that carry soil out to sea, but dump sand and gravel at the coastal plain, spreading it over choice agricultural areas. The streams aggrade or build up their beds, narrowing the gap beneath the bridges which then become dams, diverting the river, washing out approaches, and destroying more land.

Thus the preservationists, the followers of John Muir, are locking up one-sixth of U.S. resources, preserving wilderness, and exporting uncontrolled environmental destruction throughout the Third World.

We may ask why laws are not passed forbidding farming in the mountains, but laws must be enforced. If the farmer is jailed, who will feed his eight children? Welfare exists only in affluent industrial nations. With the "poverty line" now at nearly $10,000 per year, half the world yearns to be "poor" in the United States.

Only the U.S. can quit importing energy and exporting environmental destruction. Imports of oil have been reduced in the past few years and must be staged out. If from the current level they were reduced each year by 500,000 barrels per day, imports could be phased out in 10 years. This would have to be accompanied by accelerated development of coal and nuclear power and conservation in the use of petroleum.

CHAPTER 4

MINERAL ECONOMICS

Few individuals will ever buy a ton of raw iron or a hundred pounds of unfabricated copper. These quantities of metal will be purchased by many in fabricated form as an automobile. Thus metals are taken for granted, and mines are seen as horrible holes ruining the environment (aesthetically, if no other way). Not many realize that golf courses use more of the land than all of the metal mines in the country. All of those golf courses are ultimately paid for by value added on minerals. Golf courses can be sited in a wide choice of locations, however, while metals have to be extracted from those rare, restricted zones where nature concentrated them sufficiently to warrant their extraction. They have to be extracted economically (which means *at a profit* in the western world). This is essentially true in controlled market nations, even if it is not admitted.

The most significant event in the history of mining was the 2000% increase in the price of petroleum in the 1970s. Energy suddenly became very expensive. Had all prices and incomes shot up at the same rate, everything would have remained the same. OPEC announced, in effect, that they were taking a bigger piece of the pie. The rest of us were left to share the remainder. In the United States the cost of energy increased from 2% of the G.N.P. to 10% in this period. Did pensions of disabled veterans go up tenfold? They did not increase 50%. Did a $10,000 life insurance policy become worth $100,000? Among minerals only the precious metals reflected nearly proportionate increases. It was the pensioners, the people with fixed incomes, the insurance policy holders, the miners, and many others who watched their resources shrivel to feed the greed of the OPEC nations.

In the Introduction it was pointed out that the world's population is 99% dependent on "value added" to the mineral industries. This chapter will attempt to put this assertion into perspective.

Even renewable resources, food and fiber, have a cost in terms of energy and minerals. Intensive agriculture rapidly extracts minerals from the soil, thus depleting it. For high yields to continue, these minerals must be replaced. Chemical fertilizer, compounded from products mined from the earth plus energy, are applied. Soil becomes just the vehicle to carry the plant food and to support the plants while they extract energy from the sun and carbon dioxide from the air. The three major plant foods are phosphorous, potassium, and nitrogen. The first two are mined as naturally occurring minerals. The richer and more accessible deposits have already been exploited. Hence deeper mines utilizing lower-grade deposits must be developed to supply the ever-increasing demand for more food. With the requirement that an increasing tonnage be mined, more energy is consumed to produce a ton of product. Consequently, the rocketing cost of energy is dragging up the price of fertilizer and food.

There are faddists who assert that "organic farming" should be employed to eliminate chemical fertilizers. If the organic matter happens to contain the essential plant foods (potash, phosphate, and nitrogen), this will suffice. Ordinarily it requires larger quantities of organic fertilizer to produce the same results as chemical fertilizer, and therefore more precious energy to supply it. Yields would decline and labor requirements go up if it were necessary to depend on organic fertilizer. If the world population were one-tenth of what it is and people were prepared to spend a much larger percentage of their income for food and clothing (remember that the oil producers have already pre-empted a larger share) for this method, it might be adequate. With world population soaring rapidly toward five billion, the "organic" fad offers a quick trip to starvation.

Machinery is essential to make high yields of produce possible. Made of metal, and produced by the expenditure of energy, its use also consumes fuel. A metallic, fuel-gulping monster then hauls the product to the processing plant and market. As the result of this chain of economic efficiency, about 3% of the population of the U.S. actually produces all of the food and fiber required, plus 70% of the world's exportable food grains.

In contrast, in labor-intensive farming where a carabao or a mule and the farmer's family supply all of the direct energy for agricultural production, 75% of the population is needed to produce their own requirements plus the needs of the other one-fourth of the population. Sufficiency is always precarious to inadequate. Generally half of the population (and a much higher percentage of children) suffers from malnutrition, according to World Health Organization statistics.

To illustrate the economics of the mineral industries, a single commodity, copper, will be discussed in some detail. It is a major metal with world consumption of more than seven million tons per year. It is also widespread both in occurrence and production.

Copper was the first utilitarian metal, indeed, the only metal of importance to man for four thousand years. Originally it was gathered from outcrops in its relatively pure native form. When pyrometallurgy was discovered, the sulphide ores were smelted. Generally slaves mined the ore, so labor was cheap. Tin was added to make much stronger and more durable bronze. Today copper ranks third in tonnage among metals used, surpassed only by iron (including steel) and recently by aluminum. The value of raw copper produced is about $14 billion per year.

In the early 1940s at the famous copper mines in Butte, Montana, the *cut-off grade* was 3%. Any lower grade was "waste," since the metal therein could not be extracted profitably. Thirty years later a new mining method, open pit mining, had been adopted and the "cut-off" grade had been lowered to 0.3%. Assuming the average grades mined were 4.5% and 0.45%, respectively, in the first case there were 90 pounds of metal per ton, in the latter 9 pounds per ton. Looking at it another way, the miner had to process about 10.6 tons of ore in 1970 to get the same amount of copper that would have been recovered from just one ton in 1940. (The relationship is not a direct proportion because the percent of metal recovered decreases as the grade is reduced. Today a little more than one pound per ton is lost from low-grade ore in concentration.) The only thing that made it possible to reduce the mineable grade in this manner was intensive mechanization. That is, manual labor could no longer produce copper from available grades of ore at the price people were willing to pay for the product. Anaconda had two choices: quit mining copper or find a way to reduce the cost of mining and processing the ore. This was done by adding horsepower. The mining industry built a bigger mining shovel and a bigger bucket. Now shovels of 17 cubic yards and trucks of 150- to 170-ton capacity (some reach 350 tons) are commonly used. For perspective, those trucks haul as much weight as three to seven rail cars. This represents a massive increase in the use of energy per pound of copper, and a great reduction of manual labor per ton of ore. Then the price of petroleum was multiplied by 10, and doubled again.

Inevitably the price of copper increased. The average for the first four years of the 1970s was 55 cents per pound. For the last four years of the decade it was 73 cents. That is an increase of 32.7%. The copper producer's costs went up far more than that, nearly that much in some of the single years duirng the period. Demand for copper went down in the "Great OPEC Recession:" that smaller piece of pie for "everyone else" could not be stretched to cover as many automobiles, so fewer radiators were needed, so less copper was used. The copper producers shut down some of the older, higher-cost mines, and laid off the miners. That was not enough. The cost of opening new mines shot up and new developments could not be justified, so plans to increase production were shelved. Even that was not enough. If a mine had produced ore averaging 0.5% copper, it had to leave some of the lower grade in the ground and increase average grade to, say, 0.6%. This meant two more pounds of metal were recovered per ton of ore mined without increasing costs. But it wasted much ore with six or seven pounds per ton that can never be mined. This is, in effect, economic waste of scarce natural resources, forced by the economic conditions.

Monies that were normally set aside to replace worn-out and inefficient machinery, reserves for depreciation, and retained earnings were consumed in rising costs. The actual productivity of labor continued to decline and could not be offset by capital expenditures to maintain or improve productivity. Dividends to stock holders were reduced. Spare parts and supply inventories were trimmed. All corners were cut to make ends meet.

Then came a second thrust. Pollution, the environment, and ecology were suddenly *causes célèbres.* Mining companies had tried to maintain good housekeeping, as had other industries, but it was the sudden and drastic change of the rules at a time when they were bordering on economic distress that was so damaging. Some of the environmentalists ranted and announced that their objective was to shut down the industry, to prevent the opening of new mines. They drove their metal, gas-guzzling monsters hundreds of miles to protest the mining of minerals that created the leisure society, which made it possible to support these non-productive protesters. Is it any wonder some in industry concluded there was a plot to destroy the economic potential of the nation, an alien philosophy guiding this concentrated drive?

Almost all of the capital the mining companies could acquire had to be diverted to unproductive purposes, to meeting environmental restrictions. Naturally as profits plunged, tax payments dropped also. The miners could not carry their accustomed share of the burden of the gigantic government bureaucracy that was strangling them, thus contributing to the massive governmental deficits.

While many copper mines closed, others were subsidized. In some countries (e.g., the Philippines) direct subsidies were provided to mines. Some mines had small amounts of gold, silver, or molybdenum in their copper ore. The prices of these metals increased along with that of petroleum, so these by-products subsidized the uneconomic copper production. With copper at 60 cents per pound and gold at $400 per ounce, if an ore contained 0.5 gram of recoverable gold and 10 pounds (0.5%) of copper, the gold brought $6.43 and the copper (less 25 cents freight, smelting, and refining charges) 35 cents, (10 cents of which had to go to pay for environmental protection), the actual yield from the copper was $2.50. The gross revenue was actually $8.93 per ton of ore, and the subsidy from the by-product was 64 cents per pound of copper. Few mines were so fortunate.

Foreign producers did not have to pay the environmental protection charge, and their labor costs were much lower. A Filipino driving a 170-ton truck in the Philippines costs about 5% of the price of putting an American behind the wheel of the same truck in the United States. As a result, foreign producers could sell their metal at a profit at a lower price than the American operator. Manufacturers ordered their metal from abroad. Consequently the purchase of foreign copper had to be added to the deficit from purchase of foreign oil, and more American laborers were forced out of work. Anaconda Company, with its big mine at Butte, Montana, closed its smelter 11 miles away and the refinery in Helena, Montana, and announced plans to ship the concentrate from Butte to Japan for smelting and refining, passing the Tacoma smelter of ASARCO en route. They could not afford the environmental protection costs and labor demands at their own plants.

Had copper prices risen at the same rate as petroleum prices since 1970, the metal would have sold in 1982 at nearly $11 per pound. This reflects the disproportionate increase in OPEC prices.

OUTLOOK

Prior to the severe recession in the industry in 1981–1982, copper was produced by 32 U.S. mines, of which 14 produced 95% of the domestic total. In 1970 the total domestic production was 1.56 M tons. In 1978 it was 1.3 M tons; in 1979, 1.4 M tons; in 1980, 1.1 M tons. (In 1980 major losses took place because of a strike, but had there been none, shutdowns would still have been inevitable because of the poor market.) That is a picture of stagnation to slightly negative growth. On the other hand, consumption was 2.0 M tons in 1969 and 2.2 M tons in 1979, evidence of a "mature" (slowly growing) market. It also shows that 36% of the copper was imported at a cost of about $140 million. That is not much compared to the $70 billion bill for imported oil, but it contributes to the trade deficit. The U.S. Bureau of Mines estimates that U.S. production will be 2.86 M tons of copper by A.D. 2000, the world total 17.7 M tons. But with capital charges on new production in 1983 about $1.00 per pound, smelting and other charges at 25 cents, environmental protection at 10 cents, and the price at 61 cents, it is impossible to bring new mines into production. The average cost of production of old mines with depreciated equipment was 91 cents per pound. The only reason more mines have not shut down is because there are continuing costs, even if a mine is not operating. With the price below 80 cents, several found it cheaper to shut down than to bear the operating loss.

To reach the goal of world production by the year 2000 will require the investment of about $55 billion. The average debt of the American producers is very heavy. They had little borrowing capacity, and their profits averaged about 3% in 1980, surely less in 1981 and 1982. It is almost inevitable that new consumption will have to be met by imports, but not because there is any domestic copper shortage. There are many known deposits in the United States that could become commercial by the economics of 1973, now sitting idle, waiting for a change in the economy.

Big investments are being made in copper mining by EXXON, ARCO, Standard of Indiana, Pennzoil, and Elf Aquitane. There are a number of explanations: (1) Such companies have so much money they do not know what to do with it. (2) Copper companies are available at bargain prices. (3) Since large amounts of copper will be used in solar energy applications, it is probably the cheapest entry into this field. (4) If concerted action can be taken and the copper price doubled or tripled, it will be a highly profitable investment. (5) Mines are customers for large quantities of oil. (6) While energy intensive, copper is less so than the other major metals, aluminum and nickel.

OIL AND THE ECONOMY

The average price of oil was increased 9% at the end of 1980, to approximately $35 per barrel, after it had doubled in 1979. The price had already risen from $1.70 in 1970. OPEC congratulated itself for its restraint, in view of the world recession. A return to compound price increases averaging 10% or more per year is probable *unless* the marked decline in the purchase of oil by industrial nations is sustained. If the communist-controlled nations come into the market for major purchases, price increases will be even greater.

The United States has cut its oil consumption, and its imports, which had peaked at 8.4 M barrels per day in 1978 dropped as low as 3.4 M bpd in 1982. At the peak (1978 and early 1979), imports were roughly half of consumption, or 18% of total energy consumed. The European Economic Community (E.E.C.) consumed 36 M bpd, 25 M bpd of which were purchased from OPEC. Free world consumption amounted to 62 M bpd. The 14.8% drop in consumption by 1982 (to 52.6 m bpd) was partially offset by the drop in production in Iran and Iraq. The 9% increase in oil price in 1980 was determined not by compassion but by pragmatism. When economic conditions improve, oil consumption will again increase, and OPEC can "make up" with a larger increase in price, which will knock the industrial countries into a recession again (and the non-oil producing nations of the Third World into bankruptcy). A way out of this dilemma would seem to be elimination of dependence on oil for fuel through development of synthetic fuels and other substitutions. There is no relationship between price and the cost of producing oil in the Middle East, so if such a plan were developed, OPEC could lower the price enough to make synfuel uneconomic and prevent the development of alternatives (shades of *Catch 22*).

There are some indications that a permanent decrease in consumption of petroleum is underway in the United States. This is reflected in the end of the era of automotive dinosaurs. Further, a number of power plants are converting to coal.

Oil companies in the U.S. budgeted $67 billion for exploration for 1981. That is $10 per barrel consumed. They must find six billion barrels to keep reserves static. This exploration went into the wildest of wildcats, with low yields on the exploration dollar. Every reasonable prospect within the over-thrust belt of the Rocky Mountains in western United States will be rapidly tested; after that where else can we look? Except for offshore, Alaska, and the lands now closed to development (the one-sixth of the nation that may not be used for commercial purposes), there is hardly a decent prospect for 100 million barrels left. This is reflected in the concern of exploration companies; by mid-1982 seismic exploration was at the lowest level in eight years and drilling had dropped 20% from 1981.

It should be apparent that mineral economics and national economics are one and the same. Without a strong, essentially self-sufficient mining industry, the United States will degenerate into a stagnant, socialistic welfare state with a declining standard of living. We still have the option of deciding if this is the direction we choose, or if we will develop our internal energy and mineral resources. The latter course will require a high degree of discrimination on how "pure" the environment has to be and how much of the nation must remain an "untrammeled wilderness" with its resources unused. There has been insufficient direction of the effort, a lack of will, some deliberate subversion of the economy, and a strange self-flagellation complex. A decade or more has been lost, and repairing the damage will be costly.

In the future no nation dependent on petroleum as a major energy source can be great. Unless a nation is at least 90% self-sufficient in energy, it will be perpetually at the mercy of its suppliers. It can expect to be periodically knocked to its knees, hostage to politics and greed. We must realize that energy, water, and minerals are the cornerstones of any national economy.

RESERVES vs. RESOURCES

Reserves are *resources* that have been measured. Depending upon the accuracy and thoroughness of the measurement, they can be counted on for production. They are classed as "proven" or "measured" reserves when the measurement is adequate to satisfy the mining engineer. "Probable" reserves have been adequately measured to satisfy the geologist. The difference is that the engineer has to use the data to plan production so he must know exactly the shape and distribution of grade of an ore body and where waste will be encountered. It may cost ten times as much to place reserves in the "proven" category as it costs to class them as "probable". A third category is "possible" reserves, meaning that some measuring has been done, enough to justify calculation of a tonnage, but the geologist will qualify his statement of quantity and grade.

Resources, on the other hand, are technically reasonable expectations of quantities of mineralized rocks that will be developed by exploration. For example, sediments off the eastern coast of the United States are of the type known to produce oil elsewhere, and taking the estimated volume, one can calculate a quantity that is reasonable to expect. Figures that have been given for this area range from 2 to 20 billion barrels. The broad range, an order of magnitude, represents several different assumptions. (The average of that kind of estimate is 6.3 billion barrels, not 11 billion. The factor is the square root of 10.) Thus the figure for petroleum reserves of the U.S. is appreciably lower than that of the petroleum resources.

DEPLETION

There is one aspect of mining that is different from any other industry. The quantity of mineral in any deposit is limited, and it does not regenerate itself. A manufacturing plant can order its raw materials from numerous sources. The farmer can grow another crop. A mine has finite reserves; when the mineral is mined out, the mine has to close. The deposit is then said to be depleted. The mill and mine machinery may still be serviceable and can be sold at the end of the operation. For the mining company to continue in business it must find and develop a new mine. If the mine has a 30-year life, captial costs that far in the future cannot be anticipated, but experience has shown it will be far more expensive to open the next mine than the last one. Since a supply of minerals is vital to the economy, this requires special tax treatment to give continuity of supply. What may appear to be "income" is actually income plus funds to open the next mine. The system developed to provide a reserve for this purpose is called "depletion allowance." It is different from depreciation, which is the fund set up for replacing worn-out machinery. A factory has depreciation only, but a mine must depreciate its plant and provide for depletion of its means of being in business, its ore reserve. Normally this is done by permitting a company to deduct a fixed percentage of its gross sales to provide a reserve for depletion of the deposit and the unknown cost of developing the next mine.

PALEORESOURCES AND PROTORESOURCES

A mineral resource is an inferred quantity of mineral which careful geologic analysis has shown to be present but which has not been delineated. Economic conditions change, however, and a mineral that once had value may become valueless as the result of new discoveries. The classic example of this is flint. For 99% of man's history it was the only important mineral resource. Today flint is worthless. A less extreme example is the naturally-occurring nitrate deposits of Chile. After methods of manufacturing fertilizer from atmospheric nitrogen were discovered, the Chilean deposits lost much of their importance and potential value. Thus a paleoresource is a mineral substance that was once commercially valuable but through exhaustion or technical advances has lost its value as a resource. Petroleum is well on its way to becoming a paleoresource.

A protoresource is a mineral deposit or commodity which judgment leads one to expect may become an economic resource at some time in the future. The classic example today is oil shale. For 100 years the deposits in Western Colorado have been known to contain a trillion barrels of oil, more than 10 times the petroleum reserves, and there have been sporadic attempts to develop them. Today it appears that oil shale will probably be developed as an economic source of petroleum. The environmentalist lobby is fighting this development, which could result in oil shale jumping from the proto to the paleo class without ever becoming economic.

Uranium is another example of an energy commodity that leaped from obscurity to worldwide renown on August 6, 1945, when an atom bomb was dropped on Hiroshima. Harnessed to produce electricity, it is now a major and growing energy source. There are legitimate concerns about the safety and economics of nuclear power, and it, too, has had to face opposition from special-interest groups.

The history of the advance of civilization is the story of new minerals being harnessed to man's needs, one after another. Not content with natural elements, he has created ones that do not now exist in nature (e.g., plutonium). There are other protoresources remaining to be developed in the marine nodules. These too, may soon be economic resources.

COMMODITY GAMBLING DENS

The reason given for establishment of the commodity exchanges was the need for a stable market place for buyers and sellers to meet. For some years they served this function fairly well, though another middle man was added to the chain of supply.

Today the commodity exchanges have become the lairs of pirates. Instead of being a moderating influence, they have been the factor that made it possible for wild swings in the prices of commodities to take place. They have become some of the main centers where gullible investors are encouraged to gamble on borrowed money.

The example that most vividly illustrates this problem is the history of silver in 1979 and 1980. Silver had averaged $1.79 per ounce in the five years before the "oil shock." It made a new base, averaging $4.52 per ounce in the four years following the spurt of inflation in 1973 (see Figure 4). It was obvious to observers of the demand and supply of silver that the price had to move up because consumption had exceeded production by a wide margin for many years. The main source that made up the deficit was the U.S. Treasury. It sold all of the silver anyone wanted to buy at a price that was far below the cost to produce the equivalent amount. By 1978 the "Treasury Mine" was nearly depleted, and the price had to rise to the cost of production for the high-cost producers who would make up the deficiency in supply (plus a profit). Calculations as early as 1970 showed that this figure would be about $10 per ounce.

Certain individuals with immense funds and credit available to them apparently decided they could "corner" the market in silver. That is, they decided to buy enough of it to be able to control the price. Figure 4 shows the weekly average silver price during this "blow off." The price reached $50 per ounce, an increase of more than 1000%. There were single days when half of annual world production was sold, with most of this purchased "on the margin" or without paying the full price or taking delivery of the metal. The exchanges made little or no effort to curtail this speculation. To the outsider they seemed to promote it deliberately because they profited on every transaction.

At this point other "high-rollers" entered the fracas. For example, executives of Occidental Petroleum decided the price was too high, and the company started selling short, selling silver it did not own. There was massive buying and selling of paper, one against the other, neither party needing the silver. A battle of the giant bank accounts ensued, with victory to the party with the best credit line. Both sides dipped into oil wealth, accumulations of funds so vast they could think of nothing better to do with them than gambling. (See *The Great Silver Bubble* by Stephen Fay).

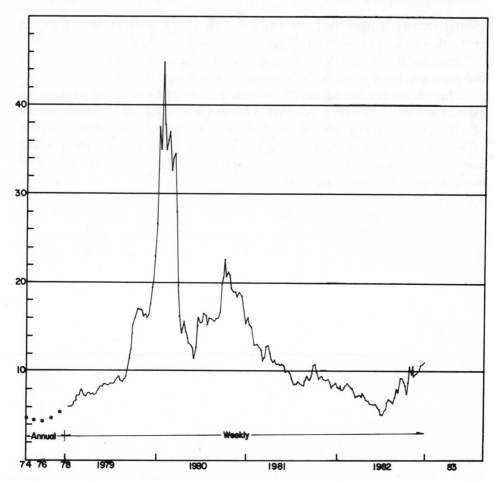

Figure 4 A graph here shows the fluctuations in the price of silver from 1978 to 1982.

After the great price increase, it was the turn of the bears; the short sellers had the advantage and the price came tumbling back down as fast as it went up. Occidental Petroleum made a "killing." At the time of writing, the price is hovering around $8.50 per ounce. This would be an "oversold" condition except for the announcement of photographic film with no silver required, which will only affect the consumption of silver used for x-ray film, so the decrease will not be large. The price can be considered to be 30%–50% too low to properly balance production and consumption.

Some may ask what is wrong with wild speculative swings. Silver is a commodity used in consumer products. In an orderly market one can contract to deliver his product months in advance. If the cost of a raw material can fluctuate 1000% in a few months with no change in fundamental factors, a manufacturer either has to have a wide profit margin for protection or face possible bankruptcy.

Iron ore is not traded on the commodity exchanges. The quantities are too great and price variation is too small to suit speculators.

The exchanges could easily be restored to their original purpose of making an orderly market. All that is needed is to institute a transaction tax of 10% on all sales where delivery of the commodity is not made, that is, 10% of the sale price, not of the margin. Commodity speculation would come to a virtual halt. The commodity exchanges would again become markets instead of gambling dens.

CHAPTER 5

ENERGY

A husky, young, well-fed man can exert about 0.5 horsepower per hour, or four horsepower hours per day. An office worker may expend one-tenth of that. A 400 hp automobile racing down the highway for *one hour* expends the energy capability of 100 laborers or 1000 office workers for a whole day. The auto would use about five gallons of gasoline, costing $7 but in the industrial nations the laborers would cost $8000, the office workers $80,000. The industrial success of the United States was the result of doing work with energy, an ever-increasing number of horsepower at the command of each worker, not an ever-increasing number of laborers.

Another fallacy has been introduced by the government relating to the "increasing productivity of labor." Any manager can testify the productivity of labor has been in a steady decline. For example, productivity per man-day in underground coal mines in the U.S. has followed this pattern: 1960, 10.64 tons; 1969, 15.61 tons; 1975, 9.5 tons; 1976, 8.5 tons (G. C. Gambs, *Energy Outlook*, Wharton Econometrics Service Energy Roundtable, 1977). Management has to buy more machines and more energy to increase production. Then a bureaucrat divides factory output by the labor force and says, "See! Labor productivity is up." In reality, productivity has been increased by increasing capital expenditures. Japan can buy iron ore from Australia, coal from Canada, copper from South America and petroleum from Iran and combine them to make an automobile that it can sell more cheaply in Chicago than one made of American labor and materials from nearby sources. That does not mean Japanese labor is so much more efficient than American (although this may be a contributing factor). They have newer blast furnaces and more efficient refineries and factories that more than compensate for the high transportation costs on all of the components. Meanwhile American industry has been forced to divert its limited capital resources to comply with sudden stringent environmental demands rather than using funds to improve productivity.

Before the oil shock of 1973, when the cost of energy was very low, the U.S. could indulge in increasingly inefficient labor. When the cost of petroleum went up ten-fold in a short period, industry was saddled with labor legislation and practices that made it non-competitive and obsolescent. Yet labor still kept up its chant of "more, more."

While the era of cheap energy has gone forever, it is still very inexpensive compared to the cost of labor, as illustrated above. Henceforth a new balance has to be struck and labor cannot expect to retain the same percentage of the total cost structure of manufacturing or mineral production. Energy-intensive industries (steel, cement, nickel, and aluminum, for example) have to charge more for their product since they cannot easily reduce either energy or labor costs.

When someone mentions energy, most of us think of the triple increase in the price of gasoline or how the bill for fuel oil shot up. These are just the fraction of the iceberg that is visible above the water. Gasoline in the United States is *underpriced*, sold below replacement cost and more cheaply than in any other industrial nation. By keeping this price down it has held the inflation index down by several points—like putting an ice bag on a thermometer.

One frequently hears the statement, "no one could have foreseen the energy crisis." This is patently false. A small group of prophets tried to get the attention of government, congressmen, and their peers in the profession as early as 1960. In 1956 M. King Hubbert accurately forecast the peak of petroleum production in the United States. It took OPEC to cudgel the world into a realization that oil is a precious commodity, too precious to burn. This is not to imply that there was anything altruistic in their act. The motive was greed.

Several months before the "oil shock," Ahmed Zaki al-Yamani, Saudi Arabian Minister of Petroleum Affairs, made the statement, "We are in a position to dictate prices [of oil], and we are going to be very rich" (*New York Times*, April 16, 1973). This shows quite clearly that a drastic increase in oil prices was planned long before the October War of 1973. The Arabian Gulf nations were merely looking for an excuse to impose the drastic price increases.

The consequences of *not* undertaking an aggressive effort to solve the energy problem in 1960-1965 were rampant inflation and economic stagnation in 1975-1980. The consequences of *not* undertaking the effort in 1970-1975 will be felt in 1985-1995, and they are likely to be much worse than the mild recession of 1980-1982. The lag between an initial research program and significant contribution of a new energy source is now 25 years or more. Atomic fusion, which has had 30 years of study, is still 30 years from utilization.

To the developing nations, many of whom are in dire economic straits as the result of the twenty-fold increase in oil price, it is the U.S., not OPEC that is blamed for the price increase (Stobaugh and Yergin, 1979, *Energy Future*). If in 1973 the U.S. had refused to pay the prices demanded, had it halted imports, tightened its belt, and undertaken a belated crash program to develop its own abundant energy resources, the price of oil today would probably be one third of its present level. The U.S. economy would be booming and virtually free of inflation. There would be far fewer nations in the economic zombie status. This is the unforgivable tragedy of the 1970s.

The energy problems that will be experienced in the next 20 years cannot be precisely anticipated. Some ideas of the energy mix for A.D. 2000 for the United States are given by E. T. Hayes (1979, "Energy Resources," *Science*, p. 233). Fossil fuels will still contribute about 79%, but the constituents will be in different proportions than at present. Petroleum will have dropped in total and even more in percentage, but the country will still need to import three billion barrels per year, and it will probably cost in 1982 dollars $100 per barrel. Natural gas use will be cut in half and coal use will have soared to equality with petroleum at 33.6%. Hydropower, which has peaked in amount, will be dropping in percentage, to 3.7%. Nuclear energy will be 11.5%. *All other* power sources will possibly amount to 6.8%, which may be a shock to those indulging in wishful thinking about solar, biomass, geothermal, or energy from ocean waves and currents. The point to note is that imported fuel will cost the U.S. over five trillion dollars during the next 20 years, money that will bleed out of the economy, leaving an anemic nation in a state of continuous semi-recession. If the expenditure drops below that figure, it will just mean the economy is in worse shape. That is a part of the cost of the shoot-the-moon circus and the Vietnam war in the Kennedy-Johnson years, the Watergate fiasco under Nixon, and the preservation-environmental binge under Ford and Carter.

Are there any ways that the United States can salvage anything from this debacle? Such a reversal would require resolute national dedication stronger than anything experienced by any nation in peace time. Taking the Colorado River water away from California and using it to produce oil from shale or coal could relieve imports by two million barrels per day. Building 100 additional 1000 megawatt nuclear power plants would save three million barrels per day. Together those steps would cut imports anticipated in the year 2000 by a little over half. By a crash coal development program to produce 2.5 billion tons per year we could wipe out *all* oil imports. That would give a healthy economy that was a net energy exporter. All three of these programs would make the United States one of the top three energy exporters. It would give time to solve the problems of nuclear fusion and of the orbital solar power plant.

Californians will scream at the suggestion that their water "rights" be cancelled. However, most of the Colorado River water consumed in California is utilized for irrigation in desert conditions where at least 90% is lost in evaporation and much of the rest in transpiration. Permitting these few agro-industrialists to monopolize and waste an inexpensive source of water constitutes a huge subsidy when it could be the basis of producing two million barrels per day of shale oil and synthetic fuel in Colorado and Wyoming, where the water originates.

Estimates of coal reserves and resources vary widely. The U.S. Geological Survey has estimated potential resources as high as 3.5×10^{12} (3.5 trillion) tons. While some of this excess above other estimates may eventually be amenable to *in situ* conversion to gas, *reserve* estimates range from 450 billion to 150 billion tons. A reasonable compromise is that the United States has 250 billion tons of recoverable coal, so the proposed rate of production would give a century to solve the energy problems of the future. Even at that there would be no time for complacence.

There are only two categories of energy likely to be significant during the remainder of the 20th century: fossil fuel and nuclear power. Other categories have little chance of being important. Possibly all others combined (hydro excepted) will not be statistically significant by the end of the century. Further, fossil fuels are likely to be dominant through the 21st century. The only visible challenges to this are the fast breeder reactor and possibly solar energy.

The fast breeder reactor creates a fuel that can be used by terrorists. There is not much danger of small groups being able to build a separator for ^{238}U and ^{235}U permitting accumulation of enough weapons-grade ^{235}U to blackmail a nation. However, plutonium is chemically different from uranium and can be concentrated fairly easily. Therefore, smart terrorists with a good laboratory *could* build a bomb, having seized or stolen the spent fuel elements from a power plant. This is why the U.S. has tried to prevent the development of the fast breeder.

Other countries do not recognize the restraint imposed by the U.S. on breeding plutonium. France, which studiously tries to avoid following American leadership, has a prototype plant in operation and is several years ahead in this field. Russia, which encourages terrorists in non-communist nations, is also well advanced in developing breeder reactors. Both of these nations can be expected to offer breeder units for sale within a few years. Nuclear blackmail may thus not be too far in the future.

The conventional nuclear reactor can never become the dominant power source. Except for the very dilute amount in the oceans, there is just not enough ^{235}U available. This factor limits use of uranium as fuel to 10%–15% of the total energy requirements of the world. However, 99.3% of natural uranium is ^{238}U, which is convertible into plutonium. Its utilization would increase the available nuclear fuel enormously. Westinghouse estimates the factor at 60 times. Thorium, is also fertile, and resources of this element are much greater than those of uranium. If the breeder is extensively developed, it could supply over 50% of the world's total energy.

MINOR ENERGY SOURCES

Hydropower: The cost of a new hydropower plant in 1980 was about $1000 per kilowatt of capacity in the small size range (1–2 megawatts), somewhat lower as the size increases. This is exclusive of construction of a dam and other facilities to make the water available to the plant. Where suitable undeveloped power sites are available, they constitute an excellent energy resource. Few sites remain in industrial nations, and nature clubs stridently oppose new power development. The snail darter, a tiny fish that is functionally extinct, was used to prevent construction of a dam and major power development in Tennessee. While the fish was found later in other habitats and the objections of the ecologists to construction overridden, the case was publicized internationally to illustrate the unconcern of the U.S. for developing nations. The U.S. was shown as refusing to develop its own resources and instead going into the world market to compete for scarce petroleum, driving the price up out of reach of needy nations. These countries looked on this as an example of arrogant use of wealth, putting a few specimens of an insignificant fish ahead of the lives and welfare of many humans.

Solar Power: The sun yields free energy, so why not utilize it for power? The trouble is, the sun is a very dilute and intermittent energy source. The availability of solar power is dependent on weather and latitude. Water cannot be boiled or a fire started without concentrating the sun's rays by focusing them on a small area. This is the massive problem in trying to predicate the energy-guzzling monstrosity called civilization on such a source. Presently the most significant use of solar energy is for heating water, which can in turn be utilized for space heating.

Hundreds of millions of dollars have been spent on solar energy research in the last few years, in the United States and in other industrialized nations. One group believes that for at least the remainder of the twentieth century solar energy will be insignificant. Another group insists that commercial development is near. A report published in *Newsweek* (July 20, 1981) showed the capital cost of developing solar power has dropped from $500,000 per kilowatt to $10,000. It further stated that a plant is being constructed in Japan to produce solar converters at a cost of $3000–4000 per kilowatt. This is called "peak power," or that delivered during the middle of a sunny summer day in mid-latitude. It does not include the battery pack to store electricity during the daytime for night use. On that basis a home with a 10 hp centralized air conditioning system would require about 25 kw of peak power, and would have to spend in excess of $100,000 to supply its needs. Reduction of the cost by two orders of magnitude (divide it by 100) is a major achievement, but the cost is still out of reach for most homes.

The *Newsweek* article cites work by Stanford Orshinsky, research supported by Atlantic Richfield and SOHIO (two of the big oil companies), where a cost of $330 per kw is indicated, representing still another order of magnitude of reduction in capital cost. If true, the same power supply would cost on the order of $12,000–$20,000 (the battery system for storage is not reduced). To capitalize the heating, air conditioning, and lighting bills for the life of a house would be very attractive at that range. The capital cost of the power supply would be one-third that of an hydroelectric plant and in the range of thermal plants, which, of course, require fuel. If these estimates prove to be valid, the era of solar power has arrived, and could conceivably produce 10%–20% of the energy requirements for some nations in the mid- to southern latitudes by A.D. 2000.

The implications of this break-through announcement could be revolutionary. General Motors announced plans to produce electric automobiles in 1985. One can foresee Los Angeles passing an ordinance that as of 1986, would permit no new vehicles burning petroleum to be registered in the city, and by 1991 would allow only electric vehicles. As the smog thins, the solar power plants on the building roofs become more efficient and soon smog will be gone forever. A futuristic application of solar energy is the energy collector that would remain stationary in space relative to a point on the surface of the earth. Concentrated energy would be sent to earth as microwaves for conversion to electricity. Constructed for electrical generation, it might become feasible in a few decades. First the space shuttle has to be perfected, then living quarters constructed in space. It may even require a moon colony with production of required materials there for export to earth orbit. This would seem to be an excellent project for nations such as Kuwait and Saudi Arabia. The timing would just about coincide with exhaustion of their oil reserves, so they would ensure a continuing supply of energy resources.

Biomass: Any combustible material of organic origin is a potential energy source. Vegetation is one such collector of solar energy, though quite inefficient. This is now the third most important energy source, after petroleum products and coal. If wastelands can be converted to tree farms or waste products can be utilized, biomass can become a locally important energy source. Because of the high bulk factor, biomass cannot be economically transported for any great distance (transport consumes energy). There is a danger that reduction of food production might result, contributing to malnutrition.

One result of expanded consumption of timber for space heat has been excessive timber cutting, with accelerated soil erosion. This is noticeable in the northeastern United States since 1973 and has long been the main factor in denudation, erosion to "bad lands," and desertification in many developing nations with exploding populations. "Given present rates of deforestation, Senegal will be bare of trees in 30 years, Ethiopia in 20, Burandi in 7." (*AGID News* July 1983). With hybrid trees in plantations now producing up to 30 tons per hectare per year and hopes that production will reach 100 t per hectare per year, this can be an efficient and growing energy source.

Gasohol: This fuel consists of 10%–15% alcohol mixed with gasoline. This is a second-stage form of solar collection. At present 110% energy input is required to get 100% out. In other words, it is an energy sink, not a source. Research on methods of dehydration of alcohol may make significant improvement. Sugar cane is used as a source of alcohol, and where this plant can be easily raised, it can be of value in producing fuel. Thus it is capital intensive and capital and energy inefficient.

Geothermal: Thermal energy from the earth itself has long been utilized. In Iceland for example, volcanic steam heats greenhouses, permitting truck gardens and fruits to be grown (hydroponic agriculture). Italy was a leader in utilization of energy from volcanic sources for generation of electricity. The United States is now the largest user of volcanic energy, and a major research project has been under way for several years at Los Alamos, New Mexico, for utilization of heat from dry *plutons.* New Zealand and Japan have major geothermal power stations in operation. Geothermal power development in the Philippines, now ranking second in on-line geothermal power production, is making great strides, and in a few years it should advance to the position of largest producer. It has many potential sources. Indonesia is also beginning to develop its abundant geothermal resources. A different method of geothermal energy utilization has taken place in the Paris basin in France. Warm water obtained from deep wells is now extensively used for space heating. It is an efficient, but limited, source.

Wave, Tides, and Marine Thermal Gradient: These are potential energy resources that will have local feasibility, but are either cyclic, irregular, or dilute. They are capital intensive but capital inefficient.

Nuclear Fusion: Some consider fusion to be the ultimate energy source. Deuterium or heavy water (^2H_2O) is present in the oceans in dilute but virtually inexhaustible amount. It is a clean energy source and results in no environmental destruction. The problem is that ^2H burns to ^4He at a temperature in millions of degrees Celsius, and no material can contain the reaction. Research on magnetically constrained plasma is promising, but far from perfected. Decades will elapse before a prototype plant is operational, and if economically competitive, fusion plants will then be constructed rapidly. This is one of the most promising energy sources for use in the declining years of fossil fuels but, because of the long lead time, needs to be vigorously pursued now. If nuclear fusion can be exploited, it will be capital intensive, but also one of the most capital efficient sources.

Geopressurized Gas: This is properly a fossil fuel of futuristic potential. In the earth there are very deep sedimentary horizons filled with water under very high pressure. Hydrocarbon gases are known to be dissolved in this water; the theory is that if drilled, the gas will "boil off" and be available for fuel. The trouble is that such wells are very expensive, and the gas is relatively dilute. Then too, pressure drops quite rapidly in a tapped geopressure zone because water is virtually incompressible. Some very extravagant claims are being made for this gas, but it will probably be a very expensive energy source. It is capital intensive but capital inefficient.

Wind: This is actually another form of solar energy and one of the oldest energy sources utilized. For centuries sails have been used in developing nations for vessels of various kinds. A major factor limiting the use of wind is its intermittent nature. Virtually every farm in America used to have a windmill to pump water for livestock and domestic use. There were many wind-powered generators with 32 volt storage battery banks to collect the wind's energy when it was blowing for use when it was not. The rural electrification program and power cooperatives replaced these units. Wind generators may be coming back to significant use, however, particularly in isolated areas. Some plants as large as 100 kw have been constructed and plans for 1–2 megawatt units are being made. A problem with large propeller type generators is that wind is commonly much stronger at higher elevations above ground and if the blade is 60 m (200 feet) in arc diameter, stress becomes significant. Some locations are natural wind funnels and where these exist both stronger wind velocity and more steady flowage can be utilized. There are places where the wind at ground level seldom drops below 60 kph (40 mph). There has even been consideration of anchoring a blimp with a suspended rotor-generator, using the cables to transmit power to the ground. One hazard is the cables would make an excellent lightning rod. Wind power will become an important source of energy in some localities.

Exotic Sources: A recent photograph on the cover of *EOS*, a professional geoscience publication, showed a night picture of North America from a satellite. The light belts on the ground resulting from electric lights were very striking. It was possible to pick out every town of 20,000–25,000 population. The first reaction was that a very large portion of the electricity generated is wasted by radiation into space. Directed luminescence should have great potential for increasing the efficiency of lighting. The purpose of the photograph was not to show the earth, but to present a magnificent display of the aurora borealis. The lights in the sky were probably 100 times greater than all of the lights on the ground. A tremendous amount of energy is streaming toward earth in the vicinity of the north magnetic pole. There might be some way of capturing this, possibly more efficiently than from solar collection. Intensity of energy flow follows the sun spot cycle of 11 years, so it is somewhat variable.

Bioluminescence and bioelectricity (the electric eel) are energy or light sources deserving greater study. Fireflies and plankton do not waste energy by converting part of their power to heat as do man-made light sources.

CONCLUSION

There are literally libraries full of volumes on the subject of fossil fuels and nuclear energy. Thus to give comprehensive coverage here is impossible. Instead the approach selected has been to try to put some of the aspects of energy use in perspective. I have mentioned, for example, the cost of doing work with manual labor vs. mechanical energy, the cost of subsidizing agro-industry in California, the effect of the energy shock in developing nations, and the alternatives that are really available, shorn of wishful thinking. It is still possible to have a viable economy if the adjustments are made within the system. With energy receiving a larger proportion of the gross national product (10% today relative to 2% in 1972) some of the other segments have had to shrink. Labor, management, food supplies, and mineral products all have to share this proportional reduction. To let inflation make the adjustments represents gross irresponsibility on the part of government, because the strongest organizations refuse to accept their proportional reduction. Consequently some segments of the economy are forced to bear a disproportionate share of the burden.

CHAPTER 6

EXPLORATION

From the seventeenth to the nineteenth centuries geographic explorers covered the entire earth, mapping and studying the physiography and ecology. While there are a few "die hards" nostalgically attempting to relive the experiences of that earlier period, exploration in the twentieth century is the prerogative of the earth scientists, seeking to discover and evaluate the mineral resources upon which civilization is dependent. They are the successors to the prospectors, a hardy group of individuals who went into the mountains with a bag of beans, a chunk of salt pork, a pick, a shovel, a rifle, and a dream of finding riches.

Today exploration is a team effort, the team being composed of a group of specialists in various phases of earth science. The leader and conceptualist (who may be the same individual) must define a target with a reasonable chance of discovery and lay out a program that will rapidly and inexpensively limit the search to a target of manageable size. This leader is usually an economic geologist with degrees in one or more of the specialties of earth science.

Today no one wants to find a small deposit. It takes little more effort to find and evaluate a large deposit than a small one, but the yield on the exploration effort, the profit, in terms of gross mineral value discovered, is much greater if a large deposit is discovered. Thus an exploration effort might be compared to an elephant hunt. This analogy will be followed in this discussion.

FIRST, GET AN ELEPHANT GUN

You do not hunt elephants with a .22 rifle, or even a .30-'06. You need a large caliber gun capable of doing the job. In exploration, success is limited by the capability of the team leader. There are men well-versed in geology and exploration methods who will never find a mineral deposit. There are men who have spent their entire career, from junior geologist to regional manager and have never been involved in a discovery. The "big guns" cost more, but if a program of $20–30 million is laid out, it should be in the hands of someone who has done it before, someone with a success record. One of the most successful explorationists, Dr. Thayer Lindsley, thought it possible that extrasensory perception might have something to do with exploration success. If this is true, there may be negative ESP also, and it would be better to entrust an expensive program to someone with a history of "good luck" than to someone who never quite made a discovery, a man who cannot hit the target when it is in front of him.

GO TO ELEPHANT COUNTRY

There are not many places in the world where a herd of elephants can be hiding with their presence unknown. The same thing applies to minerals. Virtually all of the large silver deposits of the world are in North or South America, and by far the largest percentage of these are found within 750 km of the Pacific Ocean. Therefore, the statistical odds of finding additional silver are considerably better if one heads for the silver belt. Second choice would be areas where geologic conditions are favorable, similar to the silver country. This does not mean, however, that predecessors have always been right in interpretation. The man who realized the conditions on Bougainville Island were right for porphyry copper, even though the island had previously been ignored, deserves more credit than he received. He recognized a massive bull elephant hiding in the bushes.

LOOK OUT FOR GAME PRESERVES

There are places with magnificent herds of elephants inside areas with "No Hunting" signs posted all around. The mineral explorationist will sometimes recognize signs of major mineralization, only to find a few hundred thousand acres have been declared a wilderness area, or any one of a half dozen designations which have removed one-sixth of the U.S. land mass from contributing to the national economy. To the 150 nations smaller in area than this vast, largely unused preserve, this is incomprehensible. Nevertheless, one is wasting his company's money by thinking resources are to be found in the preserves.

LOOK OUT FOR ETHNIC RESERVATIONS

Some large areas are reserved to hunting by certain ethnic groups only. In the U.S., Indian reservations may be closed to exploration, and at the very least, different rules apply. Abroad, some nations hang up the signs, "No Foreigners Wanted." Others invite foreigners, but on terms that make it unlikely that the foreign investor will be able to earn an acceptable reward for his investment. Still other nations establish rules to protect the country's interest but welcome investors willing to develop the resources.

LOOK FOR ELEPHANT SIGNS

An elephant passing down a trail leaves unmistakable signs of his passage. Examining the signs is equivalent to reconnaissance in exploration terms. This may take several different forms, depending on the mineral being sought, the terrain, and the climate.

One choice is airborne *geophysics.* This is particularly applicable where the country is quite flat, like much of Canada and Australia, but it is of limited use in the Rocky Mountains or the rugged, mountainous jungle of New Guinea. During World War II a method of mounting a *magnetometer* in a "bird" (a pod lowered from a plane on a cable) was developed for locating submarines under the surface of the water. A mass of steel 300 feet long creates an anomaly in the earth's field large enough to be detected by a sensitive magnetometer. Of course a sunken ship will do likewise, or a submerged ridge of volcanic rock, but in the open ocean it was quite effective. Essentially the same principle applies to mineral exploration. Rocks favorable for mineralization are likely to have irregular patterns of magnetization with local highs and lows. The method is directly applicable to the location of bodies of magnetic iron ore. If a substantial body of magnetite is crossed, a very pronounced anomaly will be recorded. Several other types of ore deposits have a magnetic signature of smaller amplitude. Broad, smooth *isogons* with little amplitude are not attractive. If the isogons are closely spaced and chopped off sharply, they suggest a disturbed area and may warrant closer examination.

There are other airborne geophysical instruments. *Electromagnetic* methods can be used in the air. The principle involved is sending long radio waves that will penetrate the ground and travel through it for a distance, then return to the atmosphere and to a receiver. Both transmitter and receiver are required. If the waves pass through a substantial conductor in the ground, they will be concentrated and the intensity of the signal will vary. The trouble is, *any* conductor will give a reading—a salt pond, a graphitic schist, magnetite, pyrite, or valuable suphides. Height above ground is also a variable. This method can be used on the ground where a target of limited size has been identified, say 4–5 km^2. In its simplest version, the instrument used is the treasure-finder, mine detector, or metal detector at the airline security check. In all cases it requires a transmitter and receiver that give a signal if a conductor is present between them.

A third kind of aerial prospecting is done with a sensitive scintillation counter to detect gamma radiation. There are three elements with naturally occurring isotopes that lead to gamma decay. These are uranium, thorium, and potassium. They have different energy levels that can be discriminated. Cosmic ray background can also be eliminated, so that the detector will read only variations in uranium decay products. Air absorbs gamma radiation, however, so the distance from the ground is important. Back in the early days of uranium exploration (the 1950s), planes flew along the rims of mesas and in canyons, sometimes less than 30 m from the rock outcrops. Even more effective than air in absorption of gamma rays is a few inches of moist soil. Thus the method is most effective in deserts, least in rain forest. These three methods are geophysical tools that have been widely used.

Aerial photographs were used 50 years ago for geologic interpretation, then they were extensively used for military intelligence in World War II. With the advent of sophisticated electronics and earth satellites, some new techniques were developed, including *remote sensing*. Signals are received from satellites with broad spectrum scanners, sent to earth, and recomposed into pictures, or images, sometimes with false colors to emphasize different wave lengths. The new methods involve more sophisticated methods of aerial surveying and a more elevated platform of observation and have a definite but limited use in exploration. Since they are very expensive, and companies with the sophisticated equipment need to keep it busy, the methods have been oversold, to the point that remote sensing has become a "buzz word" interpreted to include all geophysics and aerial photography. Even visual examination has been included in remote sensing. Vast claims have been made for discoveries, some of which have been known for hundreds of years. For example, on the Altiplano of Bolivia the Salar de Uyuni, a salt flat 200 km in diameter and containing at least 200 billion tons of salt (NaCl) over saturated brine of unknown extent was the source of salt for the Kechua (Inca) Indians. The presence of boron salts was described by Ahlfeld in the technical literature of Bolivia. Yet it was recently "discovered" by remote sensing and inferred to be a potential source of boron and lithium salts.

There are other reconnaissance methods used where aerial work is not applicable. The science of *geochemistry* developed to identify anomalous concentrations of metals. Rocks always contain traces of most metals. For example, diorite normally contains about 60 parts per million (or grams per ton) of copper. Copper ore in a large disseminated deposit may be 80 to 200 times as rich. If a stream cuts into an ore zone, the alluvium down stream will also contain unusual concentrations of copper. By sampling the sediment in streams and analyzing for copper and several associated elements (now as many as 33 elements may be determined in each sample), an experienced man can identify anomalies in the drainage that may warrant further examination. An anomaly will "decay" down stream; depending on the size and gradient of the river, the climate and rate of dilution it may not be detectable even one kilometer from an ore zone, so there are limitations on the method. Some computer methods of statistical treatment of geochemical data can point an arrow in the direction of an ore body.

DON'T LOOK FOR ELEPHANTS UNDER LEAVES

While a hunter would laugh at the suggestion, men looking for large ore bodies have wasted a lot of money following small showings that should have been obviously too small for a mine.

FIND THE BEAST

Assuming the reconnaissance has pointed out a target, detailed prospecting of the site follows. Probably ridge-and-spur geochemical sampling would be the first step, while the geologist is making a detailed map of the prospective area, studying the rock types and the *alteration* superimposed on them. He looks for mineralized float (rocks carrying traces of valuable mineral which have been transported by glaciers or streams during floods) and attempts to trace them to their source. It should be noted that at this stage probably not one prospect in 1000 becomes a mine.

Various techniques are used in different sequences. Soil sampling along grid lines, rock sampling, and ground geophysics may be conducted. The latter may include magnetic surveys but in the case of a disseminated copper deposit is likely to include *resistivity* and *induced polarization*. Relative resistance of the rocks to the passage of electrical current imposed at different points in the area is measured. A sulphide body is a better conductor (or has less resistance), but that does not necessarily mean copper is present. Induced polarization is a method of charging the natural battery of the earth and measuring the rate of discharge. If no sulphide is there, no charge is taken. If a substantial sulphide zone is present, the battery will take a charge and slowly leak it back.

After all the geochemistry and rock samples have been analyzed and the geophysical results studied, comes the moment of truth. Is it an elephant or not? If the prospect is recommended for further testing from surface indications, it is then necessary to explore the subsurface, initially, perhaps by trenching and test pitting, but if favorable indications continue to be found, eventually by test drilling. The money then starts to flow rapidly and the odds are still very strong that a mine cannot be developed. Some companies have drilled as many as 200 targets before finding an ore body. This is where the Big Gun pays for himself many times over in rejecting the prospects with the least chance of developing into a mine.

READY, AIM, FIRE!

Destruction of beautiful dream castles with ugly drill facts is likely to follow. Is it a discovery? Are there two or three billion dollars worth of metal there waiting for the miner to extract a few pounds (or even grams, if it is a precious metal) per ton? Drilling is the final proof. A test pattern is established and drilling depth is decided. Possibly five holes will be budgeted to 500 meters. That is a total of 2500 m at possibly $100 per meter, plus staff time, analyses, computer time, and a helicopter standing by. Money flows like water, and still the final decision may be to walk away. The senior geologist must decide on the spot whether the hole should be extended another 100 m or be stopped at 300 m instead of reaching the target depth.

The results may be encouraging or even good. A new budget must be drawn up with pattern drilling planned. More drills must be mobilized, the camp must be enlarged, supplies have to be delivered and on time (a crew waiting for a spare part is very expensive and nonproductive). To fully evaluate a disseminated copper deposit may take 20,000 to 50,000 meters of drilling, or even more. Thus the full drilling program may cost $5-$10 million and *still* the odds are quite strongly against a commercial deposit.

HARVEST THE TROPHY

Computer methods of evaluation of masses of drilling data make play out of what was formerly a tedious and lengthy procedure with a calculator. One can make a complete simulation of 30 years of mining in a matter of minutes and, based on the assumptions used (price, costs, cut-off grade, pit slopes), determine the gross sales and anticipated profit. So the exploration department turns its find over to production for development and mining. Depending on availability of capital which can be rented for a reasonable price and the sale price of the product, the property may be immediately developed for production, "put on the shelf" to wait for more favorable economic conditions, or abandoned.

LOOK FOR THE REST OF THE HERD

Ordinarily elephants run in herds, which may include a big bull, several cows, and a few calves. Similarly ore deposits are usually found in clusters. While the exploration team that finds an ore body of 150 million tons that will yield $1–$5 billion in sales deserves a lot of credit for helping the local or national economy, it should not rest on its laurels. There may be two or three additional ore bodies nearby and if some competitor jumps in and finds a bigger one next door, the pride of discovery will turn to embarrassment. What may be even more pathetic is for the mining company to put its waste dump, tailings, mill, or townsite right on top of another ore body; this has happend so frequently that it is an industry joke: the best target for new ore bodies is under townsites, millsites, waste dumps, or tailings ponds— those areas have about 95% greater probability of hiding ore bodies than virgin ground.

SUMMARY

As Edward Teller, emminent physicist and father of the atomic bomb, has said, "There are no natural resources until humans discover a use for a particular substance." After a use, there is a need. It is the sophisticated team of explorationists that discovers the supplies of mineral resources to fulfill the needs of civilized man. This team is directed by an experienced economic geologist who calls in airborne surveys, ground geophysics, geochemistry, and diamond drilling to supplement geologic mapping. He has to integrate all of the accumulated data and, through a series of go/no-go decision points, allocate increasing amounts of high-risk funds to the definition of resources essential for the commodities needed to maintain a high standard of living.

The geologist is a true conservationist, one who works in the wilderness and loves it and conducts his programs in accordance with the doctrine of intelligent use of resources with minimal damage to the environment.

CHAPTER 7

MINERAL PRODUCTION TECHNOLOGY

This chapter is included to give the reader who is not engaged in the minerals industry a glimpse of the methods used. In the case of non-metals there are generally two processes involved, mining and manufacturing. For metals, and increasingly for non-metals, there are three: mining, winning (or concentrating), and refining. The product then goes to the fabricator, which in an integrated company may be just to another division. Each of these steps will be briefly reviewed.

Throughout the mineral industries the most overwhelming event of the century was the "oil shock." From 1973 to 1980 the price of crude oil increased 1700%–2000%. Mineral processing is energy intensive, and this factor has colored the complexion of the industry. All mineral producers have had to conduct energy audits and revise their concepts of costs. Previously the major escalation had been that of rapidly increasing labor costs, about 5% per year. This had been swallowed by substitution of energy for labor, reducing the labor factor per unit of output. The escalation of energy cost has been the most difficult problem to be faced. Meanwhile the market prices of major mineral products have increased only slightly over the period. Mining companies have had to accept the major proportion of inflation imposed by the "energy shock," and this factor has thrown the minerals industries into a deep recession.

A second factor that has simultaneously battered the industry has been increasingly severe environmental regulations. In most cases, the only way these requirements could be met was by major capital expenditure. For example, on the new Hidalgo Copper Smelter in New Mexico, pollution control facilities added 67% to the capital costs. This "one-two punch" compounded a severe recession with weak demand and low prices.

No one will argue that improved environmental quality was not necessary. In the U.S., however, the regulations have been applied selectively and seemingly capriciously or punitively to the mineral industries. In Germany, Japan, and France, where environmental concerns are also strong, the governments have subsidized the changes made necessary by increased awareness of environmental problems. American industry has had to meet the costs from its own resources or cease operating.

By having to utilize all of the available capital resources to meet energy and environmental problems, the minerals industries of the United States have been unable to build modern processing facilities. Thus they have fallen behind competitively, contributing to increased imports and trade deficits.

MINING OR EXTRACTING

About 85% of the minerals in the U.S. are produced by open pit methods. This total includes all of the gravel pits and rock quarries, the huge phosphate mines in North Carolina and Florida, the iron mines in Minnesota, the large uranium mines in Wyoming and Texas, the vast copper mines in Utah, Arizona, New Mexico, Montana, and Nevada, and about half of the coal production of the country.

Second in importance is room and pillar mining accounting for about 12% of production. This encompasses about half of the coal, most of the salt, and nearly all of the potash and trona, plus a majority of the lead and zinc mines.

Table 1
Mining and Mineral Extraction Methods

Method	Product
Open pit mining	Sand and gravel
	Quarry stone
	Clay
	Phosphate
	Copper
	Coal
	Other
Room and pillar mining and longwall retreating	Coal
	Salt
	Trona
	Potash
Stoping and miscellaneous	Salt
	Uranium
	Copper
	Clay and aggregate
	Magnesium

The balance comprises solution and *in situ* mining of salt, some uranium, and a little copper. In addition, all of the "conventional mines" (the underground mining of the metals) fall in this category. A small amount of marine dredging of oyster shell, clay, and aggregate is also included, with magnesium, salt, and minor elements being extracted from sea water.

Each of these methods will be briefly described.

Open Pit Mining: As shown in Figure 5, massive, near-surface ore bodies are mined by a series of benches with "risers" commonly about 10 m high. Rock drills work on the "tread" of each step, drilling holes about 20 cm (8 inches) in diameter to about one meter below the floor of the next lower bench. A group of holes is blasted together using dynamite, or more commonly *Anfo*, (ammonium nitrate plus fuel oil). This "fertilizer" is considerably less expensive than dynamite.

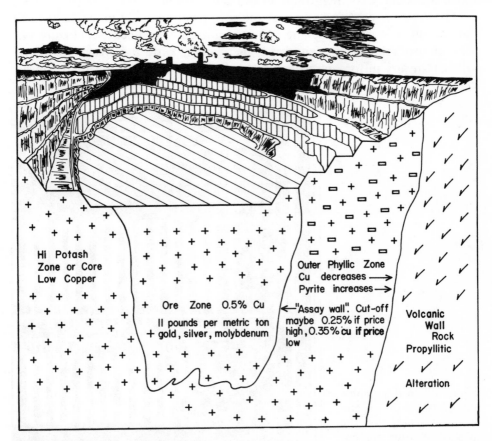

Figure 5 A schematic shows the structure of an open pit mine. Lines indicate areas that are profitable to mine.

A shovel with a *dipper* size of from 10–20 yd³ capacity loads into 70–150 ton trucks for haulage to the mill in the large operations. There may be three or four benches, or as many as 20–30. The largest open pit in the U.S. is that of Kennecott Corporation at Bingham, Utah. If one happens to be in the vicinity, it is worth taking the side trip to the observation point to look at it.

Room and Pillar Mining: The best way to illustrate the room and pillar method is by taking the "lid" off of a mine, showing the ore zone and the workings (see Figure 6a). The purpose of the pillars is to support the roof for an indefinite time. In theory the stresses will arch and transfer to the pillars. The pillars are composed of good ore or coal that can never be retrieved. The percentage that must be left for support varies with the depth of the ore bed and the strength of the overlying rocks. Ordinarily 40%–60% of the ore can be mined. In some coal mines, after the mine has been abandoned the rooms cave in and the surface is disturbed.

In mines for coal and some of the softer non-metallic minerals like salt and potash a massive machine called a *continuous miner* (see Figure 6b) cuts out the mineral bed and loads the product onto a conveyor or truck, which transfers it to a main haulage belt for conveyance out of the mine.

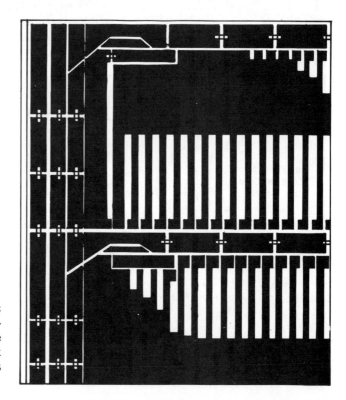

Figure 6a In this graphic representation of a room-and-pillar mining plan, the mined out areas are not shaded. Overlying rocks have been removed.

Figure 6b Jeffry 1036 Continuous Miner working in a thin coal seam. This machine, weighing 38,555 kg (85,000 pounds) will produce 10 tons per minute under optimum conditions and can work in a coal bed a little over one meter thick. Photo courtesy Dresser Industries, Inc.

A highly mechanized mine of this type produces a large tonnage at low cost with minimum personnel.

In harder rock, such as in the lead mines of Missouri, the face or breast is drilled with rotary compressed air drills from a "jumbo" which may have as many as four drills mounted on it. The rock is blasted with dynamite and loaded mechanically into rail cars or trucks for transfer to the main haulage system and eventually hoisted up the shaft. Some of these mines have hundreds of miles of openings underground. Room and pillar mining produces 98% of the coal mined from underground in the United States.

Longwall Retreating: A coal seam or a mineral bed may underlie weak ground or be so valuable that it is desirable to recover a larger percentage of the mineral (up to 90%). In this case *headings* are driven to the limit of the ore zone and the most distant ore is mined first, with the mine retreating toward the shaft. Temporary support is provided beyond the face, and as the ore face retreats the supports are moved closer to the working zone. As a result, the worked-out area collapses. Thus the surface is temporarily disturbed but is eventually restored at a level lower by the thickness of the ore zone removed. If this is pasture land or a wheat field, there is little loss of production from the surface. This method cannot be used under a town or superhighway or under a river which might break into the mine. Generally as much as possible of the waste, which has to be mined with the coal in some mines, is replaced in the worked-out area before the roof is permitted to collapse. Longwall retreating is a more expensive method than room and pillar mining, but large-scale production is possible. This method accounts for about 2% of coal mined in the United States, with the proportion slowly increasing.

Block Caving: When a valuable mineral is disseminated evenly throughout a large block of mineralized rock and is buried too deeply to permit mining as an open pit mine, block caving is a possible alternative. Copper, iron, and molybdenum are the metals most commonly mined by this method; the only industrial minerals so obtained are diamonds and asbestos. Not all deposits will "cave" properly. Figure 7 is a diagram showing the method of development. The height of a block ranges from a minimum of about 30 m (100 feet) to a maximum of 300 m (1000 feet), with most blocks in the 100–150 m range (330–500 feet). The horizontal measurements of a block vary from about 25 m (90 feet) to 60 m (200 feet) square. If one horizontal dimension is more than 1.5 times the shorter dimension, the method is called panel caving. Block caving requires an ore that is naturally well fractured. If 20% or more of the rock breaks in fragments larger than 1.5 m (5 feet), there are likely to be "hang ups" and plugging of *draw points*, so the method cannot be used. On the other hand, if the ore breaks too finely and particularly if it contains much clay, it will pack and not flow from the draw points. Low-grade or waste rock may cave with the ore and this dilution, which can be serious, averages 16%. While some mines with production as low as 2500 tons per day use the method, it is most commonly used when production of 15,000 to 40,000 tons per day is required. With large tonnage and good operating conditions, cost per ton may be nearly as low as for open pit practice. Less explosive is required.

Narrow Vein Methods: When an ore body occurs in a narrow and steeply dipping vein one of several methods may be used, depending on the strength of the ore and walls and width of the vein. Since these methods are

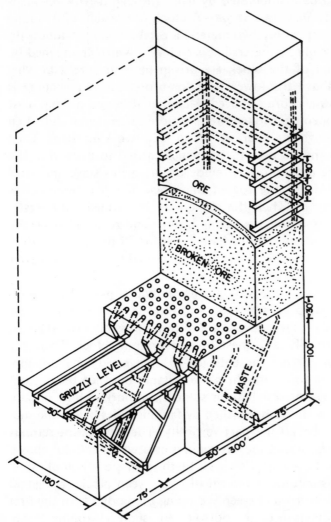

Figure 7 This diagram shows the block caving method of mining.

much more costly, the value of the ore must be greater to justify mining so these methods are less common today. Where labor costs are lower or where the product value has increased sharply (gold and silver) the following methods are used. (1) *Square set stoping*—When the ore and walls are weak, timber "sets" are used, with a framing of heavy timbers. Posts are used in four corners and cross pieces placed between them to make the sets rigid. The sets have to be carefully fitted and blocks inserted to support the ground. This method is very expensive and requires a forest for support. One variation is called the "Mitchell slice." Mitchell must have been a sadist because some of the posts used are five feet in circumference and the trees used for support have to be manipulated by hand through narrow openings by two or three men. (2) *Shrinkage stope*—A block of ore about 30 m long and the width of the vein (possibly two meters) is established as a stope with a projected height of possibly 50 meters between levels, which are opened by *drifts. Raises* at each end of the block are driven between levels. Leaving about six feet of ore above the lower drift for protection, an opening is driven between the raises and ore removed. Men then drill upward and blast the ore down into the opening. Broken ore fills more space than it did when it was in place. Just enough ore is drawn off to leave working room. Then another round is drilled and blasted, the sequence carried to the top of the block. About 35% of the broken ore is removed during this stage and after the blasting has proceeded to the top of the block, the remaining ore is drawn off from the bottom. Then the stope may be refilled with waste. (3) *Cut and fill*—In this method the ore is broken and removed from the stope with a scraper, then waste is immediately used to fill the space created, leaving enough room for miners to get in and drill the next round over head. (4) *Sublevel stoping*—When the vein is fairly wide (6 m or more) and the ground and walls are quite strong, this method is used. There is no limit on width, and it is used in large blocks too strong and coherent to use block caving successfully. Two levels are driven, possibly 100–120 m (330–400 feet) apart vertically, and these limit the mining block. From the lower level *draw raises* are driven and enlarged to an inverted cone, possibly 8–10 m in diameter at the top, with the same distance between the bottom and top of the cone. Then intermediate or sublevels are driven horizontally above the draw cones and the vein is drilled by fanning holes below the sublevel. The sublevels may be 20 m apart vertically. The lowest slot retreats first across the draw cones, and as soon as room is created for the slot above, it too is mined. This can be a fairly low-cost method where it is applicable. (5) *Sublevel caving*—This method is intermediate between block caving and sublevel stoping. It is used in wide, steeply dipping ore bodies with the first slot mined from the top instead of the bottom as in sublevel stoping. Waste caves into the area after mining. Pillars must be left to protect working areas. Under optimum conditions 85–90% of the ore is recovered with about 16% dilution. Mining by this method is quite highly mechanized. Drilling is fanned overhead and ore pulled through the sublevel rather than from the bottom.

Solution Mining: Solution mining involves injection of a special solvent into an ore bed and pumping the solution back to the surface for extraction of the solute. Some mineral deposits formed by the evaporation of saline water are subsequently covered by clay and indurated. Water is the solvent injected into the formation containing these evaporites. They can be dissolved and pumped out of wells as brine, with the salt subsequently crystallized by evaporation or used directly as brine in chemical processes. Minerals produced in this manner are common salt (NaCl), now potash (KCl) and trona (sodium carbonate). Any of the precipitates that are soluble could be mined in this manner if there is continuity in the mineral body. This method requires careful control of the plumbing system but otherwise it is quite simple.

In another example of solution mining, sulphuric acid is pumped into an oxidized body containing copper minerals or uranium ores. In this case the ore must contain a minimum of acid-soluble constituents other than the ore. If much calcium carbonate (lime) is present, the acid will be consumed in dissolving lime and costs will be prohibitively high. The dissolved metal is recovered by solvent extraction (see section on Sea Water Extraction and Evaporation).

Geothermal hot water sometimes occurs as a brine containing fairly high concentrations of heavy metals. One of the brines in Southern California reportedly contains important and recoverable amounts of gold. If production of thermal energy from those brines is feasible, gold will be a by-product. This will be mining of a natural solution.

Experimental injection of water into hot granite at Los Alamos, New Mexico, has resulted in recovery of sufficient steam to operate a small generator. This method of "mining energy" holds promise for the future in some localities.

Rather closely related is the mining of sulphur by the Frasch method (see Part II, Sulphur) by injecting superheated steam to melt the sulphur, then pumping it to the surface in the liquid state.

Dredging: Dredging is excavating unconsolidated earth, sand and gravel from beneath water by a large machine, usually floating. In mining, valuable minerals are extracted and the earth discarded. Some minerals occur in stream gravel, on the shallow portion of the continental slope, or in bays and estuaries. Most of these concentrations were formed during the Ice Ages, when sea level was 100 m or more below the level of today and mineral deposits were formed in stream beds or by streams and waves on shorelines, which are now submerged. Examples are the heavy minerals such as gold on the beaches of Nome and in the ancient stream gravels in Alaska, diamonds offshore and on the beaches in southwestern Africa, and rutile, zircon, ilmenite, monazite, and magnetite in Sri Lanka, Australia, Florida, and other places. Extensive tin placers are found on the submerged coastal plains of Indonesia, Malaysia, and Thailand where large dredge ships are used to bring the gravels to the surface for processing.

The largest tonnage of product from marine dredging is the gravel operation in the English Channel between England and France. The area was above sea level during the ice ages. Similar deposits are available in many places to relieve aggregate shortages. Modern dredges have the capability of reaching to 100 m or more in depth.

At some locations extensive reefs of fossil oyster shell have accumulated and have been dredged for making lime and portland cement. Most of the operations of this kind in San Francisco Bay, Mobile Bay, and off-shore Louisiana have been terminated because of exhaustion of deposits or by environmental authorities.

Dredging of phosphate deposits off the Carolina and California coasts could extend the reserves of phosphorous for fertilizer. The manganese nodules in the deep ocean are potential sources of manganese, nickel, copper, and cobalt that may be commercially profitable in several years (see Chapter 8). Dredging for aggregate on land continues to be a big industry.

Sea Water Extraction and Evaporation: The oceans are an inexhaustible reservoir of many minerals. The most important is water. There are no technical problems involved in recovering water from the ocean. About 90% of the cost of this process is energy, so if the energy is supplied by petroleum, the cost is now 2000% higher than it was a few years ago. Where it was marginally economic before, it is only a high cost source of water today.

The most abundant dissolved constituent in sea water is common salt (NaCl). From ancient times this essential for nutrition has been obtained by evaporating sea water. Today in dry climates solar evaporation is a major source of salt. In commercial production water passes through a series of ponds or "pans" and first calcium carbonate (lime) and calcium sulphate (gypsum) precipitate, since they are less soluble than salt. Next iron oxide precipitates, and in flying over the east coast of southern San Francisco Bay, the bright red pans where the iron drops out are very visible. The concentrated brine is evaporated to the point at which the salt precipitates but the *mother liquor* is not evaporated to dryness because some of the constituents are undesirable. In some places magnesium, potash, bromine, and iodine are also extracted from this residual liquor.

Japan has announced a plant to extract 10 tons of uranium per year from sea water. The uranium content of the ocean is 1–3 parts per billion. This should be regarded as a pilot plant, since 30 million tons of sea water have to pass through the plant daily if recovery is 80% in order to obtain this amount of uranium per year, valued at only $650,000.

Sea water is the major ore for magnesium and an important source of magnesia.

A scheme to recover gold from sea water was initiated in Germany after World War I as a proposed method of paying off the war debt. The process worked, but was uneconomic, probably because the engineers made an error in the decimal point. Average sea water contains 0.02 parts per billion; i.e., 50,000 tons must be processed to obtain one gram of gold.

BENEFICIATION

Beneficiation is the process of winnowing the valuable mineral commodity from the other (generally valueless) constituents with which it is associated in nature. In general, it is a method of concentration, preparing the product for the refining stage. In most of the methods of beneficiation the valuable constituent has to be liberated from the waste, usually by crushing the ore to a fine size. The first stage utilizes a jaw or gyratory crusher which may be able to crush fragments one meter in size. Secondary and tertiary crushers may reduce the ore to about 1 cm size. Subsequently the ore is ground in a *mill* to the fineness necessary to free most of the valuable constituents from the waste. It is then treated in one of several processes to make the *concentrate.*

Handsorting: The simplest and oldest method of concentration is to judge by eye which pieces of rock are ore and which waste and to pile them separately. Sometimes this is done by the miners underground, and the low grade or waste is never brought out of the mine. This method can only be used where labor costs are low and the value of the product is quite high. A slightly more sophisticated system is to hoist the ore out of the mine, crush it to particles less than 7.5 cm (3 inches) in diameter and screen out the fine material then wash it. The coarse fragments are placed on a conveyor belt and passed along a line of laborers who methodically remove the valuable mineral from the belt. It requires a readily observable difference between ore and waste, such as white quartz (with gold) from black rock (waste). It may be possible to concentrate the ore 10 times in this way and save the cost of fine-grinding 90% of the waste.

Photoelectric Sorting: Instead of a line of laborers picking ore from a conveyor belt, mechanical means can be used. A photoelectric cell picks up the reflection of light from the light-colored pieces, actuating an arm that shoves the fragment off the belt. Variations on this are to have the cell sensitive to fluorescent light and, in the case of diamonds, to use x-rays that cause the diamonds to luminesce. A photo multiplier tube detects the light, a small jet of air is activated, which blows the diamond off the belt.

Gravity Concentration: If particles of different specific gravities, heavy and light, are bounced together in water, the dense particles move toward the bottom of the vessel and the light particles to the top. When ore minerals such as galena (lead sulphide) occur in large lumps, an effective concentration can be made at coarse size. The device for bouncing the ore is called a *jig.* There are generally three products, a concentrate from the bottom, waste from the top, and a *middling*, which must be processed further to liberate the mineral. Another method of gravity concentration used with coarse sizes is by *heavy media separation.* This method depends on creating a dense fluid with controlled specific gravity. Just as wood will float in water, quartz with a specific gravity of 2.65 will float on a fluid with a specific gravity of 2.85, yet a lump of galena, cassiterite, wolframite, or other heavy mineral, or even a mixture of ore and quartz will sink to the bottom. The quartz waste can then be skimmed off and discarded. The dense fluid is made by suspending fine, heavy material in water by violent stirring. Usually the suspended material is magnetite or ferrosilicon, materials that can be recovered from the waste and concentrated by magnets. A third method of gravity separation is used for finer material. It is called a *shaking table*. This is a large, flat table with small ribs running lengthwise. The table has a little tilt cross-wise and it is activated by two jerky motions, one vertical and the other horizontal. The result is the waste jumps over the low ribs and moves across the table while the heavy ore particles move lengthwise along the ribs and are collected as a concentrate.

Magnetic: Finely ground magnetite can be separated from other minerals by passing a stream of ground ore over magnets. Another application of magnetic separation is in the use of a very high intensity magnetic field that will attract the iron in minerals not normally magnetic, such as biotite, hornblende, pyrite, and hematite. This method is used to remove small amounts of iron that are deleterious in ceramics and glass manufacture.

Electrostatic: This method is used on fine-grained, dry particles. Some minerals will pick up static electricity much more readily than others. Then as they pass from a belt through a field of opposite charge, the charged minerals are attracted to it and separate from the ore stream.

Leaching: Some minerals are soluble in certain chemicals, and this property can be used in concentrating the valuable product. If the net value contained is rather high, leaching may be done in vats where the desired commodity can be rapidly extracted. If the value is rather low (for example 0.4% copper as oxide, or 1–2 grams of gold per ton), it may be heap-leached, with ore piled up and sprayed with the solvent. Copper and uranium are leached with sulphuric acid, gold and silver with cyanide solution. The solution is collected and pumped to an extraction or precipitation plant. Leaching is also done *in situ* (in the ground) for copper oxides, carbonates, chalcocite (a sulphide), and chrysocolla (a silicate), and uranium.

Solvent Extraction: A rather new process for recovery of metals from solution was developed by General Mills. Copper in solution from leaching or mine water as copper sulphate in fairly low concentration is stirred with a solution of a liquid ion exchange reagent (LIX) dissolved in kerosene. The copper is removed from the water and concentrated in the kerosene fraction. The kerosene floats on the water and is separated from it. The copper is "stripped" from the extractant with sulphuric acid, and the concentrated copper sulphate solution goes to electrolysis for refining. Similarly, dilute solutions of uranium sulphate are concentrated by solvent extraction, precipitated as U_3O_8, and sent to an enrichment plant.

Cyanidation: Gold and silver can be dissolved from their finely ground ores by sodium cyanide solution. While this is a deadly poison, if the pH of the solution is kept high (basic), the poisonous gas will not be released. This is an old process and actually is a form of leaching, but it is a specific for precious metals. These metals are then commonly precipitated by use of zinc powder. A new technique has been developed recently called carbon-in-pulp. Activated carbon stirred with the gold cyanide solution precipitates the gold and the carbon is easily separated and chemically "stripped" of the gold content (or burned to concentrate the gold).

Flotation: The most important method of concentrating metal sulphides and some non-metallic minerals is by selective flotation. This is a chemical and physical process that has been developed to a high science. The ground ore is mixed with water and a frothing reagent in a vat or cell. The valuable minerals attach to bubbles and rise to the surface of the flotation cell where they are skimmed off. The chemistry can be so closely controlled that the bubbles will attach to chalcopyrite, the copper ore mineral $(CuFeS_2)$ and not attach to pyrite (FeS_2) which is a waste product with many similar properties and is always present with chalcopyrite. Other metal sulphides can be sequentially floated by changing the chemistry of the solution. It was the discovery of this process that made it possible to utilize low-grade mineral deposits. The discoverers, Francis and A. Stanley Elmore, who patented the process in 1898, should be credited with one of the great discoveries of the past century. These men made industrialization possible, yet few have ever heard of them and most are unaware of the process and its importance.

Selective Crystallization and Precipitation: By carefully controlling the concentration of solutions in the evaporation of sea water the desired product (e.g., salt) can be crystallized in a nearly pure state. A part of the process for separation of sodium and potassium chlorides depends on the increase of solubility of potassium chloride (KCl) in hot solution while sodium chloride changes little with temperature. Thus KCl is crystallized on cooling. Some minerals can be precipitated by changing the pH and others by addition of an ion which forms a relatively insoluble compound.

Calcining, Leaching, and Precipitation: Bauxite is treated with caustic soda at elevated temperature and pressure to produce soluble sodium aluminate, which is leached from the associated constituents of the ore, then precipitated as alumina (Al_2O_3) with twice the Al content of bauxite. The product is then ready for electrolytic refining. In the production of magnesia, the process is reversed, the magnesium carbonate is precipitated from sea water, then calcined, then leached and dehydrated.

REFINING

Refining is removal of enough of the remaining impurities in a concentrate or impure metal to make it commercially usable and converting it to the form required by commerce. There are three major divisions of refining: *pyrometallurgy* or fire refining, commonly called smelting; *electrometallurgy* or electrolysis, either in the fused state or with water as a medium; and *hydrometallurgy*, usually a step in concentrating the raw minerals (hence included in beneficiation) but which is also an important method of refining. There are also a few processes that do not properly fall in any of these categories, for example gaseous diffusion of uranium.

The field of refining is very much in flux at present. Some of the older methods do not meet the new concepts of environmental purity. The investment in refining plants is enormous, and the cost of trying to make them meet air quality standards may cost from $100–200 million. An estimate of the cost of making the copper smelter at Anaconda, Montana, meet environmental standards was $400 million, so the smelter was shut down and the concentrate shipped to Japan for smelting and refining. With the price of copper very low, there was no way to amortize the cost of meeting environmental standards or to build a new refining plant. Actually, Anaconda did build a new hydrometallurgical refinery using the *Arbiter process*, brought it into production, but then shut it down and put it in "moth balls." It could not produce copper competitively. This is a good illustration of *Schon's Law*: "almost nothing new works." When it is necessary to stake 10s or 100s of millions of dollars on a new, untried process, management is reluctant to do so until someone else has done it successfully first.

In mining and concentrating there are a limited number of methods that can be applied. In refining far more chemical properties can be utilized and the possible combinations of processes for each mineral are quite varied. Frequently a concentrate from an individual mine may require a process tailored to its character.

Rather than describing a flow sheet for several commodities, brief descriptions of the unit processes will be given. Under "Commodities" in Part II, the application of each process for different minerals is described.

Pyrometallurgy: Several different processes fall under pyrometallurgy. (1) *Roasting*—is heating to the point where oxidation occurs without melting. The purpose is to burn sulphides to oxides for subsequent treatment. Copper is an example of a concentrate that is roasted, partially eliminating sulphur as the dioxide. The equipment used is a tower with many grates. Rakes drag the concentrate away from the center on one level and toward the center on the next lower one. This method is highly polluting. It is difficult to make it meet environmental standards so it is now rarely used. (2) *Sintering*—is heating the ore to the point of incipient fusion, until enough is melted so that the particles stick together. This is used in preparing fine iron ore for the blast furnace and sometimes in making lightweight aggregate from clay. (3) *Calcining*—is a process of heating to drive off an undesirable constituent in a kiln. Limestone fragments are heated to decarbonation, driving off CO_2. Portland cement is usually made in rotary kilns; the "raw mix" is heated to the point where chemical reactions forming cement can occur. The product is called "clinker;" it must then be ground with gypsum to produce cement. Plaster is made by calcining gypsum in kettles. (4) *Distillation*—is heating an ore to the point where the mineral decomposes, at a temperature above the boiling point of the metal of interest, which is then collected in a condenser. Mercury and zinc are refined by this process. (5) *Matte smelting*—is the formation of an artificial sulphide (for example, copper and iron in desired proportions) in a *reverberatory furnace.* This type of furnace may be as much as 40 m (130 feet) long. It has several gas- or oil-fired burners at one end and the flame is directed across the top of the concentrate. The concentrate melts and a *slag*, which has been chemically designed to do a minimum of damage to the *refractories* lining the furnace, floats and is removed from the matte. This is an energy intensive step, and waste heat must be recovered to make it economic. (6) *The converter*—is a refractory-lined rotating drum about 4 m in diameter. A compressed air pipe girdles the converter, and at every ~30 cm, air ports called tuyeres, ~3 cm in diameter, lead into the furnace. The converter is charged with molten matte and air is blown into it. First the sulphur in the iron is burned off; the iron then reacts with the silica, forming slag, which is poured off. After slagging is complete, the sulphur in the copper begins to burn, and this continues until only molten copper remains. If the resulting metal is poured into forms, it has a peculiar blistered appearance and is called "blister copper." (7) *Blast furnace*—is one of the most massive pieces of machinery in use. It rises 75 m (250 feet) or more from the ground. It is used for reducing iron ore to metal and to producing slag from the earthy constituents. Coke, limestone, and iron ore are charged at the top by a double bell arrangement, the top bell closing before the lower is opened, so gases are not lost in charging. The furnace operates continuously. The coke produces carbon monoxide, which reduces the iron oxide to metal. An air blast is maintained to burn the coke, which melts the reduced iron and the calcium silicate slag. Both are tapped at the bottom of the furnace. Other furnaces that are similar but smaller in size are used for some other metals. (8) *The Bessemer converter*—is a pot about 3 m in diameter and 6 m high, is lined with refractory, and has holes in the bottom to admit blasts of air. It is charged with molten pig iron, and air is blown through it. Excess carbon is burned and silicon and manganese are slagged. The blow takes about 12 minutes and produces a low-carbon steel. (9) *The open hearth*—is another furnace for refining pig iron with the addition of scrap. The secret of its success was a pair of chambers with brick checker work to alternate as flues and air pre-heaters. This permits heating the iron to a higher temperature. An open hearth may produce 125 tons of steel per day. The furnace is lined with basic refractories, and a basic slag is produced. Capacity has been greatly increased by using oxygen instead of air to burn the gas. This furnace produces a superior steel. (10) *The electric furnace*—is used to produce steel of closely controlled specifications, ordinarily using scrap iron as raw material. Plants can vary in capacity from 250 kg to 50 tons per day. Electrodes of graphite are used and the resistance of air and slag to passage of electric current heats the charge to the melting point. Electricity is an expensive source of heat but it is convenient and does not contain the contaminants that are introduced by burning gas. Alloying agents can be closely controlled, making specialty steels possible. (11) *The flash smelter*—is a relatively new type of furnace used in refining copper and a few other metals. It is a reverberatory furnace designed to increase the SO_2 in the gases, making it easier to control pollution. Oxygen is used in blowing through the furnace. (12) *Continuous smelting*—efforts have been made to combine the smelting step that produces a matte with the converter stage to be able to feed concentrate in at one end and remove blister copper from the other on a continuous basis rather than as two batch processes.

Electrometallurgy: Electrolytic refining consists of immersing an anode of impure metal and a cathode of pure metal (a "starter sheet") in a solution containing ions of the metal and passing an electrical current through the solution. Ions of the metal are formed from the impure electrode, migrate through the solution and precipitate on the cathode. Copper is refined in this manner, as are several other metals. Impurities either drop to the bottom of the tank and form a sludge or go into solution and are not precipitated at the controlled current density used. The sludge may contain gold and silver and, in the case of nickel refining, the platinum group metals. These by-products are recovered by other processes. Electrolytic copper is called *cathode copper*, and is 99.9% pure. It is melted and cast into forms called *wire bar.*

Some metals cannot be electroplated from water solutions but can be refined in the molten state. Aluminum, which ranks second in tonnage of metal produced, is prepared by dissolving the alumina (Al_2O_3) in a bath of molten cryolite (a natural or artificial mineral with the composition Na_3AlF_6) and heating it by passage of an electrical current through the molten bath. Pure aluminum metal sinks to the bottom of the cell, where it accumulates and is drawn off periodically and cast in molds for fabrication. This process is energy intensive (8–10 kwh per pound of metal), but ALCOA has announced a new process involving aluminum chloride, which promises to reduce the required power by as much as 50%. Magnesium and possibly lead and zinc can also be refined by electrolysis.

Hydrometallurgy: There has been a great deal of research on processes to leach sulphide ores and by-pass the smelter. The first copper process to reach the production stage was the *arbiter process.* A plant was built at the smelter of Anaconda in Montana but subsequently shut down as not commercially profitable. The Cyprus Process (*CYMET*) was tested and abandoned but other new processes are being tested. Most of the attempts to develop a successful process for recovery of copper from concentrate involve a ferric chloride-cuprous chloride leach. Four or five different approaches are being tried, but none is in commercial operation. Theoretically sulphide leaching should be possible with less energy, less pollution, good recovery of by-products, and lower capital costs—hence the intense interest. One of the problems is that the chlorine compounds involved are highly corrosive.

Hydrometallurgy is also used in two of the processes of recovering nickel and cobalt from lateritic ores. In one of these the ore is dried and reduced to the metallic state, then leached by ammonia and ammonium carbonate. Nickel and cobalt carbonates are precipitated, then calcined to a high grade oxide. The other process involves a slurry, which is heated by steam, then leached with concentrated sulphuric acid and high pressure steam at about 250°C. The leach solution is filtered and neutralized with lime. Nickel and cobalt sulphides are then precipitated with H_2S ("rotten egg" gas). The concentrate is treated as the sulphide. These processes are energy intensive, and it was reported that by mid-1981 when nickel had dropped to about $3.50 per pound all laterite operations were losing money.

GASEOUS DIFFUSION

The process for refining uranium is unique to this metal. "Yellow cake" is a pure uranium oxide, U_3O_8, a mixture of the two isotopes ^{235}U and ^{238}U. The former is fissionable and occurs to the extent of 0.7% of the element in nature. To be used as fuel in a nuclear reactor, this isotope must be concentrated to at least 3%. Weapons-grade uranium must be concentrated to about 70%. Since the isotopes are the same element, their chemistry is identical and chemical processes will not separate them. A process depending on the difference in mass of the isotopes was developed, called gaseous diffusion. For this uranium hexafluoride (a gas) is used, and the process depends on $^{235}UF_6$ being accelerated to a slightly greater velocity than $^{238}UF_6$; when this is done, the former will pass through a semipermeable tube more readily than the latter. Each stage gives very slight enrichment, but by multiple stages the desired concentration can be attained.

CHAPTER 8

CRYSTAL GAZING

Fortunetellers have various methods of foretelling the future. One of the oldest is called *scrying*, or crystal gazing. The crystal ball was originally made of quartz. Counterfeit "crystals" made of glass are reportedly used today by some, but without the symmetry of the quartz crystal, true foretelling is impossible, according to the practitioners of the art. The crystal ball should be oriented with the "c" axis vertical, and by looking down the axis, a "sensitive" individual can observe, in rhombohedral symmetry, three divisions of 120° each, which represent past, present, and future.

This chapter is an effort to foresee some of the problems and developments that will affect mineral resources during the remainder of the century. Since most forecasts for periods as long as 20 years look amusing to ridiculous in retrospect, these extrapolations, too, may be distorted by the random factors that fate has a habit of interposing.

IS THERE A MINERAL RESOURCE SCARCITY?

With some reservations, the answer to this controversial question is no. Considering the substitutions that can be made, there should be little concern on this score. Were any non-fuel mineral to have a price increase comparable to that of petroleum (20 fold) it would be available in great abundance. Most minerals would be abundant if the price were doubled. In fact, most of them would be abundant if the high price of the period 1974–1980 were sustained. The United States will never be self-sufficient in chromium, and can have adequate production of nickel, cobalt, and manganese only if it produces nodules from the sea floor, but in almost any other mineral, price determines sufficiency.

Four metals are in such abundant supply that they can meet almost any structural demand. These are iron, aluminum, magnesium, and titanium.

Shortages of minerals can be expected, however. Abundance and adequate supply cannot be equated without the ultimate resource. The real problem is availability of a low-cost energy resource. The same answer always appears: petroleum is not a low-cost energy source and within a generation it will be shrinking as a major energy resource. The only energy supplies on which civilization can be based are coal and nuclear power, with the possibility that solar power will develop in the first half of the next century to fulfill part of the requirement.

In an article in *Science* (June 27, 1980) Dr. Julian Simon stirred up controversy with an article entitled "Resources, Population, Environment: An Oversupply of False Bad News." His view that the "oil shock" was a minor wiggle on a declining cost curve for energy, that it does not reflect an abrupt discontinuity, is diametrically opposite to this analysis. This assessment, that there is no shortage of mineral resources, agrees with his view but from a very different basis.

Simon used copper as a commodity representative of mineral resources. To prove his argument that mineral resources are infinite, he stated, "Even the total weight of the earth is not a theoretical limit to the amount of copper that might be available to earthlings in the future." It is the word "available" that makes his analysis improbable, one of his weakest points.

Extending the analogy of copper, it is pertinent to consider the energy required to recover the metal from its ore. There can be no question about the adequacy of copper for the real-time future, but some mines have reserves containing 1% copper. Some companies try to produce from mines with less than half that grade. Thus the energy per kilogram required to produce the same amount of copper more than doubles. Table 2 illustrates the relative amount of energy needed.

Table 2

Relative energy required to recover copper from various grades of ore
(Open pit mining through milling; index set at 1.00 for 1% ore)

Grade (%)	Kg/per ton	Recovery (%)	Kg Recovered	Energy Index
2.0	20	92	18.4	0.49
1.0	10	90	9.0	1.00
0.8	8	89	7.12	1.26
0.6	6	88	5.28	1.70
0.5	5	87	4.35	2.07
0.4	4	85	3.40	2.65
0.3	3	79	2.31	3.90
0.2	2	70	1.40	6.43
0.1	1	50	0.50	18.00

These data are even more impressive when shown graphically, as in Figure 8. The energy cost increases geometrically as grade declines and approaches infinity at about 0.05% copper.

Table 2 represents the energy to mine and produce the copper concentrade only. The energy cost at Chuquicamata, Chile, is roughly one-eighth of what it would be in a mine with a grade of 0.3%. The latter cannot compete in a free market as long as the high grade deposits can supply the world's needs. The energy consumed at the concentrate stage represents only about one-fourth of the total energy required to smelt, refine, fabricate, and market the copper. These steps are the same, whatever the source of the concentrate. Therefore, if society has to pay five times as much energy to mine copper from a new source, the total energy expended only doubles in the finished product. In other words, if society is willing to pay twice the energy price, the available copper will increase greatly.

It is difficult to estimate the magnitude of the copper protoresource because deposits that would average 0.3% copper have been abandoned without a thorough study. There are many porphyry copper systems that

Figure 8 An index of the energy used to produce a kilogram of copper, plotted against the percentage of copper in the ore.

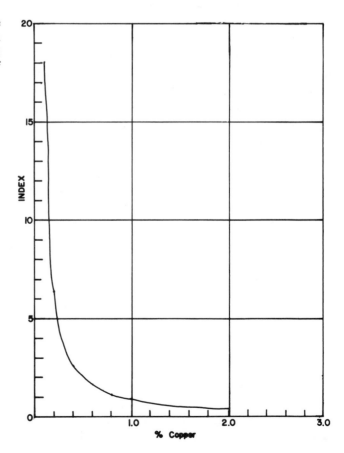

might become economic. In addition, there are basalts with zones of this grade, as well as extensive sedimentary areas carrying copper. Protoresources today, they will become reserves if the energy cost is acceptable.

In the last 20 years, few large copper deposits have been found with a grade as high as 0.8%–1.0%. The bulk of the disseminated copper deposits average around 0.5%, with many of them at about 0.4%. At 0.5%, the energy cost is 4.2 times that of Chuquicamata in Chile, which in the past had a grade of 2%. While 0.5% copper was a profitable grade in 1973 and for a short while in 1974, today no mine can operate at that grade unelss they have a subsidy, usually from by-products.

Thus there was a marked decrease in world copper ore reserves ("ore" being mineral that can be mined *at a profit*) as the result of the "oil shock." The copper is still there in the ground, converted back to protoresources. There is no shortage, even at a give-away price, because the recession reduced demand and the subsidies sustained otherwise uneconomic production. Consumption would have to increase by about 25% to cause shortages. There is very little copper that can be produced at $0.80 per pound in the U.S., but in Chile there are still substantial amounts of a higher grade that are subsidized by co-products and cheaper labor.

Thus no major supply deficit is imminent, although shortages may develop from time to time. Industrial nations will not "run out" of the major metals, though dependency on Third World nations will increase. The fallacy in many of the scare stories about scarcity is the total tonnage involved. For example, the United States is 97% dependent on foreign sources for tantalum. World production is on the order of 1100 tons, and the United Stated uses about 800 tons. This is much too small a production total to be included in the commodity section (Part II). The whole requirement could be loaded on about 15 rail cars. At $6 per ounce it is nearly as expensive as silver, and substitutions can be made for most uses. There are reports of discovery of a deposit carrying 0.4% tantalum in Canada. At this grade, a mine of 1000 tons per day of ore could supply the entire world requirement, and a small operation of 250 tons per day would supply enough to drastically reduce the price.

Thus the Club of Rome in its forecasts of a bleak future is wrong in predicting exhaustion of resources, if a low-cost energy source is available. OPEC did society a favor by effectively drawing attention to the fact that petroleum has served its time as an inexpensive supply of energy.

MINERAL RESOURCE POLITICS

It should be obvious that the one thing the U.S. should *not* do is to dissipate its limited financial resources on the mistaken premise that the

Middle East oil fields are essential to its future. There is no advantage to be gained by building up an obsolete, World War II-type military force, an ill-conceived Maginot Line, to defend them. At any point in time the clock could start ticking and in a few minutes the oil fields would be eliminated forever. It makes no difference if there are 12 or 15 task forces sailing the oceans, or bases in Egypt, Diego Garcia, or elsewhere. They are not capable of fulfilling the assignment. They might as well be armed with bows and arrows.

Assume for the moment the oil fields in the Persian Gulf have just been 90% incinerated. OPEC then consists of Nigeria, Algeria, Indoneisa, and Venezuela, with Mexico cooperating. The price of oil would immediately be boosted, probably to $100 per barrel. The United States would have to terminate all oil imports, freeing Mexican and Venezuelan oil for Europe and South America. Strict rationing would be required. The spot price of oil would start to creep up and the producers might raise the price to $175 per barrel. Then a year or so later the price would have to be doubled again to "dampen demand." Inflation would go wild in the producing countries if there were no supply of goods for the money storm to buy. Depression would sweep the industrial nations, and Third World nations would be swept by revolution followed by starvation, like that in Kampuchea under Pol Pot.

Pandora's box was opened at Hiroshima, and much that is bad and good is yet to be realized.

THE BUY-OUT BINGES OF THE OIL GIANTS

In the "hard minerals" industries, copper production is one of the largest. World production is in the range of 7.5–8 million tons per year range. At 75 cents per pound, that has a gross value of about $15 billion. There are a dozen oil companies, *each* with sales larger than the entire copper industry, and half of them are trying to gobble up the comparatively small mining companies.

In the middle 1960s one oil company decided to enter the fertilizer field. One after another, several oil companies followed like a flock of sheep. One of the oil giants built 11 large fertilizer plants around the world. Suddenly these companies realized they had to have phosphate rock. The order came down to buy it. Next they found they had to have sulphur. They created such a demand that the price tripled. Then they looked for customers but the price of their product was so high few customers could be found. "Sell the plants and fire the economists," were the next orders.

The fertilizer industry represents about 235 M tons of raw materials, 30 times larger than the copper industry, yet fertilizer was too small for the money of the oil giants. There are only two mineral industries larger than fertilizer, i.e., steel and concrete (cement plus aggregate). Steel has avoided the invasion of the oil giants by virtue of being a perennially sick industry. In concrete there are so many small producers that it would be difficult to assemble a semi-monopoly. Both of these industries are very cyclic, exhibiting wide swings with the building cycles. Thus none of the three largest of minerals industries was attractive to the raiders.

So the oil giants, with more money than they know how to spend wisely, have pounced on little copper as their victim. The results are beginning to be apparent. One measure of an efficient new mine is the capital cost per ton of ore treated daily. A recent open-pit mine in the Philippines developed by Benguet Corp., cost $6000 per ton of ore mined per day. Cuajone in Peru is reported to cost $16,500 per ton of ore mined. A proposal by an oil company to open a mine in Africa came to $300,000 per ton. It concluded the project was not feasible, but they should have been able to reach the conclusion that it was going to cost 10 times as much as any copper mine ever opened without spending $30 million to find out.

Another oil giant spent $10 million on evaluation of a small property in New Mexico, and concluded the project was not economic, so decided to call it a "demonstration mine" and open it anyway. It is not quite clear who would be demonstrating what to whom. Later they apparently "farmed out" the project to a mining company.

The following table shows who is gobbling whom.

Table 3

Mining Company Take-overs

Buying Company	Mining Company Purchased
Cities Service	Tennessee Copper
	Miami Copper
Atlantic Richfield	Anaconda
Standard Oil of Indiana	Cyprus
	Baghdad
Pennzoil	Duval
Louisiana Land	Copper Range
Standard Oil of Ohio	Kennecott
Standard Oil of California*	AMAX
Elf Aquitaine	Texasgulf
Fluor	St. Joe
Hudson Bay	Inspiration
Consolidated Gold Fields	Newmont

*Offer made but not consummated

This leaves only AMAX, ASARCO, Phelps Dodge, and Homestake of the major mining companies in the United States as independents. Eight oil companies have either purchased or are pursuing 10 of the major mining companies.

The first oil company to enter the copper field was Cities Service. A news item in June 1981 said they were offering their mining properties for sale. The article stated the value was estimated to be $500,000,000. The article went on to state that the copper operations had earned $17 million before tax in 1980. On the estimated value that is 3.4% return on investment, and assuming a 40% tax, 2% returns to the company on its half billion dollar investment. An investor who expects 15% after tax on his money might offer $68 million for the package. To yield the prime interest rate, he might offer $82 million. The sale was made in late 1983 at $75 million for the major part of these assets.

RESEARCH

There is a danger that in discussing mineral resources, one may be carried away by the propaganda generated by the industries themselves. As always, self preservation is the rule. Preserving and enlarging the market, improving the price, securing reserves that have a preferred position (geography, grade, or quality) are the first considerations.

New developments come from outside. Actions are taken at Bell Telephone Laboratories, Western Electric, General Electric, Westinghouse, General Mills, Corning, and many other firms not directly connected with minerals that are developing new organic and non-metallic products, that will have great impact on the metals industry.

For example, the world would rapidly consume known copper deposits if all communications had continued to be dependent on the metal for conducting all signals from transmitter to receiver. First came microwaves then satellites, and the cost of communication rapidly decreased. The cost of use of a channel via satellite is now reported to be 12 cents per minute to anywhere in the world. The rest of the charge is imposed by the telephone companies at each end.

This is not the place to review materials used in advanced technologies, but it is significant to mention some developments under way that may materially change some of the mineral markets.

Is it reasonable to use natural gas to generate electricity at an efficiency of 35%, then transmit it with losses to a plant where it is inefficiently converted into work? Or should fuel cells be built in the plant itself, with natural or synthetic gas or hydrogen transmitted instead? The overall efficiency in fuel cell technology can be as high as 80% if the heat is also utilized. The generators are modular, so expansion is easily accomplished. No central station with huge steam plants and turbines plus transformers and unsightly power lines is required. Westinghouse is conducting extensive research on this energy system.

General Motors (among other cmpanies) has perfected a new battery system that is lighter in weight than the lead battery on an equivalent power basis. It has a much longer life. This company announced plans to introduce electric automobiles in 1985. Assuming they are successful, such innovations will cause major changes in the mineral industries. With elimination of the gasoline engine, gasoline will no longer be a major fuel. The iron requirement will be appreciably reduced and electric motors will be installed on the wheels. The copper in the motor windings may not make up for the loss of radiator cores. With no lead batteries, lead mining will be seriously affected. Depending on which battery system is used, some metal will be in greater demand.

Even the new system of solvent extraction, so important in refining of several metals, was developed from outside the minerals industries, by General Mills.

One may conclude from such examples that the mineral industries themselves are limited in their research by mental boundaries, but outside research efforts are likely to develop new systems that will have a major impact on demand for various mineral commodities, either positive or negative. It is probable that these developments will have the effect of reducing demand for the more expensive minerals and increasing consumption of the more abundant and less expensive raw materials.

MARINE NODULES

Metalliferous nodules are found on the deep ocean floor. Many of our mineral shortages would be solved by dredging these potato-sized accretions of manganese, nickel, copper, cobalt, possibly molybdenum, and other strategic metals. They are free for the taking, just scattered on the bottom of the sea. (At least this is what the efficient public relations departments of the firms wanting to promote such ventures report in a steady stream of stories on the subject.)

There are a few problems. True, there are nodules on much of the ocean floor. The zone that seems most promising lies south of Hawaii and a few degrees north of the equator. It is 300 km wide and 2500 km long, running lengthwise from east to west. At 2.25 kg per square meter, that area represents on the order of 2×10^{12} (trillion) tons of nodules. Since the ocean basins are international waters, the first problem is ownership. This is a three-cornered argument. First, there are the industrial nations, which need the resources and are developing the technology to produce them: Japan, the United States, Europe, and Russia if she chooses. Second, there are nations that have the resources in conventional deposits on land, need to sell them to consumers and do not want competition from a cheap source. This is quite a strong block when it includes nations producing nickel, copper, molybdenum, cobalt, and manganese. They would like a high excise tax to handicap the development of nodule technology. In the third group are the developing nations with little need for the resources even though they may not have supplies themselves and lack the technological base to develop them. This group wants a high excise tax for revenue and may not be able to distinguish between a tax that will raise revenue and one that will conform to the desires of group two, who would prefer to prevent development of the nodules. A series of Law of the Sea conferences have been held; the report states that agreement has finally been reached, but treaties must be ratified.

Several countries, including the United States have announced that they will not ratify the treaty. The technological problems are the most formidable every contemplated in mining. What was thought to be a consortium ready to commence operation turned out to be a CIA mission to recover a wrecked Soviet nuclear submarine. The ocean bottom is a hostile environment and a ship on the surface has to manipulate a recovery system as much as four kilometers long when the crew cannot see what they are doing. It is like trying to pick up beer cans on Second Avenue from the top of the Empire State building at night. The long umbilical cord will be highly stressed and if the "rake" strikes an object it cannot move, it may snap off and $10–20 million of equipment would be lost.

The economic scale of the operation can be analyzed. If production is developed there will be more than one dredge, probably from three to five. The highest priced commodity to be recovered in quantity is nickel. The world uses about a billion pounds of this metal per year. If half of this is supplied from nodules by five ships, each will recover 100 million pounds. At 30 pounds per ton, this means each dredge will handle 3.3 M tons per year or, in 200 days of operation, 16.7 thousand tons per day and each dredge will sweep 7.5 km^2 per day. The dredge sweep will have to be 75 m wide and the dredge will have to traverse 100 km to accomplish this. An average speed of 4 kilometers per hour will be required to cover this area. The problems of designing such a system are formidable. If there are 30 pounds of copper and two pounds of cobalt per ton, this will amount to 100 million pounds or 45,000 tons of copper per dredge or 0.225 million tons annually from five dredges. This is only 3% of the copper market, so no great threat exists to the established copper industry. About 3000 tons of cobalt would be produced per ship (15,000 tons total), which is 53% of the world market. If the nodules contain 20% recoverable manganese (some proposals would discard this product because the price is low) this would total 4.18 M tons, 15% of world consumption. Thus it should be clear that nickel is the controlling element. If an effort were made to supply 10% of the copper market, it would flood the nickel and cobalt market and break the price, making the operation uneconomic. So development hinges on how badly Japan and Europe want an independent source of nickel. (The United States can count on Canada as its supplier.) If a 10% severance tax were imposed, a burden which would probably prevent operations, the revenue would run the United Nations for a few days but would yield no revenue to the nations with dreams of sharing riches. It would be no surprise if these deposits remain protoresources for many years.

CONSERVATION

How much use of materials is waste, whimsy, and indulgence? When this proposition is examined, there will be some reflexive objections. First it is necessary to point out that Americans have a motion fixation. There is a mistaken notion that motion is progress, a fixation that racing around in circles is "getting ahead." This may be a boy on a bicycle, a man roaring around an oversized puddle in a motor boat, or a chief executive chasing across the continent in his Lear jet. The more financial resources a person commands the more material resources he wastes.

The boy on the bike is using 10–20 pounds of metal and rubber and the energy of youth. The man in the boat is using 200 or more pounds of boat and motor with gasoline to propel it. The trailer must also be considered — another 200–300 pounds of metal and rubber. It takes an automobile to haul the boat to the lake and gallons of gasoline. Possibly another vehicle is required as well, to haul the family and supplies. This adds up to several tons of metal and is justified as "essential recreation." A cross-continent Lear jet trip requires tons of fuel and an organization at each end plus pilot and co-pilot. The justification may be an hour's conference at the other end, but there may also be luxurious "trimmings."

With today's superb communications it would cost less than 1% of the trans-continental trip for a 30 minute leisurely telephone call, with video if eyeballl-to-eyeball talk is essential.

Much of today's work force travels 30–60 minutes to and from the job. A massive amount of mineral resources is tied up in this mindless ferrying back and forth. Much of the production of industry is engaged in catering to this compulsive motion. The workers in the south side live in the north side and so on around the compass. Apparently this is a part of the motion complex. People are accustomed to commuting long distances, but it is very costly in energy and other mineral resources.

The United States has tremendous capacity to conserve resources, but little inclination in that direction. Woe to the politician that even hints the nation should "kill its sacred cows."

THE MANDA

Throughout this section of the book there has been a constant refrain: an inexpensive energy source is essential to civilization, and petroleum will no longer fill this need. The giant oil companies have more money than they know how to invest wisely. Likewise the 13 OPEC nations went on a spending binge and, unfortunately, have squandered much of the surplus funds on armaments. Their industrial oil customers are happy to supply them, since it did not take long to equip every camel with a transistor radio.

There seems to be no way to clamp a lid on the spiraling inflation caused by the greed of the oil producing nations. If Libya wants to finance a few more revolutions, it demands a higher oil price. In some countries the princes have tired of building new palaces and buying fast autos and planes. The million dollar high rollers at Las Vegas and Monte Carlo have become legend. Never before has so much wealth been concentrated among an indulged elite that did nothing to earn it.

While 1982 saw a temporary surplus of petroleum, this condition is certain not to last long. If the value of the dollar inflates, an increase in oil price is almost automatic. The OPEC nations cannot countenance a reduction in their squandering power. If prudent management of the U.S. economy (for a change) tries to get inflation under control and deflates the dollar, all of the other oil purchasers scream that the United States is jacking up the oil price, since oil prices are fixed in dollars.

There has been much talk about finding a standard, something of absolute value, a reference mark that can be the basis of the world monetary system. Throughout history gold served that purpose. Today gold is manipulated along with other commodities. While some echos from another age are still heard in the plea, "return to the gold standard," in truth this would be very difficult.

Possibly an entirely new approach should be considered. Suppose energy were monetized. How could the price of energy be increased? Is this not an absolute unit of value?

Such a plan might take the following form. A healthy, well-fed laborer can exert one-half horsepower of energy per hour, or in a day, four horsepower hours. That is a man-day of work. For this he deserves "an honest living"—a home, clothing, food, education for his children, and a bit of recreation. So the monetary unit might be called a MANDA. How could the wage be increased? He is still doing one day's work. That is the minimum wage.

If a man watches a 1000 hp motor as his days work, occasionally squirting a few drops of oil, he might get a bonus of 0.1% of the horsepower he is responsible for overseeing. On the other hand, if he operates a 250 hp truck he might receive an extra 1%, or 2.5 MANDAS. It becomes more complex when an effort is made to assign MANDAS to the 90% of the "work force" that produces nothing. What is a minister worth? A school teacher? Is there a differential between a kindergarden teacher and a college professor? Probably the former expends more energy. Is a banker or a lawyer worthy of a MANDA per day? What happens to those on welfare? Is retirement possible?

The MANDA has absolute value. Four horsepower hours are equivalent to 2.984 kwh or 10,188 BTU, or 2566.8 kilogram-calories. This is the energy equivalent of a pound of poor quality coal or one-twelfth of a gallon of gasoline. Probably it is best to leave this as a jest, because someone might take it seriously and assign to the writer of this book what he is worth!

PART II

The purpose of this section of the volume is to review briefly the most important mineral commodities so that a handy reference is available. The tonnage of world production was selected as the limiting factor for inclusion in this study. For metals, the cut-off is at cobalt with world production of 28,000 tons, equal to one shipload. Thus mercury (6500 tons) and rhenium (10 tons, or one truck load) are not reviewed. Among the non-metallic minerals, the lower limit is 500,000 tons per year, equivalent to *one* medium-sized quarry. Commodities with world production lower than these sizes are of minor economic significance. Chapters on the three precious metals, diamonds, and gemstones are included. This results in data on 38 commodities, listed in Table 4 (see page 93) according to tonnage.

In general, the publications of the U.S. Bureau of Mines are the sources of data on production, with recent figures from trade journals. The Bureau of Mines has a large staff keeping track of mineral production data, and issues several excellent publications. For the person interested in more detailed information on mineral commodities, an excellent publication, *Mineral Facts and Problems*, is issued every five years by the U.S. Bureau of Mines. The most recent volume available at the time of compilation of these summaries was for 1975 (1291 pages), but another volume for 1980 is now on sale.

A second series by the Bureau of Mines is the *Minerals Yearbook*, published annually in several volumes. This gives more current data and less background than *Mineral Facts and Problems*. There are also monthly and annual separate summaries on a number of the major commodities.

There are a number of trade journals that publish data and summaries. The *Mining Journal* is a weekly air-mail publication that reviews several of the major commodities in some detail during the year, and carries many news briefs on world-wide mining activity and news. This journal also publishes an annual review in June and covers 60 commodities plus reviews of activity in about 127 countries. It carries reviews of developments in exploration, mining, and metallurgy. Advertisements, some of them spectacular, of most of the machinery firms give further insight into the industry.

The *Engineering and Mining Journal* (known to the industry as *E & MJ*), a monthly trade journal noted for the accuracy of its statistics, publishes prices of selected commodities, articles, and an annual review in March. It generally covers 42 commodities plus area reports. There are numerous other good trade publications.

There are several trade associations that specialize in one or a few commodities (for example copper, lead-zinc, sulphur, or fertilizer). Generally these organizations have publications or periodicals in their specialty, designed to promote the use of their commodity.

In addition there are encyclopedias, handbooks, text books and sometimes shelves of books on a single commodity. Thus if anyone desires more information on mineral commodities, data are quite readily available. In no case were all of the data included here available from any one source, and much information comes from personal experience and contacts.

Commodities are divided into metals and non-metals and arranged alphabetically within each group.

Table 4 shows an estimate of the adequacy of supplies to the United States, assuming that in an emergency the United States and Canada would cooperate. There has been much discussion of strategic and critical mineral commodities. For an estimate of the adequacy of commodities to the U.S. economy, those judged "critical" are marked with "C." It is necessary to drop to the fourth *order of magnitude* of tonnage to find such a commodity. Manganese and chromium appear here. These are steel alloying metals. Some might argue that aluminum should be in this class. As far as current production goes, this is true. Nearly all of the alumina and bauxite are imported. However, the supplies of alumina from clays and other silicates are virtually unlimited, and the process for recovery is well known. If imports were cut off, there would be severe dislocation while new sources were being developed, but it could be done.

In the sixth order, another metal appears: tin. In the first six orders of magnitude of production twelve commodities are in exportable surplus, and only three are in critical supply. Only when dropping to the small tonnage commodities does the number of critical metals increase to four. In most of these doubling the price would materially improve the quantity available and dampen demand and result in substitution. Therefore scarcity is not judged to be as serious a problem as some believe.

If a commodity is in deficit status in North America, it is marked "D." Seven commodities are in this class. In general, if the supply in the United States and Canada is inadequate, the deficit can be made up from Mexico.

Table 4

*World Production of Mineral Commodities in
Millions of Metric Tons*

Rank	Commodity	Tonnage (1979)	Status*
1	Aggregate	12,000	S
2	Portland Cement	957	S
3	Iron Ore	887	A
4	Clay	306	S
5	Silica	200 (est.)	S
6	Salt	185	S
7	Phosphate	128	S
8	Gypsum	82	A
9	Sulphur	55	S
10	Manganese	27	C
11	Potash	26	A
12	Trona	18	S
13	Aluminum	16	D
14	Magnesite	11	A
15	Chromium	11	C
16	Barite	7.6	A
17	Copper	7.6	D
18	Zinc	6.0	A
19	Fluorite	5.4	D
20	Asbestos	5.3	A
21	Lead	3.5	A
22	Borates	3.0	S
23	Nickel	0.8	A
24	Zircon	0.8	D
25	Graphite	0.6	D
26	Magnesium	0.3	S
27	Tin	0.26	C
28	Molybdenum	0.103	S
29	Titanium	0.100	A
30	Antimony	0.077	D
31	Tungsten	0.046	D
32	Vanadium	0.041	A
33	Uranium	0.035	S
34	Cobalt	0.028	C
35	Silver	0.011	A
36	Gold	0.0012	A
37	Platinum	0.0002	C
38	Diamond	0.0000096	C

*North American status, including U.S. and Canada. S = surplus;
A = adequate; D = deficient; C = critical.

Thus shortages are less significant than some make them out to be.

This table serves to reiterate the conclusion that severe shortages of major minerals are unlikely within the next two generations, with the exception of manganese and chromium. Some of the other "critical" minerals are deficient to the extent of one ship load to one truck load. These shortages should be considered in their proper perspective.

ABBREVIATIONS AND MEASURES

Throughout this section on commodities metric weights are used unless otherwise indicated. When statistics are published only in the English system, such as short tons (2000 pounds) the symbol is given as "st." Sometimes statistics are given in long tons (2240 pounds); these are shown as "lt". The metric ton is 1000 kilograms (kg), or 2205 pounds. Another exception to the metric rule is for precious metals, which are conventionally weighed in troy ounces; a troy ounce equals 31.1 grams or a kilogram contains 32.2 ounces.

Abbreviations used

lt	long ton, 2240 pounds or 1.016 metric tons
st	short ton, 2000 pounds or 0.907 metric tons
ppm	parts per million (equals grams per ton)
M	million
Mmt	millions of metric tons
Km	kilometers
carat	0.2 grams
Kg	kilograms = 2.2 pounds
g/t	grams per ton
BPL	Bone phosphate of lime. Divided by 2.18 equals $\%P_2O_5$
^{40}K	The isotope of potassium with atomic weight of 40
m	meters
cm	centimeters
°C	degrees centigrade
tpy	tons per year
BTU	British Thermal Unit
kwh	kilowatt hour

CHAPTER 9

METALS

ALUMINUM

Properties and Characteristics

Atomic number	13
Atomic weight	26.27 (lightest major metal)
Specific heat	0.226
Electrical resistivity	2.669 (excellent conductor)
Density	2.70
Melting point	660°
Modulus of elasticity	10×10^6 psi (rather low);
Major minerals	Bauxite* (Al_2O_3. $2H_2O$); Kaolin ($H_4Al_2 Si_2O_9$);
	Dawsonite [$Na_3 Al(CO_3)_2$. $2 Al(OH)_3$]

*Bauxite is a mineral aggregate. See "Occurrences."

History: Commercial production of aluminum began in 1845 and the metal sold for $100 per pound. By 1886 the price per pound had dropped to $8. In that year Charles Hall discovered a method of producing aluminum from a molten bath of cryolite using electrolysis. Using the Hall process, the price dropped to $2 per pound by 1893 and continued to drop. The average from 1943–1947 was 15 cents per pound. This was the magic of the free enterprise system at its best. It changed the price from 20 times as high as silver to one-thirtieth of the price of silver, and by so doing created a mass market for the metal, now an indispensible part of our economy, second only to iron and steel in tons consumed.

Following World War II, when as a part of the "new economics" of John Maynard Keynes, planned inflation began to be felt, the price crept slowly upward. With the "oil shock" of 1973 and subsequent surging energy cost, the price rose to 75 cents per pound in 1981.

Uses: The major uses of aluminum take advantage of its light weight and high electrical conductivity. It is used extensively in power transmission

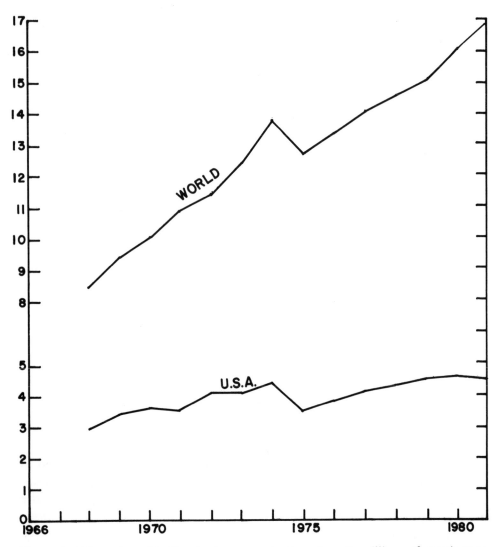

Figure 9 U.S. and worldwide aluminum production given in millions of metric tons (Mmt).

cables, but they must have a core of steel because aluminum is not strong enough to carry its own weight between transmission towers.

The largest use of aluminum is in building and construction. It is adaptable to modular construction and permits erection without heavy equipment for small buildings. Its light weight reduces the amount of steel required for large buildings.

Because of the cost of gasoline, aluminum is making great inroads in automobile manufacture. This could soon be the largest usage of the metal.

It is widely used in aircraft, but it is not suitable for the skin of supersonic planes because it does not retain strength at the high temperatures which develop.

Fabricated durable items—furniture, refrigerators, appliances, and packaging (cans and foil) are other major uses.

Because it oxidizes very rapidly, aluminum powder is used as an explosive called "Alcoa Allunite."

Occurrence: Aluminum is the most abundant metal in the world, making up 8.05% of the earth's crust. It occurs in every country in all major igneous rock types, and is abundant in shaly sediments. However, it is in tight chemical combination with silicon and oxygen, and the energy cost of breaking the bond is prohibitive. In the tropics, where it is warm and moist, a particular kind of weathering called *"laterization"* occurs on poorly-drained gently sloping terrain. Silica and some other constituents like soda, lime, and magnesia are removed in solution. This leaves concentrated alumina (Al_2O_3) combined with water in the mineral aggregate known as *bauxite*. It is actually a group of minerals: diaspore, gibbsite, and boehmite, which contain alumina plus limonite, the iron oxide which colors it buff to brown to red, titania in the form of ilmenite, and the "bad one" (silica), which is likely to be combined with part of the alumina as clay.

Bauxite is often found as small spheres called *pisolites* built up in concentric shells like tiny onions. They are generally less than one-fourth inch (6 mm) in diameter.

In the intense leaching of soils to form bauxite much of the nutrient is washed away and the soil is unsuitable for agriculture. It is likely to be distinguished by scrub jungle and coarse, useless grasses.

There are two main origins of bauxite. In Jamaica and elsewhere extensive areas with outcropping limestone erode into small hills with rather broad valleys between them, called *karst topography*. There are no rivers or streams because the rainfall leaks out through cracks and caverns. A thick coat of volcanic ash fell on this rock, collecting in the valleys, and through laterization, was converted to bauxite. The second type is weathering in place, of lava, mud flows, or hard rocks of the andesite to basalt type, called "intermediate" to "basic," chemically. That means they had less silica and more alumina to start with.

The largest known bauxite deposits, by far, are in Australia, which has become the number one producer of the mineral. Guinea, Jamaica (which used to be the largest producer), and Surinam are other major producers. Table 5 shows the production of bauxite in 1979 and 1980.

The USA is 93% dependent on foreign nations (mostly the Caribbean and South America) for its bauxite. Domestic production is almost entirely from Arkansas. There are extensive ferruginous (low grade) bauxites in Washing-

Table 5

Production of Bauxite

Country	Millions of metric tons	
	1979	1980
Australia	26	27.5
Guinea	12.5	12.0
Jamaica	11.8	12.0
Surinam	5.0	4.5
Guyana	3.0	3.4
Yugoslavia	3.0	3.0
Greece	2.7	2.8
France	2.0	1.9
Brazil	1.6	1.8
United States	1.7	1.6
India	2.1	1.6

ton, Oregon, and Hawaii.

Other mineral sources should be mentioned briefly. High alumina clays and shales occur at many places in the United States (and other countries). They are potential sources of aluminum and much research has been done on this. It has been considered a sub-economic process. A plant to manufacture alumina from the anorthosite rock that occurs east of Laramie, Wyoming, was constructed during World War II but operated only briefly. Complex political and economic factors will determine if or when the United States will become independent of foreign sources. The present direction is to export the capital and import the finished metal which will be a costly decision.

Economics: There are six main factors in the production of aluminum: (1) production of the raw material; (2) refining of alumina; (3) smelting aluminum; (4) transportation; (5) cost of power; and (6) political considerations.

Ordinarily the cost of mining the raw material is very low. The overburden must be stripped and the bauxite mined. Generally no drilling or blasting is required. The chemical refining of the alumina to 99.5% purity probably costs 10 times as much as mining. Smelting is much more costly, largely because the cost of energy has shot up since 1973. It takes about 8 kilowatt hours per pound of metal through the plant for smelting. When a power supplier announces a six-fold increase in power charges, as the New Zealand government did in 1977, (the cost of producing hydroelectric power in an amortized plant did not increase) it can turn an operation into a loss.

A recent figure for capital cost of a smelter was $3000 per ton of annual product, or for a 200,000 ton smelter, $600 million. That does not include the mine, alumina refinery, or power plant. The capital cost of a new smelter could easily amount to 30 cents per pound, the biggest single cost item. When all costs are cumulated, including royalties and direct taxes, they may easily total 70 cents per pound (May 1982). Meanwhile the price had dropped to 45 cents per pound.

Political considerations are also an important cost item. The power charge mentioned above amounts to a discriminatory tax levy. In the United States it is pretty well documented that "environmental protection" rules applied to copper production have increased the cost of production by 10 cents per pound at a time when two-thirds of the industry was operating at a loss. This was done without even documenting the need for the expensive pollution controls. Faced with this kind of administration, an aluminum company would be unlikely to go into eastern Wyoming, develop high-alumina shales and an untried process, open a large coal mine, and build a large power plant to produce aluminum. They are voting with their heels! Every aluminum producer is taking his money and going to Australia. In a few years the United States will be importing $10–$20 billion in aluminum into its pristine welfare poverty.

Costs, like water, cannot be heaped up. Money flows away seeking a lower level. If huge environmental costs are piled on fantastic energy costs in one area, plants close and money flows to a new site. One-third of the Japanese aluminum plants closed in 1978 and Japanese companies are building in Australia.

Economic necessity dictates that the prudent investor invest where the prognosis is more favorable. If Australia remembers the recession experienced during its brief dose of socialism, it should be virtually recession-proof for the next 20 years.

Production Methods: Because deposits are thin and ore is light in weight and is produced in large quantity, mining of bauxite consumes and destroys more surface area than the mining of any other metal. For the industrial nations, the environmental damage caused by mining, is conveniently exported and hence ignored. The surface is usually restored, many times to greater productivity than before mining.

First the bauxite layer must be exposed by removing the waste overlying it. This is transferred into the mined out zone. Next the bauxite layer is scraped off. No drilling or blasting is required. The bauxite must be transported to an alumina refinery, often via truck to rail to ship to rail. The bauxite is treated with caustic soda at about 400°C in pressurized vats; the alumina dissolves, and is precipitated in its pure form. One ton of ore yields one-half ton of product, and the alumina may again have to be transported, to the smelter.

Metallic aluminum is produced from alumina by the Hall process. The oxide is mixed with artificial cryolite and heated by passing electricity through the furnace melting the cryolite and dissolving the alumina. Then the aluminum accumulates in the bottom of the "pot" as the cathode, in the molten state. Carbon anodes are consumed by oxygen from the alumina, forming carbon dioxide and escaping as gas. Metal is tapped periodically, and additional alumina is added. Anodes are changed periodically; if the continuous anode system is used, however, this is not necessary.

The record of aluminum production for 1979 and 1980 is shown in Table 6.

Table 6

Aluminum Production in Western Nations

Country	Million of metric tons	
	1979	1980
United States	4.6	4.6
Japan	1.0	1.1
Canada	0.86	1.0
West Germany	0.74	0.73
Norway	0.67	0.66
France	0.40	0.43
Spain	0.26	0.39
United Kingdom	0.36	0.37
Australia*	0.27	0.30
India	0.18	

*Australia will probably move to second
 place in a few years.

Outlook: The end of the era of cheap energy was the end of the high growth rate of aluminum. The metal is so important that even after a three-fold price increase, substitution is not likely to make important inroads on its market. Many of the plants in high energy markets, particularly older, less efficient plants, are closing and new, modern plants are going to cheaper energy sources. Because capital costs are also high, it is not likely that new firms will want to enter the low-growth market.

Aluminum is ripe for any innovation or breakthrough to cut energy consumption. A well-known metallurgist stated that it should be possible to electroplate aluminum from aqueous solution. That would change the outlook for the production of this metal.

In the United States several aluminum plants were built in the Pacific Northwest to utilize the excess power of the Bonneville project. This was classed as interruptible power, subject to the demand of users who would pay more for it. At about one-fourth cent per kilowatt hour, the power cost of producing aluminum was only 2¢ per pound. With greatly increased power consumption in the region, interruptible power is no longer available, so power costs have multiplied by about five.

ALCOA has developed a new electrolytic process that reportedly will reduce power consumption by 30%, which is a major savings in this era of expensive power. It uses aluminum chloride rather than the oxide. The capital cost increases of the post oil-shock period, however, reflect increased energy cost throughout the machinery and construction stages, plus the high interest rates caused by demand for funds to develop new energy sources. When the cost of power was 2¢ per pound of metal it amounted to 13% of the sale price. Today at 2¢ per kwh (and assuming 6 kwh) it is 27% of the sale price. Old plants that consume as much as 10 kwh per pound of metal have to pay 44% of the sale price for power. With capital cost amounting to 65% of sale price for new plants (at beginning of depreciation) anyone contemplating new construction must seek the most favorable situation for new smelters. Large undeveloped hydroelectric sites relatively close to a good harbor are the best choices today.

Research is continuing in an attempt to develop a method to recover aluminum from the more common sources, such as clays and other silicates. There have been reports that metallurgists in Japan have developed such a process, which promises to be competitive with the method using bauxite.

Like all of the major metals, the severe recession of 1981 and 1982 resulted in the drop of the price for aluminum below the cost of production for about half of the world's plants. To sustain a high level of industrial activity, the price of the metal will have to rise to the range of 80–90 cents per pound.

ANTIMONY (Sb)

Properties and Characteristics

Atomic number	51
Atomic weight	121.75
Isotopes	121 and 123
Melting point	630.5°C
Specific gravity	6.62
Average in rocks	0.3 ppm
Major mineral	Stibnite Sb_2S_3

History: Antimony was one of the first metals used by man. The name probably comes from the Latin "antimonium," and is probably derived from Hamitic. A vase excavated from a site in Chaldea dated as 4000 B.C. was made of the metal. Since it rarely occurs in the native state, the art of smelting it had developed by that time, one of the earliest applications of pyrometallurgy. The Egyptians had learned to plate antimony on other metals by about 2400 B.C. Women adopted the mineral stibnite to cosmetics, with Jezebel and Cleopatra reportedly using it as eye make-up to seduce men like King Ahab, Caesar, and Anthony. Antimonial bronze was discovered probably accidentally both in the Mediterranean area and by the Incas of Bolivia and Peru. By the fifteenth century it was in use in type metal. Late in the nineteenth century consumption had risen to 7500 tons per year. The electrolytic process of production was applied in 1896 and consumption began to increase rapidly. Most of the ore came from China. Consumption of antimony rose sharply during World War I and subsequent wars. Disruption of the supply from China caused development of other sources. With limited reserves, the United States obtains much of its supply from scrap sources.

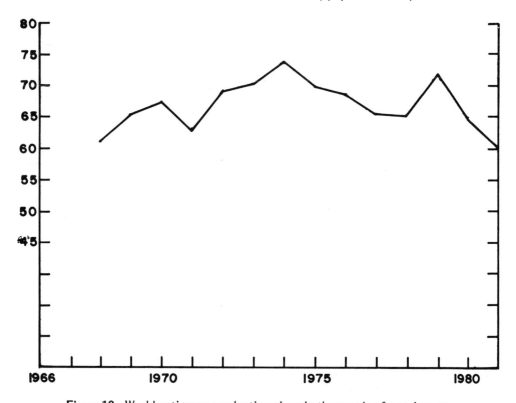

Figure 10   World antimony production given in thousands of metric tons.

Uses: Antimony is most commonly used in lead storage batteries, particularly for automobiles (this has dropped sharply since 1979), and as the trioxide in a fire retardant. Alloys include type metal (the alloy expands on cooling), solder, anti-friction bearings, cable sheaths, and pipes. It is used in decorative castings. Various compounds are used for enamel, white, black, vermilion, yellow, and orange pigments, as a vulcanizing agent in rubber and to protect fabrics from sunlight. It is used in bullets and in tracers. The oxide is the dense smoke used for smoke screens. In very pure form it is used in electronics as a semiconductor.

Occurrence: Antimony is classed as a *telethermal* metal, formed by cooling solutions emanating from intrusive rocks. Deposits are generally small and discontinuous and do not extend to depth. The only mineral mined for antimony is the sulphide, stibnite. It also occurs with lead and copper, however, and is sometimes recovered from the smelters.

Probably half of the known reserves are in China; when the metal has been withheld from the market shortages suddenly occur. With its new market orientation, China may prove to be a more stable trading partner than it has been at some times in the recent past. There are many small antimony mines on the altiplano of Bolivia; this nation generally is the second largest producer. Many of the deposits outcrop at the grass roots on the flat plain, with no surficial evidence of their occurrence. Systematic geochemical sampling would probably disclose numerous other deposits. The largest known deposits are at the Consolidated Murchison Mines in South Africa. There are important deposits in Mexico, Peru, Canada, Yugoslavia, Russia, and Thailand.

Economics: The small size of deposits and the generally low total consumption combined with ample material available and large scrap supplies has generally kept the price low. During war-time, however, demand shoots up, as does the price. There have been times when China withheld supplies from the western markets, which also causes strong surges in price. The average price during the 1960s was about 45 cents per pound, with a surge to over $1.00 in 1969. In May 1982 is was quoted $1.05 per pound. In December 1974 there were 40,734 tons in stockpiles in the USA, and the objective was reduced to zero. By the end of 1979 the stockpile remained the same and the objective had been raised to 20,130 tons.

Production: Most of the mines are small, with a few miners following the discontinuous, shallow veins. Rarely are the deposits large enough to justify mechanization. Concentration is by hand sorting or simple jigs.

World production of primary metal in 1980 was only 77,000 tons, half-way between molybdenum and tungsten, ranking fourteenth among the metals, thirtieth among all mineral commodities.

Outlook: There is a definite trend away from the use of antimony in lead storage batteries in the United States. Smaller batteries are needed for smaller cars and new developments have reduced the size and weight per watt-hour of power, so less metal is required. The "trouble-free" batteries on the market have longer life with no antimony. Thus the major market is in danger. On the other hand, the use of fire retardant chemicals is growing quite rapidly; this demand will probably balance the other shrinking market. It will probably continue to be a small miner's business without much overall change in the size of the market.

CHROMIUM (Cr)

Properties and Characteristics

Atomic number	24
Atomic weight	52.0
Isotopes	50(4.5%), 52(83.8%), 53(9.4%), 54(2.3%)
Melting point	1903°
Specific gravity	7.2
Average content in rocks	Ultramafic 2000 ppm; mafic 300 ppm; felsic 25 ppm; soils average 200 ppm; R 5–1000 ppm
Major mineral	Chromite $FeCr_2O_4$ or $FeO.Cr_2O_3$, 68% Cr_2O_3

History: The name chromium was derived from the Greek word "chroma" because of the brilliant colors of some of the compounds. It was chosen by Louis Vanguelin who first identified the new element in 1797. Russia was the early source of the ore until it was discovered in Maryland, Pennsylvania, and Virginia. These deposits were quite limited and when deposits were discovered in Turkey in 1860, they quickly dominated the market. The huge deposits in South Africa, 75% of known world resources, are now the major sources.

Chromium, one of the most vital mineral commodities, is scarce in the Americas. The United States has limited small, low-grade deposits which, if produced at high cost, would be quickly exhausted. Necessity thus ties the economies of South Africa, which dominates production, and the United States, the largest consumer.

On a tonnage basis chromium ranks fourth among metals, 13th among all mineral commodities.

Uses: The most important use of chromium is as an alloy in stainless steel, 62% of the mineral being used for this purpose. The specification for

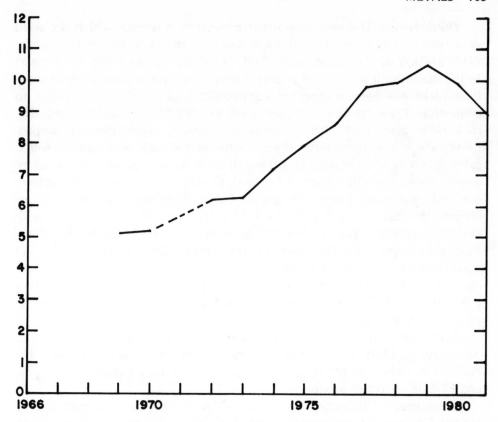

Figure 11 *World chromite production given in millions of metric tons.*

metallurgical chromite is a minimum of 48% Cr_2O_3 and Cr:Fe ratio of 3:1 minimum with a maximum of 8% SiO_2. Some chromium goes into all steels and cast iron. *Stainless steel*, with as much as 13% Cr, is specified where corrosion is likely to be severe. Chromium plating is used where a bright, resistant finish is desired, such as automobile trim.

The second use is in the mineral form for refractory purposes. The specification is a minimum of 31% Cr_2O_3 and Cr_2O_3 + Al_2O_3 of 58% with a maximum of 12% Fe and 6% SiO_2. This accounts for 18% of the total consumption, and this usage has been declining at about 3% per year. This reflects the declining importance of open hearth steel, where chromite bricks are used as a lining, giving way to electric furnace steel.

Chemical uses amount to 20% of the consumption of the commodity. The specification is a minimum of 44% Cr_2O_3 and maximum of 5% SiO_2. Uses include pigments and paints, tanning leather, textile dyes, corrosion inhibitors, catalysts, and drilling mud compounds.

Occurrence: The only important mineral is chromite, which is classed as a spinel. It is found in ultrabasic rocks of the type that make up the lower portion of the ocean crust. While it can be assumed that the amount in the ocean basins is vast, it is only where a freakish occurrence of mantle-type rocks has been trapped in continental rocks that it is available to commerce. These rocks are known as *ultramafics* when found on land. The rock types associated with chromite are dunites, peridotites, and serpentinite, which is derived from them. Higher in the rock sequence are found gabbros and basic submarine lava flows. If these rocks are highly distorted by emplacement (as in the Alps of Europe), the chromite lenses are discontinuous and cannot be mined. In South Africa there are extensive areas of ultramafics that are now near the land surface; there are also zones with extensive segregations of chromite. The zone in South Africa known as the Bushveld complex is estimated to contain two billion tons of chromite. An occurrence in neighboring Zimbabwe reportedly in dolomite probably contains 600 million tons. Thus a very small zone in these two nations contains more than 95% of the world's available chromite, a metal essential to all industrial nations.

Russia ranks third in chromite resources and conditions are favorable for discovery of additional deposits. Russia is a major exporter. Turkey, the Philippines (which is the largest producer of refractory chromite), Albania, and Finland are other producers.

Economics: Chromite is the classic example of a strategic mineral. The United States consumes over a million tons per year and it is all imported. Industrial Europe and Japan are likewise dependent on imports. The huge mineral storehouse of southern Africa has a virtual monopoly on this metal. Zimbabwe has an avowedly Marxist government, which has taken a pragmatic view of trade with industrial nations. For political reasons, the black African nations have tried to cripple the economy of South Africa, and for their own purposes, the Marxist nations have supported them. They would very much like to deprive the western industrial nations of the resources that are of vital importance, and secondarily to have them under control of a government aligned with their political philosophy. Consequently multi-faceted foreign elements will be trying to influence the government of South Africa. Arabian Gulf oil and South African minerals are the two exposed vital spots to the industrial West.

Recognizing the importance of chromium to American industry, the stockpile program built up a reserve of eight million tons by 1964. In 1965 half of it was declared surplus to be sold. By 1969 the metallurgical grade segment objective was adjusted upward from 2.5 Mmt to 3.1 Mmt. The stockpile in 1978 stood at 2,488,000 tons of metallurgical, 242,000 tons of chemical grade and 391,000 tons of refractory, or a total of 3.1 Mmt (approximately 40% of what it had been in 1964). There have been no sales since that time. A reserve of a little over two years of metallurgical chrome would seem to be inadequate for such a vital metal.

Each of the major producers has been expanding its capacity of ferro-chrome, thus increasing the value-added which is retained at the source. South Africa is thought to be producing about 60% of the world require-ment at present. This increases the foreign exchange expenditure and balance of payments problems for the importers.

For several years, during the Rhodesian crisis, sanctions by the U.N. inhibited purchases of chromite from that source. During this period some nations took advantage of the opportunity to subvert the sanctions, the USSR being a major offender. The United States in turn imported most of its supplies from Russia, a profitable arrangement for that country. In spite of sanctions the Rhodesian/Zimbabwean mines produced at record levels. Expansion is now under way with sanctions lifted.

Turkey, in desperate financial straits, is an important chromite producer. However, it raised its price above that of the world market. As a result stockpiles at the mine sites have grown. In May 1982 Turkish ore 48% Cr_2O_3 was quoted at $100–115 fob and Transvaal (South Africa) 44% at $42–48 cif. Chromium metal 99% was quoted as £3550–£3800 ($6532–$6992) per ton, or about $3 per pound.

Production: While originally some of the mines were operated as open pits, most of them are underground today. The Zwartkop mine in Transvaal has five producing seams and the ore dips 20–25°. Scrapers are used to remove ore from the face and load it into cars. It is hauled to the inclined shaft, hand sorted underground, and hoisted to the surface. Lump ore is shipped and fines are concentrated using gravity methods.

Metallurgical chromite is reduced to ferrochrome in the electric furnace. A new approach, however, has been to use a blast furnace which permits use of lower grade ore and produces stainless steel directly.

With adequate supplies of high-grade ore there is little incentive to try to develop the low-grade deposits in the Stillwater complex in Montana or the large deposits in Greenland.

Outlook: Reserves are adequate to meet demand for several centuries, but maldistribution gives southern Africa virtual control of the market. Some substitutions are possible, but for many purposes chrome-steel is essential. Chromium cladding can replace tin in some applications, depending on economic factors.

Over the period of 1973 to 1979 changes in consumption of chromite in the U.S. were as follows:

	1973 (tons)	1979 (tons)	Change per year (%)
Metallurgical	630,000	720,000	+0.8
Refractory	370,000	210,000	−3.3
Chemical	190,000	230,000	+1.1

The foregoing tabulation suggests that some modest increases in metallurgical and chemical chromite should continue. The United States will remain dependent on imports.

COBALT (Co)

Properties and Characteristics

Atomic number	27
Atomic weight	58.93
Specific gravity	8.92
Melting point	1493°C
Isotopes	59 (Artificial, 60) Ferromagnetic
Average content in rocks	18 ppm, in ultramafic to 200 ppm, range
Average content in soils	1–40 ppm, 5 ppm minimum for healthy cattle and sheep
Major minerals	Smaltite $CoAs_3$ 20.8%; Cobaltite CoAsS, 35.5%

History and Sources: While the ancient ceramists did not know the reason, certain earths contained the magic property of giving glass and ceramics a beautiful blue color. It was first used for this purpose more than 4000 years ago in Persia (Iran). When Marco Polo returned to Venice in 1295 from the court of Cathay (China) he brought back beautiful porcelains decorated with blue dragons and phoenixes. European ceramists who had not learned the secret of porcelain (kaolin and feldspar fired at 1450°C) were amazed. Actually the cobalt ore was imported into China from Persia. It was not until the 15th century that cobalt was discovered in China and was used in the "Ming" porcelains (1368–1644). Chinese cobalt contained manganese, an antiflux which helped prevent the blue from running.

In the sixteenth century German metallurgists, trying to refine copper ore from the Harz Mountains were frustrated because they could not recover the copper. They blamed it on an evil spirit, a *kobold*. This gremlin was identified as an element in 1780. The first important mining was in New Caledonia in 1860. Cobalt was found in the Sudbury Ontario copper-nickel

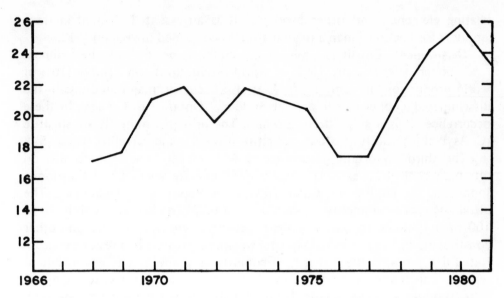

Figure 12*a* Cobalt production in the free world, given in thousands of metric tons.

ores early in the twentieth century and in the Belgian Congo (now Zaire) about 1920. Today Zaire produces half of the world's supply. Morocco, Zambia, and the USSR are other producers. In the United States small amounts are found in Pennsylvania and in Idaho in the Blackbird district.

Uses: Neutron bombardment of ^{59}Co results in ^{60}Co, the radioactive isotope with a half-life of 5.3 years. It is very useful in medicine for cancer treatment; it also has a military potential in nuclear bombs, where it could make large areas uninhabitable for many years.

Cobalt is similar to iron in many of its properties, one of them being excellent ferromagnetism. In alloys (e.g., alnico: aluminum, nickel, and cobalt) it makes the strongest permanent magnets. They have many applications in small motors and space facilities. Far less electricity is required to operate an appliance with permanent magnets than electromagnets, making battery operated hand tools possible. This accounts for 30% of the consumption.

Superalloys also consume 30% of the metal. There is no adequate substitute for cobalt in this field. These alloys retain their strength at relatively high temperature (to 650°C). Thus they can be used in the vanes of jet turbines for aircraft and on re-entry vehicles in the space program.

Chemical uses (25%) are the third important application of cobalt. This includes glazes, enamels and paints, and as a neutralizer of iron green in glass. It is the best binder for tungsten carbide for machine tools and drill bits. It is also used in other alloys for springs, dental bridges, stainless steel, heating elements, and other products. It is an essential element in trace amounts for health of man and animals. It is contained in vitamin B-12.

Occurrence: Cobalt is a by-product metal. It occurs with the sedimentary copper ores of Zaire (50% of world production) and Zambia (10% of world production) in central Africa. It also occurs in major amounts in the disseminated copper-nickel ores at Sudbury, Ontario, in Canada. In these occurrences it is a sulphide or arsenite. The principal minerals are smaltite ($CoAs_2$), skutterudite ($CoAs_3$), cobaltite ($CoAsS$), and carrollite ($CuCo_2S_4$).

The third important occurrence is with nickel in laterite formed on ultrabasic rocks by weathering in a tropical climate, such as New Caledonia, Indonesia, the Philippines, Cuba, Dominican Republic, or Guatemala. The ultrabasic rocks commonly contain 0.15 to 0.25% nickel, and with it, 50 to 100 ppm (0.005% to 0.01%) cobalt. Selective removal of silica and other constituents in the process of lateritic weathering results in a residue concentrated 6–8 times. If the nickel is of commercial grade, it may be possible to separate cobalt as a by-product. However, if the process for recovering nickel is to produce a nickel matte (sulphide), the cobalt cannot be separated. Likewise cobalt is lost if the ore is smelted to ferro-nickel. It is only in the chemical winning methods as practiced in Cuba and in Japan that cobalt can be recovered.

For the future, cobalt occurs with nickel and copper in the manganese nodules on the ocean floors. When production of nickel from this source becomes competitive with laterites, cobalt can be produced with it.

Economics: Cobalt has no economics of its own. Its cost allocation is dictated by accounting policy. Supply is inflexible and totally dependent upon production of the metals with which it occurs. World production of cobalt metal has averaged about 20,000 tons; mine production (not recovered for lack of market or stockpiled for future recovery) is somewhat higher (Fig 12). Thus it is a minor metal with consumption only twice the tonnage of silver. When Zaire was invaded in May 1978 by what were supposedly Katangan rebels wanting to separate that province from the country, production of the mines was brought to a sudden halt, shutting off about 50% of the supply of the western nations. Panic ensued among the consumers to whom it was an essential metal. The result was a price explosion, as shown in Figure 12b.

The invasion was quickly repelled with some outside assistance, and the mines were not badly damaged. Many of the expatriate experts and their families were killed by the invaders. As soon as possible most of the rest of the foreigners needed to manage the operation fled. Thus copper production, and with it cobalt, declined steeply.

Other copper producing nations were not unhappy about having production curtailed in one of the most productive nations at a time of market glut.

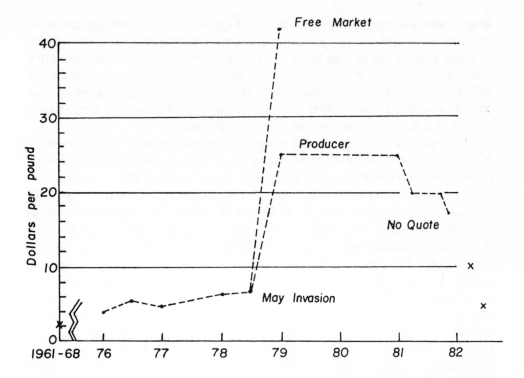

Figure 12*b* The price of cobalt, showing a sudden surge on the invasion of Shaba in May 1978.

They could produce at a high level and still not depress the price. For cobalt users, however, it was a crisis of supply.

Meanwhile the U.S. government price controllers were, as usual, out of phase. A large stockpile of this strategic metal had been built up in the 1950s. In 1965 it stood at about 46,200 tons. Then the policy changed. "We don't *need* all of this cobalt"—and the government began to sell it. The stockpile was to be reduced to 17,300 tons. Over a 10-year period 27,700 tons were sold, somewhat exceeding one-fourth of U.S. consumption. Of course, this overhead supply held down the price and suppressed development of other sources.

Supply problems in Zaire in early 1976 resulted in increased stockpile offerings. The government then realized that cobalt was a strategic metal. If Zaire were to be cut off it would be in great demand. Sales were reduced in April and halted at the end of August (2300 tons were sold in eight months). On October 1 with the level at 18,500, tons a new strategic stockpile objective of 38,744 tons was announced. The government ordered the purchase of 20,200 tons, to bring the stockpile back to the 1965 level. Sell when there is a surplus and force the price down, buy in a shortage and force the price to gyrate wildly upward, and the poor taxpayer is whipsawed again. Is it any wonder Europeans think the U.S. government is irrational? Of course this was a relatively minor piece of mismanagement compared to the great gold and silver rip-offs. At least the cobalt selling was controlled, while with gold and silver it was, "Come and get it, dollars for dimes, as long as they last." For gold the bargain was restricted to foreigners.

To look at the economics of opening a laterite mine solely on the basis of cobalt content, assume the rock had an original grade of 100 ppm cobalt. Laterization concentrates the grade 6.3 times, to 0.063%. A process will recover 80%, yielding one pound of refined metal per ton of ore. An estimate of the capital cost in 1980 would be about $30,000 per ton of daily through-put. That means the price has to be $12 per pound to repay the capital. That money has to be rented from someone, and at an interest rate of 14% this amounts to $11 per pound the first year. Operating costs would be about $12 per ton (pound) or a total of $35 per pound, just to break even. The prudent mine operator would have to add a big chunk for escalation, experience showing this to be expected and knowing it would be about seven years from the time evaluation started until the mine would be in full operation. Then the owners and stockholders want something for their investment and risk. If a price of $50 (1982) per pound could be reasonably assured for 1989, the cobalt mine might be a sound investment. At that price there is no cobalt shortage. But what if the United States decides again in 1987, that it does not *need* all of that cobalt in a stockpile?

Production Methods: Since cobalt is almost never mined for itself, but as a by-product of other mining operations, reference is made to operations of nickel (laterite and magmatic segregation) and bedded deposits under copper. It is separated in the refining process from these other metals because it is an impurity.

Outlook: For probably two-thirds of its uses other metals can be substituted, or there is promise of substitution. In carbide tools and some special alloys, however, no adequate substitute is known. Since it takes time and costs money to make substitutions, a switch to an alternate material, once made, is likely to be a permanent loss of the market. The market for any material is a function of price. Diamond cutting tools can replace tungsten carbide, so even this market is not secure. If the January 1980 producers' price of $25 per pound had remained, the market would be reduced and life of reserves proportionately extended. In mid-1982 there was no published price with sales reportedly being made at $10–$12 per pound, dropping below $6 by the year's end.

One other factor comes into play when there is a major price escalation. Secondary recovery becomes more efficient, again reducing the market for new metal.

To illustrate the futility of trying to forecast, the U.S. Bureau of Mines in 1970 forecast the price of $1.85 per pound would continue (barring shortage) to A.D. 2000 and between 26,800 and 38,900 tons per year would be consumed (world) at that time. Since the price has already increased 3.5 times (less inflation), consumption might be lower than the lowest estimate by that year. No fundamental shortage is foreseen through the twenty-first century. It is probable that cobalt will be recovered from the marine manganese nodules early in the next century.

COPPER (Cu)

Properties and Characteristics

Atomic number	29
Atomic weight	63.54
Isotopes	58, 59, 60, 61, 62, 64, 66, 68
Melting point	1083°C
Specific gravity	8.95
Average in rocks	70 ppm; mafic 140 ppm; felsic 30 ppm; soils 20 ppm; range 2–100 ppm
Major minerals	Chalcopyrite $CuFeS_2$, Cu 34.5%; Bornite Cu_5FeS_4, Cu 63.3%; Chalcocite Cu_2S, Cu 79.8%; Native, Malachite $CuCO_3$ $Cu(OH)_2$, Cu 57.4%, Cuprite Cu_2O, Cu 88.8%

History: Copper, occurring in the native state, was one of the earliest metals used by man. The archeological records indicate that tools were made from it about 10,000 years ago, during the neolithic period. Knives and spear points were some of the first products, used for fighting and hunting. Because of the beauty of the metal it was prized for decorations and jewelry.

Pyrometallurgy probably was discovered as the result of copper oxides being contained in stones in a camp fire which happened to come in contact with hot charcoal. An inventor may have noticed the beads of metal the next morning and concluded that he could make this valuable metal out of the blue stones. If he was an entrepreneur, he may have set up shop, charging a leg of wild ox for a knife. These developments took place in the Middle East, and were a factor in development of civilization.

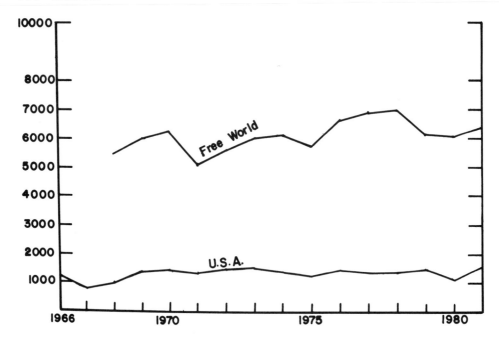

Figure 13 Copper production in the United States and in the free world, given in thousands of metric tons.

The history of copper is discussed in some detail in Chapter 1, the use of this metal giving its name to two of the cultural periods in human progress, the Chalcolithic and the Bronze ages. Copper was mined on the Sinai peninsula as early as 3800 B.C., with the Egyptians being the first to develop the extensive use of the metal. In the fourth millenium B.C. copper was discovered on Cyprus, and the deposits were so extensive that the island became a prized territory for all of the empires of the Mediterranean region. This was the main source of the metal during Roman times and it is from the Latin name for the island, Cyprium, that the term *cuprum* was derived, and later anglicized to copper. The symbol Cu comes from the Latin name.

Bronze was discovered in both the Mediterranean region and later, independently, in Bolivia and Peru. Very sophisticated medical instruments and the operation known as trepanning (repairing smashed skulls) developed in South America.

Native copper was used by American Indians long before the arrival of Columbus, the deposits in upper Michigan being one of the main sources. Copper was mined near Simsbury, Connecticut, in 1709. Additional deposits were discovered in Vermont in 1820 and the mines of the Indians in Michigan were found about 1840. Western ore bodies were discovered and developed around 1860 with U.S. production rising to 30,000 tons by 1880. The huge deposit at Bingham, Utah, was opened in 1906, the first porphyry copper deposit to be exploited as such.

A major mine was developed at Kennecott, Alaska. After the deposit was depleted, the company had set aside reserves for depletion and was prepared to return the capital to the stockholders. At a meeting it was decided not to dissolve but to buy another mine. The property purchased was that of Utah Copper Co. at Bingham, Utah. This was the beginning of the modern Kennecott Corporation.

Uses: Copper ranks fifth among the metals in tonnage consumed. Its uses are many. By far the most important is in electrical applications. It is used in motor and generator windings where its high electrical conductivity gives it an advantage over most metals. It is used in transformers, bus bars, switch gears, and in electrical wiring. It is extensively used in communications equipment including cables and television transmitters and receivers.

Copper's second important use is in construction, particularly in plumbing and hardware and decorative purposes. It is important in non-electrical industrial applications such as the alloy with nickel for tubing in sea water desalination plants. It is used in heat exchangers, pollution control, and liquid waste disposal. Automobile radiator cores are made of copper; it is also used in air conditioners, heaters, gas and oil lines, and bearings and bushings.

Military uses rank fourth, and the price usually goes up during a period of military spending. This is one of the incremental uses which can rapidly increase consumption. Coinage, jewelry, chemicals, pigments, brass and bronze wares, and a multitude of minor uses also demand copper.

Copper is essential to plant growth; if the soil content falls below 10 ppm, good growth is not attained. On the other hand, if a large amount of copper is present in the soil it is toxic to some plants. In the Philippines there is a variety of fern that requires about 2000 ppm in the soil for growth. Its presence is a good indicator of copper.

Occurrence: There are hundreds of copper minerals and dozens of settings for copper deposits. By far the most important mineral is chalcopyrite and the large portion of this mineral and of copper production comes from porphyry copper deposits. Other minerals in the same environment are bornite, also called "peacock ore" because of its brilliant colors, and chalcocite, which is the main mineral in the near surface zone of secondary enrichment.

The term porphyry refers to a rock which has an intergrowth of distinctly large and small crystals. Porphyries are considered to have intruded as molten rock or magma from depths of tens to hundreds of kilometers. To form the texture of a porphyry, it should have approached to within about three kilometers of the surface before crystallizing as rock. The texture of mixed coarse and fine crystals is thought to indicate fairly rapid cooling.

Certain types of rocks are more likely to occur with copper than others. These are diorite, quartz diorite, and granodiorite; late stage porphyries in these rocks are essential for copper development. In addition, quartz monzonite porphyry or quartz porphyry is highly favorable.

A "porphyry" in the sense of mineralization is a massive system that may total hundreds of billions of tons. Only a small portion carries an economic grade of valuable constituents, usually near the center of the zone. Characteristically a large volume contains a fairly uniform dissemination of chalcopyrite, even though low in grade, thus another name for this type of deposit is "disseminated copper." Average size is about 120,000,000 tons containing 0.5% copper. Today, however, that would hardly be ore unless it contained some gold, silver, or molybdenum.

In the high deserts of Arizona, Chile, and Peru where erosion is slow, the copper and iron sulphides oxidize, forming sulphuric acid and metallic sulphates. The copper solutions trickle down to the water table which may be 300 m below the surface, where reducing conditions exist and the copper is precipitated as a sulphide again, commonly chalcocite. The zone just above and below the water table thus becomes enriched from two to ten times the grade of the original mineralization. This is called secondary enrichment and if it forms a substantial zone, it is called a chalcocite blanket. These enriched zones have been the only economic deposits in some mines and constitute an important source of copper.

Second in importance to the deposits in igneous rocks are the stratabound deposits. These occur within strata of sandstone, shale, or limestone, often limited to a single stratigraphic layer. It may be bedded, hence covering an area of even hundreds of thousands of square kilometers, such as the Kupferschiefer which extends across Germany into Poland. There are the extremely important beds in Zambia and Zaire where the metals precipitated from the sea with the sediments. Stratabound deposits can also be found in discontinuous lenses introduced after the sediments were deposited. One of the earliest known copper mines which was rediscovered and put back into production was of the stratabound type. A deposit known as King Solomon's Mine in Israel in the Negev desert was this type. Another form of stratabound deposit is known as *kuroko* (black ore), named from the classic occurrences in Japan. The copper and other metals are deposited directly on the sea floor around a center of surfacing igneous rocks. Sometimes massive sulphides (largely pyrite) have formed reaching 500 million tons. Ancient deposits of this type are found in eastern Canada, Australia, and elsewhere. Yet a third type of copper deposit is found within sediments. This is the replacement type, usually in limestone. Hydrothermal solutions dissolve part of the limestone and deposit copper and other minerals in its place. This may be in the same system as a porphyry and represent some of the richest portions of the zone. On the ocean floor at centers of volcanic activity hydrothermal solutions in hot springs, sometimes deposit large masses of copper and zinc sulphides. Juvenile deposits of this type have recently been photographed deep in the ocean near the Galapogos Islands. Large, ancient deposits of this type occur at Cyprus, the world's first large mine.

Frequently in the halo of a porphyry, in an outer zone of alteration, veins of copper and other minerals are found. They may be of appreciably higher grade than the porphyry, but the cost of mining is much higher. Veins provided the only source at Butte, Montana, for many years; the low-grade ore in the open pit was developed many years later. There are also veins that have been mined around the huge deposit at Bingham Canyon, Utah.

A large occurrence of native copper (free metal) is found in Michigan. Sometimes the masses of metal are so large they cannot be mined. They cannot be blasted or cut by a torch. These deposits are within sediments also.

In the Sudbury district of Canada in the magmatic segregation deposits nickel and copper sulphides and platinum group elements have settled into a narrow zone and are rich enough to be mined. These deposits are very extensive and are the world's main source of nickel (see discussion under nickel).

One other type of deposit is called "supergene." This consists of a group of minerals formed by weathering of sulphide minerals. They are the colorful minerals found on outcrops—malachite and chrysocolla (the light blue-green minerals), tennorite (a black mineral), azurite (deep blue), cuprite (red), and native copper. Sometimes these minerals are found directly over the primary sulphides of the type from which they are derived, or sometimes they are transported a short distance and redeposited. They constitute a minor but significant source of the metal.

Economics: Copper was used as the illustration in Chapter 4, Mineral Economics, so this discussion will be short. The price of copper averaged 11.7 cents per pound from 1920 through 1946. For the next 8 years it averaged 23.7 cents, and for the next 14 years 33.7 cents. The next step upward commenced in 1969 and the five-year average was 53.2 cents. In 1974, immediately after the "oil shock," the price increased markedly with the average being $1.014 per pound in 1980. Thus in the post-war period, the price of copper quadrupled while the price of oil increased by 17 times. It is the relative deflation compared to the cost of energy that has upset the copper economy. (All prices are based on U.S. refinery charges). In May 1982 the price was 76 cents per pound, only 50% above the pre "oil shock" level, subsequently dropping to the 60–65 cent range.

Free world copper production was slightly above 6 Mmt for the period 1978–1980. A 10% increase was programmed for 1980–1982. Several very large projects are underway or awaiting more favorable conditions. Thus oversupply is virtually assured for the next five years. As mentioned in Chapter 7, the copper producing nations are subsidizing the economies of the industrial importing nations, much to the delight of the latter.

In spite of being the world's largest producer, the United States is not self-sufficient in copper. In 1946 when the initial stockpiling program was established, the objective for copper was set at 1.25 Mst. In 1950 it was raised to 2.1 Mst and dropped to 1.1 Mst in 1953 to 1.0 in 1959, to 0.77 Mst in 1963 and to zero in 1973. In 1960 there were actually 1.15 Mst in the stockpile. The reductions in the 1960s were adjusted to the excess demands of the Viet Nam war. By 1974 the stockpile was essentially eliminated. Subsequently the advisability of building it back has been discussed. Meanwhile Japan and France have undertaken stockpiling programs.

There have been many international meetings on the proposal to establish an international copper agreement, but they have all ended in bickering over some detail that has prevented agreement. The basic reason for this is undoubtedly that the consuming nations are happy with the present arrangement, where the taxpayers in the developing nations are subsidizing the consumers. Any agreement would probably increase the price of the commodity.

Production: Most of the world's copper is produced from large open pit mines using shovels with a *dipper* capacity of 40 tons for loading from several benches and trucks of up to 250 ton capacity to haul to the crusher. Mills have increased greatly in diameter, to the height of a three story building. Flotation cells now exceed 1000 ft³ in volume, the size of a small room. This trend toward the gigantic is designed to get the maximum benefit from scale, and may have reached or exceeded the cost-benefit ratio.

Some deposits have been excavated to depths where open pit mining is no longer feasible and to continue operating would require conversion to the block caving method of underground mining. This is generally a more expensive form of mining, particularly if the ore must be hoisted from a shaft. A definite trend toward this method of mining can be foreseen as surface deposits are exhausted, but not many ore bodies of this type have been found, primarily because they would be uneconomic today.

Room and pillar mining is used in the sedimentary deposits that are flat-lying, and stoping methods are used on veins and steeply dipping beds.

After milling at the mine site, the ore is either smelted on site or shipped to a smelter. The concentrate generally averages 25%–30% copper, so a lot of waste is shipped. Concentrates may be roasted or may go directly to a reverberatory furnace where enough sulphur is burned off to form a copper matte composed largely of copper, iron, and sulphur, with precious metals dissolved in it. Slag is drawn off and sent to waste piles. The molten matte goes to a converter where air is blown through it to oxidize the sulphur, which is released as SO_2, and iron, which separates as a lighter slag. The product is fairly pure "blister" copper, which is either fire refined or poured into anodes for electrolytic refining.

In the refinery process, anodes are hung alternatively with thin, pure copper starting sheets. Precious metals collect in the sludge and are recovered later. The copper product is at least 99.9% pure and is melted and cast into shapes for subsequent fabricating processes.

Free world production of copper in 1980 was 6,050,000 tons, down slightly from the two previous years. World production amounted to about 7.6 Mmt. Free world consumption dropped 4.4% to 7.18 Mmt, the difference representing withdrawals from stockpiles and refining of scrap.

Outlook: Copper is the victim of technological success. During and shortly after World War II, copper was in short supply and there were dire warnings about exhaustion of reserves. By 1960 the geology of the porphyry copper deposits was being unravelled and important discoveries were made in Canada, Peru, Chile, Papua New Guinea, the Philippines, and of course in the United States. Engineers met the production challenge by building equipment of larger size so that the cost of winning the metal from the lower-grade ore remained low.

This should be a scenario for improved profits, but with an excess of discoveries came an excess of production, followed by national policy in Chile, the second largest producer, to sell at any price to maintain cash flow. Thus for the past 10 years copper has been a depressed industry with only two brief spurts in price which permitted reasonable profit for a short spell and encouraged more over-production. Today more than half of the mines would shut down if it were not for the subsidy they receive from co-products that have increased in price—gold, molybdenum, and silver.

The impact of the big oil companies that are now invading the copper industry en masse is discussed in Chapter 8.

The outlook for copper is for at least another five years of adequate production and low to modest profits, unless the highly paid oil company futurologists know something about the business that the operators who have spent years studying it do not.

Copper is known as a war metal and in antiquated systems of warfare that used cannon and rifles, increased war-time demand drove the price up. The greatly increased military spending announced in 1981 appears to emphasize this type of ordnance, which could put pressure on copper supplies in 1983 and beyond, resulting in more attractive prices.

Without a war scare the consumption of copper is not likely to increase as rapidly as the economy as a whole; and with 30 large copper deposits in the United States alone awaiting favorable economic conditions, new production can easily be brought into being in time to meet requirements.

GOLD (Au)

Properties and Characteristics

Atomic number	79
Atomic weight	196.97 very malleable
Hardness	2.5–3.0
Electrical resistivity	2.44×10^{-8}
Color	Golden yellow
Density	19.2 (the same as tungsten)
Melting point	1063°C
Minerals	Native element, as tellurides

History: Gold! What magic, myth, and mystery that word conjurs. It has a beauty unequalled by any other metal and it never tarnishes or rusts. The chemical symbol, Au, is from the Latin word *aurium,* "shining dawn." It was probably the first metal used by man. Nuggets found in stream beds were first used as trinkets. Gold has enriched history and mythology through the tales of rich King Croesus, King Midas and his golden touch, and the golden fleece of Jason. King Solomon was one of the first rulers to have an extensive department of mines; his exploration program was very successful. His fabulous gold mine has recently been rediscovered in the Arabian peninsula and the new operator, Consolidated Gold Fields, estimates there is as much gold remaining as was removed by Solomon.

In a recent effort to verify and trace the story of Jason, the author went to Turkey and studied references to gold deposits known today, but could find none at Jason's supposed destination at the eastern end of the Black Sea. There is another clue to the location of the realm of King Aeetes. He had a bull that spouted flames and black smoke and occasionally blew up. This seems to be a reference to use of petroleum to power a mechanical bull, the first "tractor," to plow his fields. Naturally it had to be shaped like a bull because bulls always were used for plowing. Jason was brave enough to drive it around the field once. It was probably a mechanical monstrosity, and poor metal resulted in frequent explosions of the petroleum fuel. The only place reasonably accessible to the coast where an oil seep is known is from a spot in Turkey on the south side of the Straits of Bosporus; placer

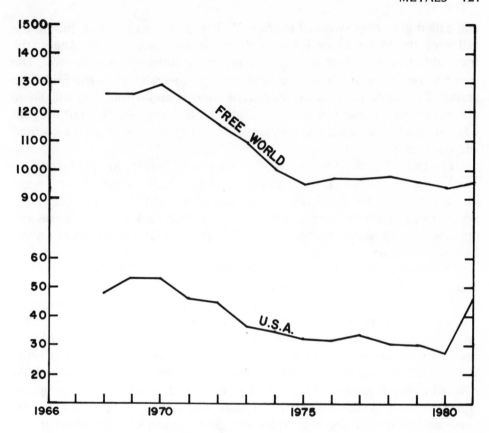

Figure 14 Gold production in the United States and the free world, given in metric tons.

gold *is* found on the coast north of the strait but on the *west* end of the Black Sea. It is just possible that the rascal Jason made up the story about the long journey east to throw other adventurers off. Like modern prospectors who "strike it rich" and do not have the ground pegged, he did not want to disclose his find. King Aeetes probably gave him the golden fleece, a sheep skin that had been used to line a sluice box to collect gold, as a dowry for his daughter. He was probably glad to get rid of the witch, and it was not long until Jason regretted taking Medea as a wife. There probably were no more than three or four ounces of gold caught in the sheepskin.

Spain discovered the new world and proceeded to undertake the most wanton pillaging in history. Galleons spent years transporting the Incan loot to the court of Spain. Pirates and "free-booters" preyed on the galleons, and tales of buried gold or sunken treasure ships have roused the imagination of many boys. Pizzaro and his "tanks" (armored conquistadors on horses) started the rape of the Quechua Indians of Peru and Bolivia under their religious leader, the Inca, or high priest. The Inca worshipped the sun as God and called gold the "sweat of the Sun." Where observed by the author in the valley of the Murmantani River high on the east slope of the Andes, the Inca mine workings were in fossil placers on the hillside above the river. The tunnels were very small, barely large enough to crawl through. From the graves of some of the miners, they were midgets about four feet tall. There are reports that these midgets were bred for this purpose. Much of the gold was low grade, but slave labor was free and they could raise their own food and coca leaves.

The United States has had its gold rushes—to Sutter's Mill, California, in 1849, and to the Canadian Klondike in 1898. Later some of the miners joined the Army for the Spanish War. The miner soldiers panned the mountain streams of north Luzon, Philippines, and then took their discharges and remained in the Islands to develop the rich mines at Baguio and southeastern Luzon at Paracale.

Probably 90% of the gold ever mined (or about 125,000 tons) is still in use or buried in hoards, like Fort Knox.

Uses: Half of the gold laboriously mined is taken out of one hole, refined, and buried in another hole. The person who has a lot of it says he is "rich." A pack rat in the abandoned mining camp with a collection of pine cones, string, and metal foil thinks he is rich, too. Ah, but gold has *intrinsic* value. That means it has value because it is just *naturally* valuable! As covered under *Economics*, the U.S. Treasury tried to refute this assumption and gave away $500 billion before admitting defeat. Therefore the most common use of gold is to hide it, bury it, guard it, and know you have it.

Table 7

Weights and Measures of Gold

1 ounce Troy[1]	= 31.1 grams
1 ounce Troy	= 20 penny weights = 480 grains
1 ounce Avoirdupois	= 28.35 grams
1 pound Troy	= 12 oz = 373 grams
1 pound (Avoirdupois)	= 16 oz = 454 grams
1 pound feathers (Avoirdupois)	= 1.2 pounds of gold (Troy)
Karat[2] (measure of gold purity) 24 k	= pure
Fineness (measure of gold purity) 1000 fine	= pure gold
750 fine	= 75% gold (18 k)

[1] The Troy system of measure for precious metals and drugs was introduced in Troyes, France. Now used only in the United States.

[2] Not to be confused with jewelers gemstone carat, which is a weight of 200 milligrams (the weight of a carob seed).

Jewelry and ornamentation constitute the second important use of gold. This, too, is a form of hoarding. Because it is inert and durable, it has been extensively used in dentistry. With the tremendous increase in price, however, it is hardly safe to have it in your mouth. Also, it has been reported that morticians have their own gold mines.

Gold has become important in electronics. It does not corrode and is the best electrical conductor. It is so good for this purpose that the Defense Department used it in its missile control systems. *That* was a usage where the Air Force did not dare risk failure. Another system that is considered fail-safe is the mercury switch. They were installed to connect the gold conductors. What the designers forgot was that mercury has a relatively high vapor pressure and gold readily amalgamates with mercury. So at one point fairly early in the missile race, about 97% of the U.S. weaponry was immobilized and no one knew it. Luckily, the missiles did not short out and fire by themselves.

The space age has developed a minor usage of gold, for applications where its resistance to corrosion is important. There is a hint that modern society has only rediscovered this. In the first chapter of Ezekiel from the fifth century B.C. the prophet describes five visitors from space wearing space suits that appeared to be made of "burnished brass," sparkling in the sunlight. He had probably never seen gold before, since he was a slave working in the fields of Babylon.

Occurrence: Gold occurs in two categories of deposits, lode and *placer*. *Lode* deposits are primary and are generally thought of as *veins*. This is a filling of a large fracture in the earth with a relatively rich concentration of minerals, some of which are valuable to man. The fractures are formed when the earth is strained beyond the strength of the rocks, failing by rupture which may be expressed as an earthquake. Hot mineralizing solutions seep, flow, or squirt into the fracture, dissolving some rock, replacing some rock with new minerals (alteration), and precipitating other minerals, some of which contain metals. In a gold lode the most common mineral is quartz with pyrite, iron sulphide being second. Pyrite is called "fool's gold" since novices think it is gold because of its brassy color. Gold commonly occurs with lead, zinc, and copper, either as the major or minor product. The gold occurs largely as tiny specks invisible to the naked eye. The rising hot water contains a small amount of gold. An atom drops out here and there, nucleating a tiny gold crystal. If a large amount precipitates, it is a gold lode. If you can see it, it is fairly rich. Many things affect whether or not it is commercial "ore," but 15 grams (half an ounce) per ton is generally a good grade. Veins are commonly vertical to steeply dipping, but can be even flat. A lot of little stringers (very narrow, criss-crossing veinlets) is a "stock work" and if large, may be ore even at a much lower grade (2-3 grams per ton).

Gold is most frequently found in the "free" or elemental form. It is quite inert chemically, reacting only with *aqua regia* (nitric plus hydrochloric acid) froming a soluble gold chloride. It is also found in nature in the combined form as a family of tellurides, combined with the element tellurium: krennerite, calaverite, sylvanite, and a few others. These are important ores of gold.

By far the largest quantity of gold is in ocean water, either in solution or suspension. One estimate is 0.02 parts per billion (50,000 tons contain one gram), but in the total volume of the ocean this amounts to 28×10^6 tons. (Other estimates range from one-fifth to 50,000 times as much.) There are bays adjoining gold areas where the water is concentrated 2000 times in gold and recovery might be feasible.

Now suppose a vein containing gold is exposed at the surface by erosion of the mountain. The quartz is broken up, and releases gold, which travels down the hillside by creep and washing until it enters a stream. Being heavy, it works its way into the stream bottom during floods and becomes concentrated in the stream gravel. This is known as *placer* gold. The early gold discoveries were placers, but prospectors quickly learned to follow the precious metal to its lode source which rarely is a "rich strike." Since the work of mining has been done by nature, placer deposits of much lower grade are commercial. In developing nations where wages are low, one gram per ton (mine a million grams to get one) is good, especially when gold is $11 per gram ($340 per ounce). However, most placer gold is produced by large dredges producing 5,000 to 10,000 cubic meters per day. By this system, at $11 per gram and 1982 costs, 0.2 grams per cubic meter may be profitable. In fact, less than 0.1 gram would "pay," such a small amount that when trying to evaluate a deposit of, say, 40,000,000 cubic meters, it cannot be accurately sampled by any means.

Gold occurs is almost every nation, but in most the amount is subcommercial. There are tremendous deposits in South Africa in the famous Rand district, and the mines, now very deep and hot, supply about three-fourths of the newly mined gold of the western world (see Figure 14). Russia ranks second, with the exact amount undisclosed, but probably about 200 tons per year. The United States is a major producer, with names like "Homestake" in South Dakota and the "Mother Lode" of California being well known. Another very large producer is the Carlin mine in Nevada, discovered in 1960, noted for "invisible" gold, so fine that it can only be seen by a microscope. Most of the U.S. gold is now a by-product of other mining operations, particularly porphyry copper deposits. Other major producers are Australia, Canada, Peru, Ghana, the Philippines, Papua New Guinea, and China.

Economics: It is difficult to discuss the economics of a myth. There is a story that President Roosevelt wanted to demonetize gold in 1933 but Bernard Baruch told him a parable about discovery of a Roman hoard consisting of gold and paper money. Although buried for 2000 years, the gold still had value. Consequently the price of gold was raised 50% and Americans were forbidden to own it. That was one way of forcing his countrymen to trust in printing press money.

The U.S. Treasury has tried hard to convince the world that there is no relationship between gold and money. Its staff has at times become almost apoplectic, as when President de Gaulle of France said, "I don't believe you," and took them up on their offer to sell all of the gold anyone (non-American) wanted to buy at $35 per ounce. The Treasury even bragged about getting rid of that worthless hoard Roosevelt had stashed away for *real* paper money, backed by the credit of the U.S. government. In effect, they gave it away. As in all price fixing schemes, when foreigners (only) realized they could buy Cadillacs for Volkswagen prices, there was a run on Fort Knox. They bought a dollar's worth of gold for a dime, the biggest giveaway in history. No one was allowed to take inventory, but at one time the government said it had $40 billion worth of gold. At $35 per ounce, that would amount to 35,543 tons. Now it has about 9000 tons. Assuming 25,000 tons were dumped, that would be worth $500 billion (at $620 per ounce) but went for $28 billion. A handsome giveaway to foreign speculators. The government could have given $2500 worth to every citizen, instead. A better measure of worth might be what it would cost to buy it back. The price would shoot up to astronomic levels. (Remember, we bought it at $35 per ounce last time.)

That pretty well establishes the fact that the "worth" of gold cannot be measured in terms of a battered and shrinking piece of paper. So let's try another standard. For many years two grams of gold would buy a barrel of crude oil. When the paper price of oil increased to $30, the price of gold rose also: 30 × 15 is $450 per ounce. The price over-shot the mark, but then settled back down. At a projected price of $60 per barrel in 1987, gold should be $900. There is no doubt that energy *is* an absolute standard of value.

A third measure would be the cost of producing an ounce of gold. That integrates the cost of fuel, electricity, and the man that controls the energy expenditure. If mining costs are going up 30% per year (a figure given for Arizona in 1979 and 1980) the price of gold has to increase about 2% per month.

How to get off this debilitating treadmill is the question of the decade. Under similar circumstances Rome elected Caesar and Weimar Germany elected Hitler.

Production Methods: Most of the gold is produced by underground mines, following small veins, or, in South Africa, "reefs." Depending on grade, the "pay zone" may be 1–10 feet (30 cm to 3 m) thick. This involves extensive hand labor. A stoper or drifter (a large air drill) is used to sink holes into the gold-bearing rock, which are loaded with dynamite and blasted into small lumps. It falls or is scraped into a chute, from which it can be loaded into a rail car or truck. It is hauled to a shaft, elevated to the surface in a skip, and fed into a crusher.

After the rock is reduced to a size to release the gold, it is put through one of two processes. Either gold is leached by cyanide solution and then precipitated, or it goes to a flotation circuit where the gold and other minerals are floated by bubbles and a concentrate is smelted to recover gold and other minerals.

The gold may also be widely dispersed, permitting large-scale methods of mining to be employed. Carried to an endpoint, associated minerals may be the major product and gold the by-product as in the large open-pit copper mines. Mining gold as a by-product is the second most important method. Still another method of recovery of low-grade gold is to pile the mined ore in heaps and pour cyanide solution over it. Great care must be taken to avoid contaminating the environment with deadly cyanide.

Yet another method used for mining placer gold is by large-scale dredging of stream gravels with a massive digger mounted on a barge, capable of digging (with the new bucket wheel dredges) to 50 m. The coarse gravel is screened out and dumped, and the finer sizes are treated by gravity methods to recover the gold. There may be significant by-products such as zircon, rutile, ilmenite, scheelite, or tin.

Under Keynesian economics, gold was almost a dirty word. The devotées of Keynes held sway from the administration of Roosevelt through that of Johnson. However, no system could withstand the economic mismanagement of the period from 1962 to 1968 (a war on top of "normal economics"). Europeans, seeing chaos coming, bought gold furiously (at $35 per ounce), shutting down the London Gold Market. In 1968, to try to restore order, the abortive and short-lived two-tier price system was created. The official price of gold became $42.22 per ounce and a "free market" price was allowed, since it was in existence anyway. It amounted to accepting chaos. In 1971 President Nixon ended the "great giveaway" which he had inherited. The governments pledged to use the "official price" after the Smithsonian Agreement in 1971, but South Africa, producing 70% of the gold, refused to abide by the agreement and sold its production to the market. The price of gold went up, and in 1973 (after the IMF meeting in Nairobi failed to solve the problem) the United States abandoned the two-tier system, which meant the U.S. could sell gold at market price, like other countries were doing. Americans were still forbidden to own gold, but the "sharpies" with Swiss accounts were into the speculation on the other side of the Atlantic.

All of this points up that the market chaos preceded the Yom Kipper War and the OPEC war in petroleum pricing. Gold broke loose from the traditional 15 bbl per ounce ratio *before* OPEC overacted.

In late 1974 the price of gold reached $197, anticipating a buying spree when, for the first time in 42 years, Americans could own gold legally. When no buying spree developed, speculators liquidated, and gold dropped back rapidly to about $110 per ounce. Oversold, it became cheaper than petroleum.

The petro-gouge knocked world economics into a tailspin. While the petro-riches were rolling into the OPEC countries, the less developed countries suffered and some became economic "basket cases." Japan swallowed a big dose of devaluation, suffered, and began to recover. Hunger and even starvation wracked the third world. The United States tried to pretend nothing had happened, and was shocked when double digit inflation hit.

When the radicals in OPEC began clamoring for more price increases, Saudia Arabia and some others tried to moderate the demands for further price increases. Several of the Gulf states could not spend the money that was rolling in so fast; a price increase would only compound the problem. The only thing of "value" was gold, then underpriced, and a beautiful situation offered itself. The OPEC countries could buy gold and make it increase in price by just increasing the price of oil. Thus oil and gold prices began to spiral upward.

The average man could not speculate in oil, but he could in gold, so late in 1979 and early in 1980 a "blow-off" occurred. Gold shot up to about $900 per ounce. At that time, oil was $42 per barrel on the spot market; in relation to the price of gold, oil should have sold for $60. As usual, the speculators got buried and the professionals made money on the down-side.

To the cynic it made sense. The average American thought the constitution had been amended to guarantee them three gas-guzzlers per family and all the gasoline they wanted to squander. They refused to countenance a limitation, and would dump any politician who asked them to accept the new reality. But by early 1980 the pinch in the pocketbook began to tell. Americans bought fewer over-sized American cars. Detroit was aghast. After a generation of telling the public what it wanted, they could no longer dictate.

Outlook: While some economists think it is a short-term coincidence, the prices of gold and petroleum seem to be linked loosely together. OPEC can control the volume of petroleum exported to protect the price. By mid-1982, speculative unloading had dropped the price of gold below the historic ratio, thus it should soon rise. To break the strangle-hold OPEC has on the world economy, two things must occur. (1) The United States must again become a net energy exporter. (2) It must be accepted that petroleum is too precious to burn. Down the road about 30 years it must be accepted that coal, too, is not for burning.

We have witnessed a "run" on the "energy bank" in the twentieth century, squandering in 80 years deposits made over half a billion years. Gold is the "fever gauge," telling us how sick the economy has become. Until there is a dramatic decrease in dependence on fossil fuels, the disease will get worse and worse.

It is conceivable that a tremendous up-surge in gold production could occur, flooding the market. This would break the gold-petroleum tie, but would not solve the energy problem.

It is possible that gold production could be greatly increased. It is reported that the geothermal brine in the Salton Sea (California) has a high gold content, and full development of the geothermal energy would yield an amount on the order of present world production. A second possible source is the ocean itself, which contains significant gold (0.02 ppb). Until now, the cost of extraction has been too high to make the process economical. If local concentrating systems should result in build-up of gold (for example, desalination plants), gold extraction could become feasible.

Alchemy: The subject of gold cannot be concluded without a discussion of transmutation of metals. Man has dreamed of instant riches by changing a common metal like lead, copper, or mercury into a precious metal, particularly to gold. The predecessor to chemistry, alchemy, was built up largely for the purpose of transmutation. Whole libraries developed on the subject.

One of the earliest references to transmutation was a law decreed in China in 175 B.C. prohibiting this practice. In A.D. 300, the Roman Emperor Diocletian ordered burning of all books in Egypt on "making of gold and silver." In 1317 Pope John XXII issued a papal bull fining anyone found "commercializing the transmutation of gold." He himself was supposed to have practiced transmutation and "manufactured" 200 gold bars. When he died in 1334 his vault yielded 25 million gold florins. He wrote a book on the subject, "Ars Transmutatoria."

In England in 1404 Henry IV made "multiplication of metals" a crime and ordered all gold made in this manner turned over to the government. In the fifteenth century George Ripley, an alchemist, contributed 100,000 pounds (45 tons of monetary pounds) of gold *yearly* to the Order of St. John of Jerusalem at Rhodes to finance the fight against the Turks. Another alchemist was supposed to have financed a crusade and another reportedly paid off the British national debt. Reports of transmutation and specimens purporting to be "proof" continue to the present, with examples in the British and Austrian museums.

Is transmutation possible? The scientist says "No, not without a neutron accelerator." Mercury has isotopes 196 and 198, bracketing the 197 of gold, but lead isotopes are considerably heavier. So is it all myth or fraud? No one has demonstrated transmutation under controlled tests and until they do, it is best to doubt. Should anyone want to pursue the subject of gold, the technical side is covered with thoroughness in a Bulletin 280 of the Geological Survey of Canada, *The Geochemistry of Gold and Its Deposits*, by R. W. Boyle. In the back are 86 pages of references, with about 35 references per page. This does not begin to cover aspects of gold, other than the geology and geochemistry of the element.

IRON (Fe)

Properties and Characteristics

Atomic number	26
Atomic weight	55.85
Isotopes (order of abundance)	56, 54, 57, 58
Artificial	53, 55, 59
Melting Point	1530°C
Average content in rocks	Av. 4.65%; Mafic 8.56% Felsic 2.7%; Soils Range 1.4%–4.0%
Major minerals	Hematite Fe_2O_3 (Fe-70%); magnetite Fe_3O_4 (Fe-72.4%); limonite $Fe_2O_3 nH_2O$ (Fe var.); pyrite FeS_2 (Fe-46.6%)

History: Iron is the metal of civilization. Fifteen times more iron is used than its nearest competitor, aluminum. Its use was first recorded in Egyptian weapons about 2000 B.C. The first source was from meteors, hence it was very scarce and ranked as precious. Iron is mentioned in Genesis; Tubal Cain is noted as an instructor in working of copper and iron. This may have been a later insertion because the period appears to antedate records of use.

The Greeks used and prized iron, obtaining it from the coast of Turkey. The cultural stage called the Iron Age began about 1000 B.C. This is discussed at some length in Chapter 1. Iron was probably accidentally discovered in a camp fire; it was produced in forges with charcoal in the Middle Ages. The blast furnace evolved between the fourteenth and sixteenth centuries in Germany. Iron making was introduced in the American colonies

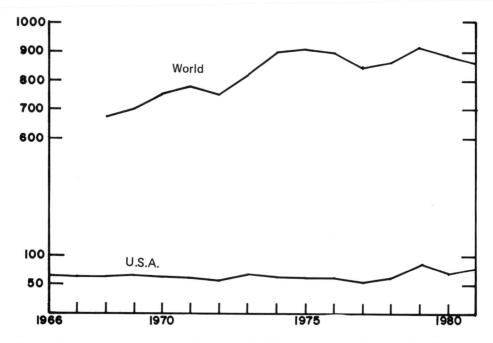

Figure 15 Iron ore production in the United States and world, given in millions of metric tons.

in Virginia in 1610. This initial plant was wiped out by an Indian raid in 1622. Another plant was built north of Boston in 1650.

The discussion of iron cannot be separated from steel, an alloy of iron with at least one other element. The first steel was probably discovered accidentally, the result of leaving a tool in a fire with charcoal for an extended period. The absorbed carbon converted the tool into carbon steel, much harder than iron.

The crucible process was developed in 1740 in England. Charcoal was used until the forests in the vicinity of the plants became depleted and coal was introduced about 1850 but the superior properties of coke were soon discovered. The Bessemer process was developed by Sir Henry Bessemer in England and William Kelley in the United States about 1850.

The Lake Superior iron ores were discovered in 1845. This led to rapid development of a steel industry which was the cornerstone of industrial America. The electric furnace was invented in France in 1892, and this has led to a decreased use of the open-hearth furnace. Today there are about 750 Mmt of steel produced in the world. Every developing country considers a steel plant an essential symbol of progress and tries to obtain one, whether or not it is within their technological, financial, or resource capability.

During World War II the steel industries of Germany and Japan were wiped out. Their plants were replaced with the newest designs with benefit of large size. This has given these nations an economic advantage when competing with obsolescent plants in the United States and other nations.

Uses: The uses of iron and steel are so widespread and well known in construction, transportation, machinery, and appliances that they will not be discussed.

Occurrences: In the United States the Lake Superior district in Minnesota seemed an inexhaustible source and provided the needs of a developing nation. The high-grade hematite ores were eventually depleted and the low grade taconite composed of magnetite and silica were developed for pelletizing and sintering. American geologists discovered and developed large deposits in Canada and Venezuela, which now provide imports. The Canadian and Lake Superior ores are found in metamorphosed pre-Cambrian sediments. Exploration in other ancient continents has disclosed very large deposits in other regions. Western Australia is now known to have immense reserves and has become the principal supplier to Japan's large steel industry.

Brazil has discovered huge reserves and is developing its own steel industry and exporting ore to the United States and Europe. In far western Brazil and eastern Bolivia there are large untapped deposits of rather low grade hematite. Very large deposits of excellent quality were found in Liberia, and the ore is exported.

Iron ore is found in France, West Germany, the United Kingdom, and Sweden. All but Sweden are now importers. Russia has huge deposits in the Ural Mountains and is today the largest steel producer. The huge Kursk magnetic anomaly is reported to contain 40×10^9 tons of high grade ore and 10,000 times as much low grade ore.

There are also iron deposits in limestone, some large enough to support a local iron industry but they do not compare in size to the pre-Cambrian deposits.

Economics: Japan has no resources for manufacture of steel. It imports its iron ore from India, Brazil, and Australia, its coking coal from Canada and Australia, its manganese from Australia, and then ships its product to world markets. There is a steel mill in Pueblo, Colorado, that ships its iron ore from Sunrise, Wyoming, and its coking coal from southern Coloado. Yet a keg of nails or a roll of barbed wire from Japan can sell for less in Denver than the same product from Pueblo. Somehow the economic perspective has become distorted.

In 1980 U.S. steel production dropped 18% to 100.8 Mmt, reflecting the rather deep recession. Industrial countries except Russia and Japan, the No. 1 and 2 producers, also dropped; but several of the developing nations are hard pressed to keep up with demand. South Korea is increasing production as rapidly as it can, but consumption is rising even faster, estimated at 12.5 Mmt in 1981, with imports of 3 Mmt required. Mexico is another dynamic growth area for steel, with production of 7.1 Mmt in 1980 and demand in 1990 estimated at 26 Mt, nearly 300% above the past year. This reflects the capital growth resulting from rapid development of its oil fields.

The steel industry, in need of modernizing, has had to divert the scarce funds available to it to meeting the stringent new environmental demands. The capital is spent but there is no improvement in production and only an increase in operating costs. Obsolete plants with about 3 Mmt of capacity were retired in the United States in 1980, which is one way to give an apparent improvement in operating economics. The price of steel is far less than any other metal, so substitution can take place only on the basis of superior properties, like lighter weight. Concrete is the only material that can compete on a price basis.

Production: Iron and steel constitute the heaviest of the heavy industries. Equipment used is massive and tonnages handled are greater than in any other industry except concrete.

Mines are generally open pit, and to haul 100 Mmt of ore to steel mills hundreds or thousands of miles away requires a constant flow of ships and trains, plus mountainous stockpiles at both mine and blast furnace.

Years ago the standard ore supplied by the Lake Superior district contained 51.5% Fe. Those reserves are largely depleted, but instead of dropping the grade, the blast furnaces largely require a higher grade, which is supplied by beneficiating the taconites, which are low grade siliceous iron deposits in the form of magnetite. After being ground, the iron ore is separated from the waste by magnetic separators. Since this material is not usable in the blast furnace, in the United States it is frequently pelletized in "flying saucers" with bentonite clay as a binder. The *green pellets* are then fired to a hardness that permits handling. The pelletizing is done at or near the mine to minimize the shipment of waste. The grade of ore now averages about 59%, which has resulted in a major increase in the capacity of the blast furnaces and reduced energy consumption. In some plants in America and in other countries the fine ore is sintered by heating to the point of incipient fusion, where it agglomerates. The porous product has much better reacting characteristics in the blast furnace.

The blast furnace is a massive piece of equipment that may rise as high as a 25-story building and produce as much as 1500 tons of iron per day. It is loaded from the top with coke, iron ore, and limestone, the latter to form a slag which melts at low temperature. Carbon monoxide from the partial combustion of coke permeates and reduces the ore to iron. A blast of hot air (or oxygen in modern practice) is blown in through tuyeres near the base of the furnace, the name coming from the air blast. The blast melts the iron, which collects in the bottom of the furnace and is periodically tapped and cast into pig iron, then hauled directly to the steel plant for further processing. The other main product is slag, which is composed of calcium, aluminum, and silicon oxides. This may be utilized as aggregate, railroad ballast, or with additional limestone added, manufactured into portland cement. Both sulphur and phosphorous are deleterious in steel and must be strictly limited in raw materials or treated to eliminate them in processing.

In 1856 Henry Bessemer invented a way to make mild steel rapidly by putting the molten pig iron in a converter and blasting air through it. This is done in a batch process of about 20–30 tons at a time and takes 12 minutes. Molten "spiegel" is then added. This consists of iron with 20% manganese; its purpose being to remove the oxygen trapped in the converter.

Shortly after the Bessemer process was invented the open-hearth process was developed. This process uses scrap iron and molten pig iron and may hold over 200 tons of material. The process requires several hours and, in this case, high phosphorous materials can be used because the phosphorous is removed in the slag. Following the pouring of the steel into billets, it is rolled or forged into desired shapes.

The electric furnace is used extensively to produce closely controlled compositions for specialty steels.

Some of the newer developments are continuous casting and direct reduction of ore to *sponge iron*, which is used in place of scrap in the open hearth process. This process is gaining rapidly, particularly in developing nations where the capital cost of a blast furnace is prohibitive and quantities produced are not so large.

No mention of refractories has been made, but large quantities of different compositions are consumed to protect the metal that must contain the molten iron and steel. There are acid and basic refractories, the former being largely silica, and the latter magnesia or chromite. When the refractory has been largely consumed, the unit must shut down for relining.

Outlook: Steel reflects economic cycles very precisely with all of their peaks and valleys. These cycles are in fact exaggerated in the United States by the efforts of foreign producers to sell in U.S. markets at times of reduced demand and withdraw from it when their own demand is high. While the steel companies may be blamed for failure to scrap old plants and build new ones, it must be remembered that the price of the commodity is one of the lowest in modern society and consumption is so high (one-half ton per capita per year) that there is strong pressure on the companies to keep prices down. As a result, capital formation is low and investment interest is even lower. Some method of keeping this vital industry strong must be developed, possibly through low-interest loans to subsidize the expense of environmental protection and for modernization. Companies are castigated in their home communities until they decide to close an obsolete plant; then, when they are faced with economic distress, pressures are exerted to force the continuation of an uneconomic operation. It is no wonder the steel companies feel trapped in a no-win situation.

LEAD (Pb)

Properties and Characteristics

Atomic number	82
Atomic weight	207.19
Major isotopes	207, 208, 206, 204
Artificial	198, 199, 200, 201, 202, 203, 205, 209, 210, 211, 212, 214
Melting point	327.4°C
Specific gravity	11.34
Average content in rocks	Basalt, 6 ppm; granite, 19 ppm; shales 20 ppm; soils 10 ppm
Major mineral occurrences	Galena (by far the most common mineral) PbS (80% Pb)

History: Because it is easily won from the mineral galena, a mineral of widespread occurrence, lead was one of the earliest metals to be utilized by man. The earliest specimen, dated at about 3000 B.C., was a figure found near the Dardanelles. Castings for art work was the earliest use. Lead is very resistant to corrosion, has a low melting point, and is inexpensive to work. Pipes made of lead were found in ancient Egypt and lead sheets were reportedly used in the hanging gardens of Babylon, one of the seven wonders of the ancient world.

Lead was a very important metal to the Romans. One aspect was the presence of silver in the famous mines at Cartagena, Spain, wrested from the Carthaginians. The mines were an important source of the financing for the expansion of the empire. Lead pipes were extensively used in Rome. There was no knowledge of lead poisoning, so this may have been an important health hazard among the patricians, who were the only ones to have access to it.

With the fall of Rome, lead mining went into eclipse, along with other vestiges of civilization, coming back slowly with the industrial revolution, with mines in Spain, Greece, Ireland and Yugoslavia.

One of the first industries in the New World was lead mining and smelting, established in Virginia in 1621. Lead bullets were needed by

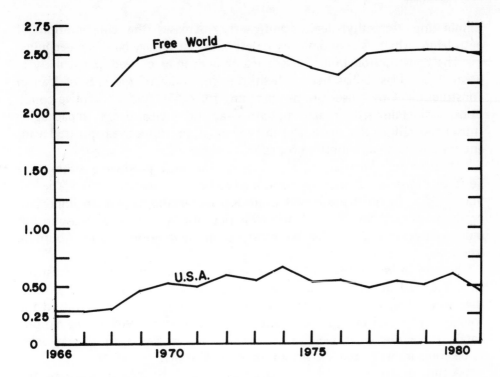

Figure 16 Lead production in the United States and the free world, given in millions of metric tons.

hunters and Indian fighters. Volume increased slowly and world consumption was only about 30,000 tons per year through the 1830s, with the United States representing about 10% of total demand. Discovery of the great lead district of southeast Missouri in 1867 made the United States self-sufficient in this metal. During the twentieth century this district was the major American producer. Since lead is not easily corroded, a large portion of the metal is recycled through scrap.

Uses: By far the largest consumer of lead is the electrical storage battery, using about 65% of the metal in the U.S. While new methods of storing electricity are in the developmental stage, lead batteries have been greatly improved, with their weight reduced and energy capacity increased. Most of the electric vehicles in use (except those in mines) use lead storage batteries.

The second important use is as a gasoline additive in the form of tetraethyl lead. This increases the octane rating, making the gasoline suitable in high compression engines. The lead enters the atmosphere with the combustion products and, under some conditions, may reach deleterious proportions. Legislation in the United States requires the phase-out of lead additive.

Eliminating tetraethyl lead significantly increases the consumption of petroleum, which is economically deleterious. This usage has been declining.

The construction industry is a major consumer of lead, particularly in waste lines. Plastic has been substituting for some of the uses of lead in construction. Other uses are as sheathing for cables under corrosive conditions, as shielding from radiation, both x-ray and nuclear decay, in packaging (tubes and radioactive materials) in typemetal, in protective paint (red lead) and, of course, in ammunition for sporting weapons.

Occurrence: Missouri is first among the lead producing states. The Southeast Missouri district has continued to be an important source. The Tri-State region in northwestern Missouri-Kansas-Oklahoma was an important producer of lead and zinc. A third district, also in Southeast Missouri but more centrally located and the most recent to develop, is the Viburnum trend.

Second in importance is Idaho, primarily in the Coeur d' Alene district. Here the lead minerals contain much silver and, in some instances, silver is the more valuable commodity in the ore. Colorado and Utah rank third and fourth in production and these four states produce over 90% of the nation's total. A new district is beginning to develop in west Texas, which may prove to be comparable to the Viburnum trend of Missouri.

Australia is the second ranking producer and the largest lead exporter. Reserves are thought to be very large. Canada, Peru, Mexico, Yugoslavia, and Morocco are the next largest producers.

The important lead mineral is galena (PbS), occurring in cubic crystals which are sometimes quite large. There are two major settings for lead or lead and zinc deposits. Most important as far as production is concerned are the deposits in sediments, usually replacing limestone. Controversy over the origin of the solutions which deposit the minerals has been very strong for years. According to one school, they are of hydrothermal origin, that is, there are igneous rocks somewhere in the vicinity of the deposits and the lead- and zinc-bearing solutions migrated from the intrusives into and replaced the limestone. They are classed as epithermal or telethermal deposits, meaning from low temperature solutions. The second concept is that the deposits were formed with the sediments or shortly thereafter by solutions indigenous to the sedimentary formations themselves. This is further subdivided: some believe the deposits formed directly on the sea floor, shoreward from an algal reef which provided a confined, saline basin; others say that connate water bearing the metals in solution was squeezed out of other formations into the limestone which they replaced. These bedded deposits are called *mantos*, the Spanish word for blankets.

The other type of occurrence is in the zones where an affiliation with igneous rocks can quite conclusively be shown, as in the western United

States. In Idaho, for example, the deposits are in large, persistent veins, cutting across other rocks. Sometimes the deposits are along the contact between an igneous rock and limestone. These deposits are usually poly-metallic, with the common associations being lead, zinc, copper, silver, gold, cadmium, and small amounts of other metals. While galena is the most important mineral, production also comes from cerrusite (the carbonate) and anglesite (the sulphate) and less commonly from bournonite and boulan-gerite.

Economics: Lead is the heaviest of the common metals. The price has fluctuated widely, rising steeply over the last 40 years. In 1940 it averaged 5.18 cents per pound and in 1979 it was 52.64 cents, the all-time high. The price had tripled from 1940 to 1973 and, following the oil shock, the price tripled again. By mid-1982, it had fallen back to 27 cents per pound.

Since mining is done largely underground, costs are relatively high and because of the weight of the metal, transportation costs are high. Therefore a fairly high-grade deposit is required to operate profitably. Probably at today's costs, the net smelter return from about 6%–8% lead would be required to open a new deposit. This could be partially paid in co-products. If it carried two ounces of silver per ton, the lead grade could be somewhat reduced.

One of the worst mistakes one can make in evaluating a deposit of lead or any other base metal is to take the assay values of the contained metals and multiply them by the metal prices. That is not the way it works out at all. If you are selling lead concentrate and it contains zinc, you will not only not get paid for the zinc, but will be charged a penalty for having it there. There are other penalties, such as arsenic and sulphur, and deductions, probably 20 pounds of lead, which the smelter claims is lost in smelting. You get paid for only a part of the gold and silver, and always at a fraction of the current price. The mine operator is likely to get paid only about half what the metal values indicate. A smelter return is a shocking experience.

All ores must be concentrated and the concentrate shipped to the nearest smelter. Transportation alone can consume 10% of the metal value received.

With the recent environmental restrictions in the United States there has been a tendency to increase the amount of imports. About 55% of consumption is recycled lead scrap, however.

The United States produces about 600,000 tons of metal from mines and imports 200,000–250,000 tons. The stockpile has had the usual ups and downs. In 1964 there were 1,378,000 tons in the strategic and supplemental stockpiles and 1,350,000 tons were declared excess as of May 1965. In 1979 the stockpile objective was 865,000 st and the inventory was 601,000 st. Lead mines are well dispersed and largely underground, and annual total scrap (including exports) is about 950,000 st, so the strategic position is quite good. Canada and Mexico are both exporters.

Production: Nearly all of the lead mined in the United Staes is by underground methods. The sedimentary deposits of the Mississippi Valley are nearly flat-lying and lie at fairly shallow depths, so they are mined by room and pillar methods, leaving minimal pillars and attempting to select low grade for the pillars. Many of the beds are 3–4 m thick, so rubber-tired vehicles can move through the haulage ways with little difficulty.

In Idaho the lead-silver veins are steeply dipping, and stoping methods are used. The walls are quite strong, and the stopes were formerly left open. After a time, however, they sometimes collapsed suddenly, forcing out the air with explosive violence, through a narrow drift, doing much damage. Now abandoned stopes are back filled.

In the mines where lead predominates, with little zinc, gravity methods of concentration are commonly used. If zinc is significant, flotation is necessary to separate the two minerals, and a clean separation is difficult. Both lead and zinc smelters penalize for the other metal.

Concentrates containing about 70% lead are first sintered in the Dwight-Lloyd hearth to remove sulphur and give the concentrate physical characteristics suitable for smelting. The next step is to feed the sinter together with coke into a blast furnace. The lead oxide is reduced to metal and cast into bars as "chemical lead." Where there are few impurities and no precious metals which can be economically recovered, this product is satisfactory for most uses. Western and foreign concentrates that contain sufficient gold and silver are refined. First the bullion is "softened" by drossing, a step of carefully controlling the temperature so that copper, tin, antimony, and arsenic separate, rise to the surface, and are skimmed off as *dross.* Precious metals are removed by the Parkes process, adding zinc metal, which preferentially alloys with gold and silver and rises to the surface as the melt is cooled. The crusts are then skimmed off and treated to recover the metals. If bismuth is present in excess of limits, the lead may have to be electrolytically refined.

Outlook: World consumption of lead possibly peaked in 1977. The reasons for this involve several industrial and environmental considerations. With batteries being by far the largest usage, the down-sizing of automobiles and engines requires less battery. The increased use of mass transit for short land and jet travel over long distances will tend to reduce use of automobiles. If the development of electric vehicles proceeds as announced by General Motors with batteries using no lead, the market could decline to a much lower level over a period of about 20 years.

The second major use of lead as a gasoline additive is also under attack. Theoretically it is to be phased out in the United States. Other countries are not interested in matching the environmental passion of the United States, particularly because the alternative methods of producing high-octane gasoline are more expensive and yield less gasoline per barrel of oil. Thus on a worldwide basis, decline of use of lead in gasoline will not be as sharp as previously anticipated.

The third market, construction, has seen substitution by plastics and as building codes requiring lead in waste lines are changed, this use will decline further.

The price rise in 1979, with lead approaching the price of copper, has been attributed to heavy buying on the western market by Russia. This unexpected demand created a shortage. Subsequently the price dropped to 35–40 cents. The United States, Canada, and Australia have the bulk of the world reserves (58%) and Europe, both east and west have limited supplies, with eastern Europe having about 13%. The overall outlook is for slight but steady decline in the demand for lead.

MAGNESIUM (Mg)

Properties and Characteristics

Atomic number	12
Atomic weight	24.312
Stable isotopes	24(77%); 25(11.5%); 26(11.1%)
Melting point	650°C
Specific gravity	1.74
Average rock content	Ultrabasic (20.4%); basalt (4.6%); granite (0.1%)
Major minerals	Magnesite (28.7%); dolomite (13.8%); seawater (0.13%)

History: Magnesium is the third most abundant structural element, 2.06% of the earth's crust. It was not differentiated in minerals from lime compounds until the mid-eighteenth century. The metal was produced in 1808 by Sir Humphrey Davy. By the late nineteenth century some magnesium was produced by electrolysis. Production increased rapidly for use in aircraft in World War II because of its weight, dropping back after the war.

Uses: Magnesium powder burns with a bright white light and was used in flash photography and in star-shells to light up battlefields at night during World War I. It is the active ingredient in flash cubes, much safer than the old pan of powder.

The property which gives magnesium its greatest value is its lightness. It is the lightest of the major metals, two-thirds the weight of aluminum. In its pure form it is not strong, but alloyed with aluminum or other metals

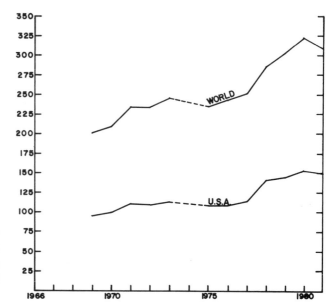

Figure 17 Magnesium production in the United States and the world, given in thousands of metric tons.

it has very desirable properties. It loses strength at slightly elevated temperatures, thus cannot be used in the exterior of supersonic aircraft. With the great emphasis on energy conservation, during the past three years magnesium has surged ahead while most metals have been in recession. A new all-time peak was reached in 1980, surpassing the production level of 1943 for the first time with 256,000 tons. It is thus tied in tonnage produced with tin for 10th place among the metals, behind zirconium and well ahead of molybdenum. With its great advantage in weight, it is surprising that its consumption is only 1.5% that of aluminum.

Magnesium is used in die castings and this area is growing rapidly. Any application where lightness is an asset is subject to magnesium substitution unless high strength or corrosion resistance is a factor. Engine blocks are made of magnesium in Europe and transmission covers, pistons, and truck bodies are other increasing uses. Because it is high on the electromotive series, it is used to provide *cathodic protection* to other metals. In this use the magnesium corrodes instead of iron, for example.

Because of its chemical activity, magnesium is used to reduce the oxides of other metals such as beryllium, zirconium, uranium, and titanium. Uses of compounds are covered under Magnesite, an important non-metallic mineral.

Occurrence: Magnesium is an ubiquitous metal. It is readily available to all nations in sea water. This is the most important ore and the supply is inexhaustible. In addition there are many brines with a high content of $MgCl_2$. For example the Great Salt Lake contains enough magnesium to supply present world demand for 600 years. Brines in connate waters are another large source.

There are huge magnesium resources in the ocean crust, in the ferro-magnesian or ultrabasic rocks. These are found in extensive amounts in the ophiolites, segments of ocean crust trapped in the continents, in the form of silicates, olivine, serpentine, and other minerals. Magnesium cannot now be extracted competitively from these rocks. A recent plant using asbestos waste (serpentine) has been announced in Quebec using a new process.

Magnesite (covered under non-metallic minerals) is formed by alteration of serpentine or limestone. It is the carbonate, and used as a refractory, not as an ore of the metal to any extent.

Dolomite, a double carbonate, $(Ca, Mg) CO_3$, is a sedimentary rock that occurs in huge deposits in many countries. The name comes from the Dolomites mountains in Italy. It is largely used in the "dead burned" form as a refractory.

Economics: The price of magnesium has increased from 35 cents per pound in 1968 to $1.01 in 1979, to $1.15 in May 1982, the recent raises reflecting increases in cost of energy and labor. This compares to about 45 cents, the cost of aluminum, its closest competitor. Both metals are produced by electrolysis, so they are both energy intensive.

With no exploration cost and ore in the form of sea water available everywhere, the controlling cost factor is cost of electricity. Any coastal city with cheap electricity can compete. Cost of production should increase more slowly than for most mineral commodities. With larger tonnages becoming available, the larger plants have the benefit of economy of scale, not available in the past, and prices are likely to be more stable than for most metals.

Production: Nearly half of the world's production of magnesium comes from the Dow Chemical plant at Freeport, Texas. It recovers magnesium from sea water. The second largest plant is that of Norsk Hydro (Norway) with a 50,000 ton capacity. Producing only 140 tons per day, this is a "large" plant. Amax purchased the third largest plant, that of NL Industries, utilizing the brines of Great Salt Lake, Utah. While designed for 40,000 tons, it had never exceeded 25,000 tons. Amax hopes to bring it to design capacity, and is considering doubling or tripling that level as demand grows. American Magnesium is producing 9000 tons and expanding to 27,000 tons using brine at Snyder, Texas. Northwest Alloys (ALCOA) has a plant at Addy, Washington producing 22,000 tons and expanding to 30,000 tons. Thus there appears to be adequate capacity to supply the growing demand.

Russia produces about 75,000 tons of magnesium, 25% of world supplies with much of it used in production of titanium. The plants in the Urals use an evaporite mineral, carnallite as the ore mineral, $MgCl_2.KCl.6H_2O$. Other producers are Norway with 14%, Canada, Brazil, Japan, India, and Yugoslavia.

The Dow process consists of mixing sea water with milk of lime, $Ca(OH)_2$, resulting in the precipitation of $Mg(OH)_2$, which is thickened, filtered, and neutralized with hydrocloric acid to produce a rich magnesium chloride solution. This is evaporated and fed into electrolytic cells, where chlorine is released and molten magnesium is tapped off. Formerly this process required 8-9 kwh per pound of metal produced. There are reports power consumption has been greatly reduced, possibly by as much as 50%.

The silicothermic process uses dolomite as the ore. It is calcined, mixed and ground with controlled amounts of ferrosilicon, then briquetted. It is then heated in a retort, and magnesium vapor condenses and is removed from the furnace. The ALCOA subsidiary uses this process.

Outlook: Magnesium should be one of the most dynamic of the mineral commodities through the remainder of the century. A particularly strong surge in demand is probable for the period to 1985 as land transportation systems strive to reduce weight to the minimum in order to decrease fuel costs.

The United States is almost totally dependent upon foreign sources of alumina but completely self-sufficient in the raw materials for magnesium. For strategic reasons it would appear desirable to increase the proportion of magnesium in the light metal category materially. It would be within probability for U.S. consumption to increase 10-20 times by the end of the century.

The province of Quebec has been experimenting with a method to recover magnesium from the wastes of asbestos production which is composed of the very common mineral serpentine. Reportedly costs are as much as 30% lower than conventional processes. Sulphur dioxide is required in this process. A plant rated at 30,000 tons per year is reportedly under construction. If this is successful, any of the ferromagnesium silicates should be amenable to magnesium production. By utilizing the wastes from asbestos processing, this source of environmental pollution is removed, and a deleterious substance yields a useful product.

MANGANESE (Mn)

Properties and Characteristics

Atomic number	25
Atomic weight	54.94
Isotopes	55

Specific gravity	7.2
Melting point	1244°C
Average in rocks	Av. 1000 ppm; mafic 2200 ppm; felsic 600 ppm; soils av. 850 ppm
Major minerals	Pyrolusite MnO_2 (63%); manganite Mn_2O_3 H_2O (62%); Psilomelane-hydrous oxide, rhodochrosite $MnCO_3$ (47%)

History: Manganese was first isolated in 1774 through the efforts of the Swedish chemist, C. W. Scheele, and his assistant, J. G. Gahn. The name probably came from the Latin word for magnet, "magnes." The oxide was used for production of chlorine. Its value in steel-making was recognized in the middle of the nineteenth century but was not used extensively for this purpose until the end of the century.

Among the metals manganese is second only to iron in tonnage consumed, rating tenth of all mineral commodities. While the United States has

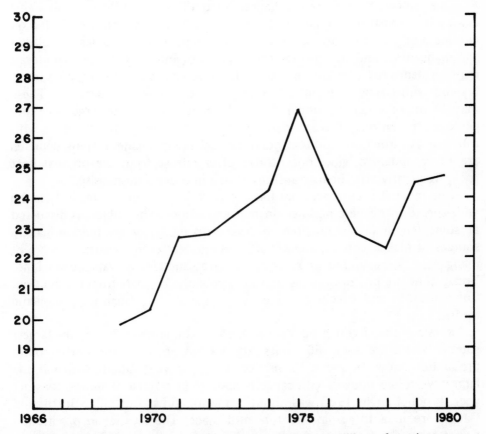

Figure 18 Manganese production in the world, given in millions of metric tons.

substantial low-grade deposits, the element is readily available from several sources in high grade form, so most of the requirements are imported.

Uses: About 95% of the manganese is consumed in iron and steel making, being required for deoxidizing and desulfurizing the steel but also as an alloying agent. This is largely in the form of ferromanganese and secondarily as silicomanganese. The balance is used in chemicals, glass (for removing the iron green), and in dry-cell batteries.

Occurrence: Manganese occurs predominantly as various oxides with the carbonate and silicate being widely distributed but of minor importance. It is a common constituent in hydrothermal ore deposits although too low in abundance to be considered an ore mineral. It occurs commonly with gold and is an active ingredient in enrichment of gold deposits. In a zoned mineral district, for example Butte, Montana, rhodochrosite occurs with zinc and it was mined during World War II when foreign ores were difficult to obtain. Still further from the center of mineralization, various oxides are distributed.

One important origin of manganese is from fissures on the sea floor. This is a hydrothermal occurrence, but the manganese oxides are precipitated on cooling and dilution with sea water. Commonly silica precedes or follows the manganese, and the two may be layered or intermixed. These minerals may be deposited directly on the sea floor volcanics or they may be interlayered with clastic sediments, forming pseudo-sedimentary deposits. These may be quite small or, under favorable conditions, quite large. In older geologic formations (Precambrian), they are frequently interlayered with iron ore. All iron formations contain appreciable manganese. Many deposits are of secondary origin, concentrated after release from the original host rock, frequently after being transported to a new depositional site.

One mineral occurrence that has received much publicity recently is the wide-spread manganese nodules on the ocean floor. This subject is discussed at some length in the chapter on crystal-gazing. They are predominantly sources of nickel, copper, and cobalt, and may not even constitute an ore of manganese, since abundant reserves of cheap metal are available on land. Today they are protoresources that are probably 10 years from production. Concentration and precipitation of the minerals is probably by biogenic means.

Russia is the largest producer, with the Ukraine being by far the largest source. There are some 60 mines, using both open pit and underground production, now at about 12 million tons per year. South Africa is the largest western producer, with capacity soon to be rated at 9 million tons per year. Production in 1980 was about 5 million tons. Australia, Brazil, and Gabon are in a three-way tie for third place. The Australian production comes from the Groote Eylandt mine on the north coast. This is a rather recent development, and production is scheduled to increase from two to three million tons. Reserves are approaching half a billion tons. With measured reserves of about 1.2 billion tons of ore for the world, this mine is in a dominant position. Total world resources are estimated at four billion tons, with the United States having very small tonnages of low-grade material and very little production.

Economics: The price of 48% Mn ore has increased from about $30 per ton in 1968 to $82 in 1982. The grades and prices are highly variable, however. The eight largest producers account for 96% of world production.

Manganese ranks second in tonnage among the metals. The supplies are abundant and of high grade, thus keeping the price low and limiting beneficiation. There is excess capacity at present, and new mines and expansions are planned, so surpluses are likely to continue for some time.

With the market tied directly to steel production, manganese follows the strongly cyclic pattern of that product. Consumption and price have been depressed for the past three years. In 1964 there were about 13 Mmt of manganese of all types in government stockpiles with 5 Mmt declared surplus. By 1980 3.07 Mmt remained in stockpiles.

The price of ferromanganese moved up about 25% in 1980 reflecting the major increase in transportation costs. Union Carbide, the largest producer in the United States, sold its operation to Norwegian and Canadian interests.

Production: Most of the mines are fairly small and operated as open pits. Underground mines normally use the room and pillar method. Beneficiation of the simplest kind is employed in most operations, such as washing and screening, or heavy media separation. Because the price is low, costs must be kept at a minimum. Most of the manganese is consumed as ferromanganese, which is produced in a blast furnace similar to that used for making pig iron.

Outlook: The United States will not become an important manganese producer unless it develops the manganese nodules on the ocean floor. This element is essential to steel-making, so developing a sizeable stockpile is the prudent course. Competition is presently keen for the markets and some countries have subsidized the manufacture of ferromanganese, thus keeping the price at a level that it was unprofitable for domestic manufacturers. The government has offered inadequate protection for domestic producers and consequently most of the production has been sold to foreign companies. There is a strong tendency to develop ferromanganese at the source rather than to ship the ore containing less that 50% metal.

Since little elemental metal enters the market, the public is quite unaware that it ranks second in world production among the metals and is essential to all steel. (The fact that 100% of American consumption is imported, is also not realized.)

MOLYBDENUM (Mo)

Properties and Characteristics

Atomic number	42
Atomic weight	95.94
Isotopes	98, 96, 92, 95, 100, 97, 94 (decreasing abundance)
Artificial	91, 93, 99, 101, 102, 105
Melting point	2620°C (unusually high)
Specific gravity	10.2
Average rock content	1.3 ppm; soils av. 2 ppm range 0.2-5 ppm
Major mineral	Molybdenite, MoS_2 (60% Mo)

History: The mineral molybdenite was identified as molybdenum sulphide in 1778, and the metal was separated in 1782 in Sweden. It was a very minor metal until World War I, when the United States was cut off from its traditional supplies of tungsten and the importance of molybdenum as a replacement in hardening steel resulted in rapid development of the

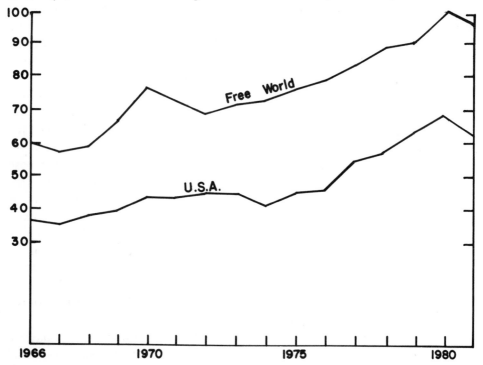

Figure 19 Molybdenum production in the United States and the free world, given in thousands of metric tons.

huge deposit at Climax, Colorado, and the important deposit at Questa, New Mexico. It has been said that without the molybdenum deposits the United States would not have been able to manufacture armor steel and artillery, and might not have won World War I.

The name of the element comes from the Greek word *molybdos*, meaning lead. The early mineralogists thought molybdenite and graphite were forms of lead and were perplexed because they could not refine the metal from them.

Molybdenum is in the same group in the periodic table of the elements as chromium and tungsten. All three are important alloying elements in steel.

Uses: Molybdenum is a minor metal with its consumption always given in pounds instead of tons. Its major use is an alloy in steel about 80% going to this purpose. It gives hardness, strength, toughness, and corrosion resistance to the products. Much of it goes into transportation equipment, heavy machinery, and tool steel. It is particularly useful in applications requiring strength at high temperature. The purified form of the natural mineral is used in lubricants, which are resistant to high temperature. Compounds are useful as pigment and as catalysts in cracking petroleum in refineries. The metal has several electrical and electronic applications.

Occurrence: The most important mineral is molybdenite, found in very large, low-grade disseminated deposits. The largest are underground mines at Climax and Henderson, Colorado. Climax was the first large producer of molybdenum in the world. There is another mineral in this deposit, molybdite, a yellow oxide that could not be recovered for many years; metallurgical improvements now permit its recovery, however. These two deposits are mined by AMAX and a third, Mount Emmons in Gunnison County, now under development by the same company, is on a straight line with the other two. AMAX has been conducting an extended study of another deposit on the opposite direction, on Jack Creek in Jackson County, Colorado. If this band is broadened, it includes the mine in northern New Mexico at Questa. In fact, virtually all of molybdenum of the western world is found in a band in western North and South America, from Quartz Hill, Alaska, probably the largest, to the deposits in Chile.

A second type of occurrence is as a by-product of the disseminated copper deposits in the same belt of North and South America. The molybdenum content is very low (for example 0.015%), but since the rock is already mined and ground to powder, it pays to add another extraction process and save it.

Economics: Molybdenum has had steady growth in consumption at about 4% per year for 15 years and has not been affected by the economic cycles. Steel, however, has fluctuated widely and has had little growth. The reason molybdenum has consistently outpaced steel and most other metals is the rapid growth in demand for the high-strength specialty products. This reflects the desire to reduce the weight of automobiles and other vehicles to conserve fuel.

With surging demand, productivity has steadily increased, but has not kept pace. Thus prices have moved up rapidly (but not as rapidly as petroleum prices). The price per pound in concentrate in early 1969 was $1.68 per pound and in May 1982 it was $7.90, a five-fold increase. Shortages have existed for most of the last five years.

Whenever one commodity surges rapidly ahead of others, many new companies try to enter the field. Western production in 1979 was 195 million pounds and announced increases will bring it to about 259 million pounds by 1984, with further large increases later in the decade. Molybdenum is probably entering a period when the market price will drop back to the producer price level. If historic growth continues, there will be 20% excess capacity in 1984, and the over-supply will persist through the end of the decade.

While there has been a surge of discoveries of molybdenite properties, the grade of the new discoveries is low. This will probably result in post-ponement of production of some deposits, in view of greatly increased capital and operating costs. If not, molybdenum has had seven fat years and may be facing an extended period of lean years.

Production: Since all of the major deposits are low grade (3–10 pounds per ton), large tonnage methods are essential for profitable operation. Open pit methods are preferred because operating costs are much lower, and consequently lower grade ore can be mined. If the deposit is deeply buried, like the Henderson mine of AMAX, block caving and hoisting is required. In the case of by-product molybdenum from the porphyry copper deposits, operating methods are identical, and 45% of the production is of this type.

Milling methods are conventional flotation yielding a product with about 90% MoS_2. The sulphide is then roasted to molybdic oxide (MoO_3) which is refined to the pure product. Ferromolybdenum is prepared by combining the oxides of the two metals and reducing them in an electric furnace. Normally the alloy produced is 60% Mo and this product is a convenient form to add to steel in the furnace to produce the desired alloy. On the other hand the purified MoO_3 can be briquetted and added in that form to produce the desired steel grade.

To prepare metallic molybdenum, either MoO_3 or ammonium molybdate is reduced with hydrogen. The product, metal powder, is pressed into bars. The extremely high melting point prevents melting the metal except in small amounts for special purposes.

Outlook: Since a major share of the molybdenum is a by-product of copper mining, this segment is totally dependent on the economics of copper. When production drops, the primary producers are the only alternative supplier and they do not have flexibility in capacity. The by-product molybdenum is subject to the labor problems of copper, historically less stable then the primary moly mines.

Demand for molybdenum should continue on its growth curve of 4% for many years. The demand for high quality steel is continuing to rise. Moly in catalysts for production of synthetic fuels is sure to grow rapidly and for applications of corrosion resistance, molybdenum is essential. For example heat exchangers using sea water for cooling, gas turbines, nuclear power plants and solar collectors will all increase the demand for moly. Virtually all applications should continue on a rather rapid growth pattern.

Known reserves of molybdenum have been rapidly increasing in the last few years and any shortages that develop should be short-lived and the result of factors such as labor problems. As new producers enter the field, prices will have to rise to accommodate the increased capital costs, improving the profit margins of established producers. The severe recession of 1982–1983 curtailed production of molybdenum, forcing mines to close. Assuming economic conditions improve, this metal should return to its former growth trend.

NICKEL (Ni)

Properties and Characteristics

Atomic number	28
Atomic weight	58.71
Isotopes	58(67.8%), 60(26.2%), 61(1.2%), 62(3.7%), 64(1.2%)
Melting point	1455°C
Specific gravity	8.9
Average in rocks	100 ppm; ultramafic 1200 ppm; felsic 8 ppm; soils 40 ppm
Major minerals	Millerite, NiS(64.7%); niccolite, NiAs(43.9%); pentlandite (Fe, Ni)S(22%); garnierite H_2(Ni,Mg) SiO_4. nH_2O (variable)

History: Since meteoritic iron contains nickel and this was the only early source of iron, nickel was accidentally used 3000–4000 years ago. There are conflicting reports as to whether or not the center of the Islamic religion in Mecca is a large iron-nickel meteorite—the Ka'aba stone. Copper ores in Saxony, Germany, caused a lot of trouble in metallurgy because of the

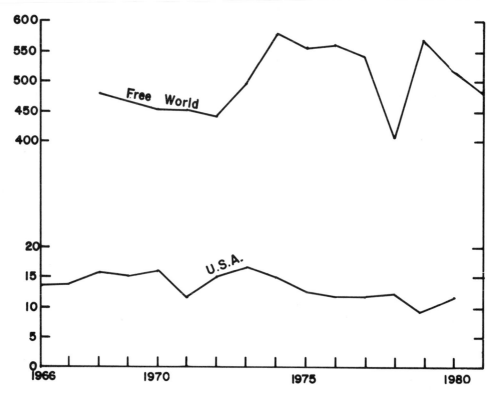

Figure 20 Nickel production in the United States and the free world, given in thousands of metric tons.

mineral niccolite (NiAs) contained in them. The miners thought the devil was playing tricks on them and called the ore *kupfernickel* (devil's copper, "Old Nick" being the name for the devil). Nickel silver developed in this area, an alloy of copper, nickel and zinc which was widely used for decorative pieces that looked much like silver but did not tarnish. The pure metal was prepared by A. F. Cronstedt in 1751, and he named it nickel.

Nickel had no commercial importance until after 1820, when Michael Faraday prepared an alloy similar to meteoric iron, initiating the nickel-steel industry. Faraday also developed the laws of electrolysis for plating one metal on another, but apparently did not actually plate nickel. Nickel-steel armorplate was developed in France. The lateritic deposits on New Caledonia were opened in 1875. Mining in the Sudbury district in Ontario commenced about 1885 but the size and importance of the district was not recognized until the French engineer Garnier (the mineral garnierite was named for him) studied the deposits in 1890. International Nickel, the world's largest producer, was formed in 1902 to exploit these deposits.

The only significant property in the United States is a laterite at Riddle, Oregon, opened in 1954. There are other low-grade nickel laterites in northern California that may be developed in the future.

Uses: Half of the nickel produced today goes into stainless steel, a market that has been growing rapidly. Other steel alloys make up much of the rest. It is particularly useful in corrosion-resistant applications and in the chemical and petroleum refining industries. Copper-nickel alloys are particularly resistant to salt water corrosion. The metal and some of the salts are used as catalysts. The nickel-zinc battery holds promise for growth in transportation.

Occurrence: The average nickel content of crustal rocks is about 0.01%, or 100 ppm. The ultra basic rocks, however, carry about 0.12% and when they are weathered (laterized) in a tropical climate, the nickel is concentrated 8–16 times and can constitute ore deposits. The lateritic ores are found where ultrabasic rocks, segments of the ocean crust, are thrust to the surface and weathered in a tropical environment. Most of these occurrences are within 15° of the equator, in Guatemala, Colombia, the Dominican Republic, New Caledonia, Indonesia, and the Philippines. One deposit is being mined in Oregon, the only American producer. The deposits in northern California reportedly contain 0.8% Ni, half or less the amount in successful operations at present, but rich enough that by recovering by-products of chromium and iron, they may be commercial in the near future. They constitute a strategic resource.

The largest known occurrence of nickel as a sulphide is in the Sudbury district of Ontario. The origin of the Sudbury massif is controversial. Some say that in the Precambrian a large meteorite struck the earth at tnis point and the magma rose at the point where the crust was penetrated. The advocates point to shatter cones in the surrounding rocks as evidence for this theory. Following emplacement, as the rock crystallized, the heavier minerals settled and collected throughout the massif in a rather thin zone containing about 1.5% nickel and copper (each), plus the platinum metals and some gold. Cobalt is also a minor constituent. This district produced over half of free world's nickel in 1977 (231,000 t), but production fell drastically in succeeding years, because of long strikes, but also because of a marked drop in demand.

In South Africa the Merensky reef, the major source of platinum, contains significant nickel sulphides as a by product. Australia produced 80 million pounds of refined nickel in 1979 and in addition, shipped concentrate to Japan and elsewhere; thus it ranks as one of the largest producers. There are important sulphide deposits in the ultrabasic rocks of Western Australia. Major Russian deposits are also sulphides, with one of the largest at Petsamo, an area seized from Finland after the Russian invasion in the 1930s. Russia has some lateritic deposits also.

The largest occurrence of nickel is probably in the manganese nodules on the ocean floors. The grade ranges from a few tenths of a percent to 1.5%.

This is the most valuable constituent in the nodules and the economics of production will be based on this constituent, with the other metals constituting co-products. The manganese nodules are discussed as some length in Chapter 8.

Economics: Nickel sulphide deposits are less costly to mine and process than the laterites. It is unlikely that new major districts will be discovered to command a major segment of the market. Thus the lateritic deposits constitute the major resources for development in the immediate future.

One of the more recent laterite plants was that built by Falconbridge in Dominican Republic. The plant cost $200 million, and would cost about $600 million to duplicate today. The large excess productive capacity built in the 1970s has resulted in a hiatus in building new plants. Demand has grown on a 6.5% trend line for 30 years but appeared to break off to a flatter slope about 1975. Nevertheless, consumption is still increasing at about 4%, greater than the world economic trend. In a few years the capacity will be straining to meet demand. In May 1982 the producer price was $3.20 per pound, with the free market price at $2.40, indicating that there is probably substantial discounting.

Nickel laterite plants are capital intensive, estimated at $17 per pound of annual capacity. Thus a plant capable of producing 50 million pounds would cost $850,000,000 (in 1982). If that money had to be borrowed at 15% and amortized in five years, the capital cost alone would be $5.95 per pound the first year. Even if the money could be found at 10% and amortized over seven years, the cost would be more than $4 per pound. Thus it is quite apparent nickel prices have not discounted current construction costs, and the price can be expected to double in a few years (constant dollars). Doubling the price would make little difference in consumption, since the competing ferroalloys are all more expensive today.

Extraction of nickel from lateritic ores is energy intensive, with energy making up to 60% of the total operating cost, reportedly even higher in the Philippines where the laterite grade is only about 1.1% nickel. Thus a source of low-cost energy available to an operation would be a great asset.

Hanging over the head of the nickel market is the threat of production from the marine nodules. At today's price, these, too, are probably not competitive. If the international agreement to mine is reached and no exhorbitant royalty is set, any substantial price move would probably result in several dredging operations being started, each equal to about 10% of present world consumption. This is a stand-off situation that may result in a price blow-off in a few years. This is discussed at greater length in Chapter 8.

Since the United States is largely dependent on foreign sources, the stockpiling program was used to accumulate a reserve. By 1964 this amounted to 220,000 st, about half of world production for a year. In May 1965 162,000 st were declared surplus, and in February 1971, the stockpile objective was reduced to zero. The United States imports 99% of its foreign nickel fron Canada, which is almost as secure a source as domestic production.

Production: The lateritic ore bodies are normally thin (5–15 m) and cover the tops of hills and ridges. They may contain 50% moisture and they tend to become fluid when disturbed. Sometimes they will not support the weight of machinery. Shovels or drag lines are used for loading onto trucks for transfer to another conveyance to the plant site. There is no way to concentrate this material, so the entire tonnage must be treated. There are several alternate routes for treatment. One involves producing a nickel matte in a blast furnace of low height with gypsum added to provide the sulphur, coke for heat, and limestone for flux. The matte is either cast into anodes for electrolytic refining, which permits cobalt recovery, or roasted, briquetted, and reduced to metal. In a second process, the ore may be dried and charged into an electric furnace with a reducing agent. This is refined by desulphurizing with soda ash then blown to remove silica and chromium as a slag. Lime is added and a final blow removes calcium phosphate and carbon. The ferronickel contains 25%–30% nickel.

There are two chemical processes, and these hold more promise for the future because they are less energy intensive. One involves leaching with ammonia, which dissolves nickel and cobalt and gives an ammonium carbonate precipitate. The carbonate is calcined to nickel oxide containing cobalt, which is sintered or reduced to metal. The other process is an acid leach with concentrated sulphuric acid and high-pressure steam at 245°C. Following the leach, the ore is neutralized with lime, and by carefully controlling the pH, impurities are precipitated and nickel and cobalt recovered separately. In this process other metals (if present in significant amounts) can also be recovered. Precipitation is in the sulphide form, by H_2S. The nickel is then oxidized and reduced to nickel powder.

Outlook: The demand for nickel is sure to continue to grow as the need for special steel products, copper-nickel alloy, and possibly nickel batteries, will grow more rapidly than the economy as a whole. The industry has been suffering from overbuilding of capacity, which has kept the price below operating costs at some plants. When new plants are built to supply forseeable demand, a whole new cost factor will have to be faced, requiring at least a doubling of price in current terms. A shadow over the industry is whether or when the marine nickeliferous nodules will enter the market. Each unit will probably amount to about 10% of world production. If several become operational at about the same time, severe dislocations will again occur.

PLATINUM (Pt)

Properties and Characteristics

Atomic number	78
Atomic weight	195.09
Isotopes	190(0.01%), 192(0.8%), 194(32.9%), 195(33.8%), 196(25.2%), 198(7.2%)
Melting point	1769°C
Specific gravity	21.46
Average in rocks	Detectable only in ultrabasic rocks, range about 0.01 ppm.
Major minerals	Native platinum (% variable with other minerals in group) Sperrylite $PtAs_2$

History: When the Spanish came to South America, they found the Indians of Ecuador using many articles made of platinum. The Spanish called it platina, "little silver" (which gave the element its name) and generally discarded it in their placer gold operations. The Spanish government did not like to have it brought to Europe because it was easy to make counterfeit gold-plated articles. It was first imported into England in 1741. The existence of the other platinum group metals, iridium, osmium, palladium, and rhodium, was discovered about 1803, and ruthenium was recognized in 1844.

Platinum mining began in Colombia in 1778 and it dominated world production. With the discovery of the metal in the Urals in 1819, this source displaced Colombia from top position. Recovery in South Africa started in 1920 and in Canada in 1924.

Uses: In 1979 the use of platinum as a catalyst in automobile exhaust systems reached 25% world-wide, the largest use of the metal. In the United States, this use accounted for over 60%, reflecting the greater concern for environment and clean air in this country than in the rest of the world. Formerly the largest use was for jewelry in Japan, where it is preferred to gold.

Platinum is widely used as a catalyst in the chemical industry and in petroleum refining. It has further use in this industry, where corrosion resistant metals are important. It is extensively used in electronic applications where reliability is very important, for example in aircraft spark plugs. It is used in production of synthetic fibers and fiber glass, and in dental appliances.

Platinum is quite inert; virtually all of its uses are in the metallic state. It occurs naturally as an alloy with the other members in the group; in many of the uses these metals are interchangeable or specific alloys are used. The catalytic automobile muffler uses three of the metals in alloy— platinum, palladium, and rhodium.

Occurrence: Platinum occurs as a natural alloy in varying amounts with palladium, iridium, osmium, rhodium and ruthenium. The metals are found in ultramafic rocks frequently associated with nickel and copper in the magmatic segregation deposits. This is the form in Canada, third largest producer, and for a major part of the production in South Africa, the largest producer. Within the same basic rocks it has been found that sometimes a thin line one to two meters thick carries a particularly high concentration of the platinum group metals, in the range of 15–30 g per ton. The Merensky reef in South Africa is such an occurrence; a similar occurrence has been found in the Stillwater complex in Montana. Deposits of this type are extensive. Russia is second largest producer from two districts: Noril'sk, in Siberia; and on the Tura River on the eastern slope of the central Urals. The Stillwater deposit might contribute a major amount of U.S. requirements, but reports that Montana has instituted a 30% severance tax indicate that mining will be postponed indefinitely.

In the past, important amounts of platinum were derived from placer deposits. The only production in the United States came from the dredge operated by Goodnews Bay, Alaska. This deposit was considered depleted, but with the much higher price it is being reactivated and will operate for a few more years.

Economics: The excuse given for the existence of metal exchanges in London and New York was that they made a stable market for the buying and selling of metals. The prices of precious metals in 1979–1981 proves they have ceased to serve this function. The ease with which metal one does not own can be sold and purchased has at least become a barometer of political unrest, and may be a factor in exaggerating financial panic.

The action of the platinum market in 1979 and 1980 illustrates the effect. Producers fixed a price and tried to maintain it to protect their customers, but when the price shot up from $300 to $1047 per ounce in March 1980, producers gradually increased the price to $475. Three weeks after it peaked, it plunged again, losing half its price. The exchange itself is now the *venue* for speculators to fleece the sheep, a factor that makes it impossible to stabilize commodity prices.

U.S. consumption rose sharply in the late 1970s, reflecting the environmental ruling limiting carbon monoxide and nitrous oxide in automobile exhausts. This peaked in 1979 at 1,300,000 oz. Automobile production in the United States then dropped 25% in 1980, and smaller autos with smaller mufflers dominated the market, so consumption sagged.

The Japanese jewelry market, which came to a virtual halt in late 1979 and early 1980 as the prices gyrated wildly, recovered toward the end of the year as the price became less erratic, ending the year at about $600 per ounce. It had dropped to $466 by May 1981, $317 a year later.

The United States has about 658,000 ounces of platinum (a half year's supply) and a 17-month supply of palladium in stockpiles.

Production: In Canada and in some of the South African mines platinum is a by-product from nickel mining. It is concentrated with the nickel and when that metal is electrolytically refined, the sludge contains the precious metals. Platinum, palladium, and gold are dissolved with aqua regia, the gold is precipitated with ferrous sulfate, then platinum is precipitated with ammonium chloride. The palladium is precipitated separately and each is reduced to sponge, which is then melted. The other four platinum group metals are then recovered from the sludge.

A new source of palladium, rhodium, and ruthenium is the nuclear reactor. These elements are a by-product of the burning of uranium, plutonium, or thorium. They can be recovered.

About 80% of the world's supply comes from South Africa and Botswana. Russia apparently produces about 15%, and Canada 4% of world demand.

Outlook: The demand for platinum in the automobile market follows the economic cycle. In addition, strong efforts are being made to find a satisfactory, less expensive catalyst. If diesel or electric automobiles or mass transit systems make inroads on the need for the gasoline engine, this segment of the market could fall sharply. The other uses in the chemical industry are growing at a faster rate than the economy as a whole. While platinum will probably have a rather slow growth in the next few years, there should be an increase in the latter part of the decade.

The conflict between the physical and economic environment is sharply illustrated by platinum. There is no production in the United States at the present, and purchases at the present level represent an outflow of about $600 million. Large deposits have been found in Montana; they can be developed commercially in today's economy. The claimants have applied for permits to mine, but the anti-mining groups have blocked the development of mines to this time.

SILVER (Ag)

Properties and Characteristics

Atomic number	47
Atomic weight	107.87 (two isotopes, 107 and 109)
Isotopes	107(51.4%); 109(48.6%)
Electrical resistivity	Lowest of metals
Thermal conductivity	Highest of the metals
Melting point	1050°C
Density	10.5
Average rock content	Basic 0.3; acid 0.15 ppm; black shale 5–50 ppm; soil 0.1 ppm
Major mineral	Argentite; in galena (lead sulphide)

History: The biggest event in the history of silver occurred in early 1980, when the Hunt brothers of Dallas, Texas, apparently tried to "corner" the silver market. The price went shooting up to nearly $50 per ounce then came crashing back down to $10. It came close to being a financial "panic." No one knows how much it cost the Hunt family to play its game, but two

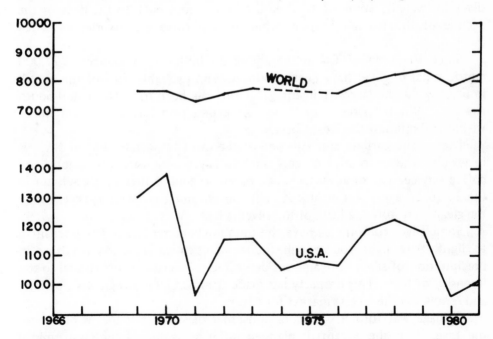

Figure 21   Silver production in the United States and the world, given in metric tons.

large organizations reportedly had a combined profit of about $600,000,000 on short sales, so some group lost at least this much.

Silver, like gold, has a mystique called "intrinsic value." It was probably the second metal to be used by man, and it was known in the Paleolithic period. The name silver is derived from Germanic sources. Ancient forms of the word were *soelfor* (old English), *silabar* and *silbar* (old high German), *silfr* (old Norse) and *silubr* (Gothic). The ultimate source was in the Far East. In early Roman times *Luna* (moon) was used for the name, and a crescent was used as its symbol. Later the Latin name *argentum* was adopted and Ag became the chemical symbol. The moon and moonlight have been associated with silver in many cultures. In Spanish, silver is called *plata*; this name is applied to all money in some Spanish-speaking countries.

It was mined and hoarded by the Incas of Peru before the Spanish conquest where it was known as the "tears of the moon." Possession of silver has always been a measure of wealth, and in many cultures the reserves of families were kept as silver jewelry worn by the women. It could be used as a dowry, it could be moved readily, and in an emergency it could be sold readily. This has been particularly true of the Middle East and South Asia. Probably the largest hoard of silver in the world is in India, with estimates ranging from one to five billion ounces. Since labor has almost no value in this region, jewelry of beautiful workmanship is sold at the market value of silver by weight. Some of the hoard of India goes back to the days of the decline of the Roman Empire, when expenditures for luxuries exceeded income.

Since the time of Columbus about 25 billion troy ounces (777,000 metric tons) of silver have been produced, and probably 70% of this is still in use. By far the largest percentage of this has been from North and South America. Ninety percent of American production has been from mines within 700 miles of the West Coast.

Uses: The earliest and still one of the most important uses of silver is in jewelry and decorative objects, such as silver tableware, candelabra, and coffee service. The disadvantage, compared to gold, is that a little sulphur in the air (or in eggs) will tarnish it badly so polishing is necessary; every time the gleam is restored, a little of the silver is lost.

Some silver compounds have the unique characteristic of being sensitive to light. Any light source will induce a chemical reaction resulting in precipitation of silver. The amount deposited is inversely proportional to the intensity of light. This property has made commercial photography possible, and represents the largest market for silver.

Coinage was formerly a major consumer of silver, but that is no longer the case. With the advent of planned inflation, value of the coin rapidly deteriorated below the value of the metal contained. Consequently over the past 20 years, silver coins have essentially disappeared.

Electronics has been a rapidly increasing market for silver, based on its excellent conductivity. During World War II when there was a copper shortage and the Treasury had so much silver it did not know what to do with it, copper buss bars in factories were replaced by silver, loaned by the Treasury, which released the copper for use in weapons. Catalysis has been a rapidly growing market.

Occurrence: Silver is found in veins or disseminated in low grade deposits. It most commonly occurs as a sulphide, argentite being the most abundant mineral. Ruby silver or proustite is a complex of silver, arsenic, and sulphur. It commonly occurs with gold in telluride minerals (petzite and sylvanite). There is a long series of other silver minerals that occur in minor amounts. In silver veins lead is almost always present, although lead does not always contain significant silver. In disseminated deposits, silver is commonly found in volcanic regions with lead and as a very low-grade by-product in the porphyry copper deposits in North and South America.

When silver-bearing veins are weathered, the native element is sometimes freed, forming masses or wire silver. The elemental form is less common than native gold, and it is not as spectacular as native gold, since it is almost always tarnished to a dull black.

About 80% of all the silver ever mined has come from the New World, and that percentage will continue. The largest silver mine today is the Timmins, Ontario operation of Kidd Creek Mines (formerly Texasgulf Corp.), also a large producer of copper and zinc. In the United States the Coeur d'Alene district of Idaho is the largest producing area; the Comstock lode in Silver City, Nevada, was also famous.

The copper mines in Arizona (and elsewhere) produce much of the silver, strictly as a by-product. Likewise, many of the mines are primarily lead-zinc mines, with silver dependent on the market for the major commodity. Thus it is impossible to rapidly increase silver production.

Mexico has been one of the greatest silver-producing nations; Potosi and Pachuca are great names in the silver game. With the increase in price, low-grade deposits have become commercial and Mexico will probably be the number one producer for a long time. Peru is also an important producer.

In Bolivia Potosi was a very rich area, later mined for tin, and now potentially a large producer of low-grade silver. Pulacayo and several other districts likewise were formerly major silver centers. Today Bolivia is a minor factor in silver production and at the same time the one country that could raise silver production fairly rapidly. The problem is euphemistically called "political instability." No nation has had so many revolutions. The miners, who for the most part mine tin, are under the dominance of left-wing groups, and powerful enough to upset any government.

In situations like that in Bolivia, one must dig deeper for the "real" reasons. The Altiplano or high plain of Bolivia is 11,000–13,000 feet above sea level. The mines are on or above the altiplano, even about 17,000 feet. It is difficult to get a bulldozer or compressor to work at that altitude, and engines need superchargers. It is also hard on men. They have found a super-charger, too—coca, the source of cocaine. Americans in La Paz suffering from altitude sickness or suroche, ask for a cup of coca tea in the finest hotels, and this plus an oxygen bottle give wonderful relief for the common splitting headache. (It is very important not to drink; alcohol reduces the oxygen-carrying capacity of the blood; there is not much oxygen to begin with, so collossal hangovers are the rule until one is acclimatized).

The miners and Indians living at high altitude normally chew coca leaves, which increases their capacity to work; it is still a debilitating, addictive drug. After fifteen years use of coca the reasoning portion of the brain is seriously damaged. Thus a labor leader can easily arouse emotional reactions, and another government falls. Anyone who says cocaine is not a dangerous drug is naive. Bolivia is a nation limited by addiction. Thus its riches in silver are likely to remain in the ground indefinitely.

While the great silver belt of the world is the western side of the Americas, Australia has also produced much silver. In antiquity the Cartagena region of Spain financed the empire of Hanibal, then of Rome, and later Spain itself. There were other important producers in the Mediterranean and in the Far East, but little is known in Africa.

Economics: In the nineteenth and early twentieth centuries silver had limited uses. It was popular for tableware, and gradually photography began to be significant. Miners discovered bonanza deposits in the New World, however, and production exceeded demand. Inevitably, the price remained low. Political pressure from the western states of the United States resulted in extensive coinage of silver, but still the supplies piled up. There was a panic in 1893, in the West called the Silver Panic because the Sherman Silver Purchase Act of 1890 was repealed, resulting in a falling silver price and the closing of many mines.

During the Great Depression, the price of gold was set at $35 per ounce, but the price of silver fell as low as 35 cents per ounce. Again political pressure built up, and a new Silver Purchase Act was passed. The Treasury purchased silver first at 65 cents, then after 1946 at 90 cents per ounce. They offered it for sale at 92 cents, but there were no buyers. The government profited by issuing silver certificates which used the arbitrary value of $1.29 per ounce. The difference was called *seigniorage.* The silver dollar also had silver content based on a price of $1.29 per ounce. Coins of smaller denomination were based on silver at $1.38 per ounce, the subsidiary coinage price. These stepped values later became important.

The government built up a huge surplus of silver—two billion ounces, plus over a billion ounces in coins. When the war-time inflation was added to costs, however, silver (and gold) mines started losing money. Political pressure built up for an increase in price, to no avail. The government offered all anyone wanted at 92 cents, but the cost of producing rose well above that and mines closed.

Meanwhile demand for silver rose sharply. Silver was "cheap" at the government-fixed price, so every bride wanted a silver table service; there were many post-war marriages. Photography became a very popular hobby. X-ray pictures became a lucrative sideline for dentists, doctors, and hospitals, so this usage soared. Electronics became a much more important field, requiring increasing amounts of silver.

The Treasury's silver hoard began to dwindle, but still it continued to sell at 92 cents and by this time it would have required a price of about $2–$3 per ounce to warrant new mines. Speculators began to buy silver to hoard. It was obvious that the price would soon go up, since world consumption exceeded production by about 50%. Finally, in November 1961, the Treasury was told to quit selling at 92 cents (the statutory price). In 18 months the price rose 40%, to $1.29. It stayed there because all of those silver certificates were a promise to sell at $1.29 per ounce, and all of those silver "cartwheels," so popular at Las Vegas, had $1.29 worth of silver in them. Meanwhile it would have taken a price of about $5 per ounce to build up production and dampen consumption to the point of balance, so the Treasury was still conducting a great giveaway, and speculators continued to add to their hoards. A sack of 1000 silver dollars was *very good* collateral, and banks would loan at tax-deductible bottom rates. The run on the Treasury accelerated. There was nothing like something for nothing. In 1965 silver was essentially demonitized.

Next the Treasury repudiated the silver certificates—in effect said its promise was no good. Almost immediately the price jumped to the value of silver fixed in subsidiary coinage. This was only a 9 cent rise. It was obvious the price had to go to $4–$6 per ounce to balance demand with newly mined supply.

With the price at about $2 per ounce, other factors came into play. India was estimated to have about five billion ounces of silver, and a series of crop disasters tempted holders to sell. Other hoarders began to sell; again soaring demand was met at a price that did not justify opening new mines, which by 1970 would have required $6–$8 per ounce. Thus silver remained a bargain, but it was hard to guess just how long the price would stay so low. In 1973 the price ran up to $5 and speculators unloaded, driving it back down. The U.S. Treasury threatened to sell the last remnants of the great hoard it once held, an overhead supply which contributed to the price drop.

Mining costs advanced 30% in 1978 and again in 1979, running the price which would be required to balance demand with newly mined supply to about $12–$15 per ounce. It was a speculator's dream. Any consortium with access to a few billion dollars could accumulate and force the price up, profit handsomely, and get out. To increase supply by opening adequate new mines has a time lag of 10–20 years; thus silver could carry a high price for some time.

The story of the Hunt family and its cornering of the market is so recent that it needs no reiteration. One question has been answered. Why did they keep forcing the price up beyond reason? They apparently kept on buying all the way up. As a result, they were outsmarted by speculators. Sometimes people get carried away by their own propaganda. In this case the Hunts were reported to be saying silver could go to $75 per ounce. The price plummetted and the "bears" had their day. A false boom of this type generally has a return ticket—a bust.

The fundamental factors behind the silver price increase are as follows: (1) At no time in 20 years has newly mined silver equalled consumption. The world has been living off its bank account. (2) Most of the world silver production is the by-product of other metallic production, and is thus inflexible. (3) Production can only be greatly increased when deposits carrying one to two ounces per ton of ore can be mined at a profit. That is the only geologic source capable of filling the gap. Assuming that no co-products exist in amounts sufficient to affect economics materially, a mine of 10,000 tons per day recovering one ounce per ton will yield 3.5 million ounces per year. The capital cost is likely to be $150 million (or even double that). At 15% interest, the cost will be $6 per ounce the first year, and if the company wants to amortize in five years, amortization is $12 per ounce. Mining will be at least $10 per ton (or per ounce). Obviously $20 per ounce will not be economic, but if *two* ounces per ton can be recovered, the picture is quite different. Ten of these mines recovering two ounces per ton would be required to begin to strike a balance. One property of about these dimensions has been announced, a deposit discovered by ASARCO in the Callico Mountains of Southern California. Since the preservationists have begun a battle to prevent its being mined, even this may not be a resource. To undertake exploration to develop such a mine requires at least 10 years lead time. ASARCO has another important discovery in Montana.

That leaves only one way to balance supply and demand. Price must go up sufficiently to bring about an end to hoarding and consumer demand decrease. A major part of the market is not very price sensitive. The biggest segment, the decorative and jewelry side, is subject to price fluctuations. For example, if a young bride needs tableware, she can get a service for 12, 10 pieces each (total set, 144 pieces) made of bronze, a beautiful, lustrous, golden color, for just about the same price as a place setting of five pieces in silver. Today the silver is so valuable it is considered burglar bait. She can get a handsome set of stainless steel for even less. Thus the market for silver tableware is definitely price sensitive.

While photography is considered insensitive to price, Kodak and Dupont, two of the largest manufacturers of photographic film, have long conducted research for substitutes for silver. A recent announcement indicates an organic material has been discovered that is suitable for some applications, particularly x-ray photographs.

Production Methods: Most of the deposits containing silver as a major or dominant part of the value of the ore are mined from veins where it was deposited by rising hydrothermal (hot water) solutions. Veins are mined by various stoping methods. Some mines are open stopes, where the ground is firm with little tendency for walls to cave; others are cut-and-fill stopes, where ore is mined out overhead and the space is back-filled with waste or low-grade rock; others are square-set stopes, where the ground is weak with a high tendency to cave. This last requires large amounts of timber, which is now very expensive. Ore is hauled to a shaft and hoisted to the surface, where it enters the milling circuit.

Most of the silver is so intimately associated with lead, zinc, or copper that processing follows the normal milling practice for sulphide ores— namely, flotation of the sulphides, hopefully with the depression of pyrite. The concentrate then goes to a smelter and the silver metal separates from molten lead or goes with copper anodes to the electrolytic refinery where it is left in the sludge and salvaged. Since gold is always alloyed with silver, gold refineries also produce silver. An alternate method of recovery of silver is through cyanidation (cyanide solution). The metal is dissolved from the rock, and precipitated.

Outlook: Keynesian economics resulted in uncontrollable inflation with serious distortion in price levels. Some segments, including precious metals, raced ahead of others. Sources of supply of silver that could eliminate the gap between supply and demand within 10 years were not apparent, so price increases were obviously necessary to curtail demand. By mid-1982, the price of $5.75 per ounce had to double, which it did by January 1983. The estimated "proper" price level for silver (early 1983) is $13, plus or minus $2. Outside the range of $11–$15, the price is too low or too high.

Most of the new mines will be opened in Latin America, where resources are greatest and the mining industry is welcomed for its economic contribution rather than obstructed by preservationist opposition. If a hundred million ounces have to be imported into the United States at $20 per ounce, two billion dollars would leak out of the economy.

In 1982 a Japanese firm announced development of a new electronic camera comparable in size to the popular cameras, using no film. The cartridge is not light sensitive, requires no development, and with an adaptor, can instantly be shown on ordinary TV sets. This may rapidly decrease demand for silver in photography, driving the price to the lower end of the range stated.

TIN (Sn)

Properties and Characteristics

Atomic number	50
Atomic weight	118.69
Major isotopes	116, 118, 120 (10 in all)
Melting point	231.9°C
Density	7.286
Specific heat (cal/g)	25°C 0.053
Average rock content	Acid (igneous), 45 ppm; soils 10 ppm
Major mineral occurrence	Cassiterite, SnO_2

History: Tin was the fourth metal to be used by man and the second to be of major utilitarian importance. It was never used alone, however, but was the first metal to be deliberately alloyed with another. Copper plus tin constitutes bronze, the alloy of greatest importance for 4000 years, from about 3500 B.C. It gave copper such superior properties that nothing could compete with it in weapons and in consumer products.

When Jonah decided to flee from the orders of the Lord to warn the Ninevites of their impending doom, he decided to run away, to the ends of the earth, Tarshish or Tartesus. Some place this in Cornwall, near the tin mines operated by the Phonecians. The use of tin in the Bronze Age is discussed more fully in Part I, Chapter 1. The Romans used tinned copper.

Tin was discovered in the Malay Peninsula before the arrival of Europeans (A.D. 1509). Deposits were easily worked. In the nineteenth century this led to widespread tinning of iron to prevent spoilage of food in cans. The market grew and the price was relatively low.

Uses: The largest usage of tin is in tin plate for containers (cans, etc.), representing about 37% of U.S. consumption. It is extensively used in transportation: for motor vehicles in bearings, coatings, and solder; aircraft, in bearings and high-impact alloys in landing gear; and boats, in bearings and antifouling paints. The third use is in machinery as an alloy (brass and bronze in bearings, fittings, castings and stampings) and in solders, claddings, or dippings. Significant use is in chemicals in dyes, perfume, polyurethane, glass, toothpaste, fungicides, and biocides. Recently plate glass has been

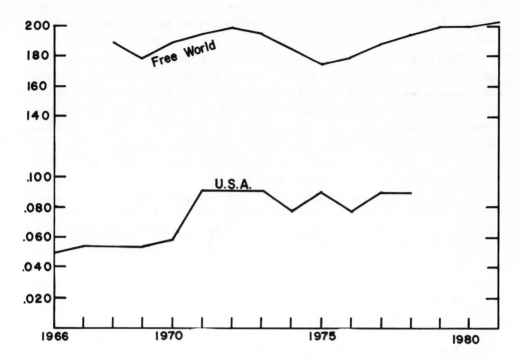

Figure 22 Tin production in the United States and the free world, given in thousands of metric tons.

manufactured by floating molten glass on molten tin. Pewter is an alloy of high tin, low lead contents, used in tableware.

Occurrence: By far the largest reserves and production of tin are in Southeast Asia, containing 65% of world reserves and 58% of production. This includes Malaysia, Indonesia, Thailand, Burma, and China. The second region is Bolivia and Brazil. Europe is third, with most of the tin occurring in the USSR and the United Kingdom. Africa is fourth in production, with Nigeria and Zaire dominant. North America has very minor reserves and production, making the United States totally dependent on imports for primary tin.

There is only one important tin mineral, cassiterite (SnO_2), which has a specific gravity of 7 and hardness of 6–7. It is most commonly black to dark brown, depending on the amount of iron contained in the crystal. Low-iron cassiterite may be medium brown to honey yellow, and can be a spectacular gemstone.

Cassiterite is a high-temperature mineral found in veins and in replacement deposits. It is sometimes disseminated or in *stock work* deposits, and is associated with tungsten or molybdenum. In Mexico it occurs in rhyolite flows. It is always found in the more acidic rocks like granite. Production is largely from veins in Bolivia but from stream or marine placers in other countries.

Economics: Four nations so dominate world tin production that they can control production and price. These are Malaysia, Indonesia, Thailand, and Bolivia (in order of current production). There is a market for nearly all these nations can produce, and the only moderating factors are the large stockpile held by the U.S. government and the relative ease with which substitutions can be made. The price is commonly quoted in Malaysian dollars (ex Penang) per *pikul.* A pikul weighs 133⅓ pounds or 60.5 kg. A *pikul* is divided into 100 catties. It was the maximum load the shippers could force a man to carry. Since the price increased from $1.01 per pound in 1960 to the $8.70 range in 1980, United States consumption varied from 82,000 tons in 1960 to a peak of 86,000 tons in 1966 to 62,000 tons in 1979, reflecting the price-sensitivity of demand in some categories.

The major tin-producing nations wanted to stabilize the price for internal economic reasons (Thailand and Bolivia are largely dependent on tin for foreign exchange), so they invited other producers and consumers to join in the International Tin Council. The first agreement took effect on 1 July, 1956 and the term of each agreement was for five years. The sixth ITA went into effect on 1 July, 1982, after much negotiation.

The ITA provided for a buffer stock of tin with must buy, may buy, neutral, may sell, and must sell price ranges. This was quite effective in moderating price fluctuations, and it was considered a model of international agreements. However, the inflation following the "oil shock" of 1973–1974 upset the price range system. In early 1976 the price was stable at about 3000 British pounds per metric ton, but by 30 June is was 4680 pounds, and by 1 November, 1979 it was 7890 pounds per ton or $8 (U.S.) per pound. The buffer stock was exhausted. By 8 July, 1982 the price had dropped to $5.18 per pound, and a surplus was again accumulating.

The average cost in tin "pump mines" in Malaysia to produce a pound of tin in the last half of 1980 was $5.17. Of this cost, 35% is needed for energy. These mines produced the bulk (56%) of the nation's output. The average price in 1980 was $7.71 per pound. The government export tax came to $1.77 per pound, or 23% effective. These figures indicate a small profit of 77 cents or 10% of sales and a 70% income tax equivalent. The recession of 1980 resulted in decreased consumption and surplus production of tin for the first time in several years. The result was a sharp drop in price to $5.80, and an average loss on sales of 62 cents per pound produced after tax on the June 1981 price. This is an excellent illustration of the unfavorable result of a direct or severance tax on sales. If income tax is used, when a price drops, both profit and taxes drop in unison. An operator can try to cut costs and continue to produce, but with a severance tax he rapidly faces catastrophic losses on a price drop, and must close down, creating unemployment in addition to loss of revenue. With a drop of this scale, probably two-thirds of the pump mines have to close with a drop in national production of 37%. Industry considers this a vicious type of tax that results in the waste of low grade reserves, as they cannot be produced without a loss.

The United States has no tin deposits of significance. Since tin has some uses for which there are no substitutes, it was included in the strategic stockpile that was established in 1946. Tin purchases amounted to about 350,000 tons before a "new look" said that amount was not necessary. Amidst complaints of the producing nations, the United States started selling. By 1 July, 1965, the stockpile was reduced to 321,634 lt, and by 31 December, 1968 to 257,765 lt. By October 1979 government inventory was reduced to 203,700 metric tons. Sales were most intense in years when there was a significant deficit of production. Hence the market disruption was minimal, but it had a major impact in preventing development of new mines to meet the overall requirements. Meanwhile the cost of developing new mines has inflated as fast as the price, so the next generation of production must have even higher prices to warrant the capital investment. Congress authorized sale of another 35,000 lt in 1980. There are indications the stockpile will be reduced to about 100,000 tons. Spendthrift administrations like to do this because there is a false "profit," of an inflation increase, which masks part of the deficit spending.

In Malaysia tin is produced by private enterprise and taxed very heavily to provide foreign exchange. One result of this has been an apparent decline in Malaysian production and a surge in tin sales out of Singapore, tin smuggled in from Malaysia. The taxes allow some profit for miners, but this is on amortized equipment and is inadequate to justify the greatly increased capital costs to bring in mines in lower grade areas. Either the price will have to go up markedly, the tax level will have to be lowered, or Malaysian production will actually drop in the near future.

Bolivia had been the number two producer until 1979, when it dropped to fourth place. Bolivia nationalized the tin mines in the 1950s and transferred production to COMIBOL, a government corporation staffed with executives many of whom had no mining or executive experience. For a time production held up, until spare parts in inventory were consumed. Then mines began closing and were cannibalized to keep other mines operating. Bolivian mines are largely lode (vein) mines, and higher in cost of operation than dredges, even when operated according to sound economic principles. With funds that should have been reserves for new equipment siphoned off into other government agencies, with too large an executive staff, and with politicized, left-wing labor unions that demanded in the labor agreements an amount of coca leaves to be furnished to the miners, it is not surprisng that it has been a declining factor in world tin production. Bolivia is basically rich in minerals, but because of constant political unrest, inefficient operations, and high transportation costs, it will remain an impoverished nation for years to come.

Indonesia has reserved new tin mining operations to the government and has rapidly increased production from 17,425 tons in 1969 to 30,000 tons in 1979. A new zone has been discovered on Sumatra that will be brought into production. Improved dredge designs permit operations on the submerged ancient stream channels that were formed on land when the Ice Ages withdrew water from the oceans. With the largest reserves and resources, it will be an increasingly important factor in world tin production.

Thailand also has reserves and other resources equal to those of Malaysia, so production should increase. Brazil and Burma are the only other nations with resources adequate to greatly increase production.

Production Methods: Since cassiterite is a hard mineral resistant to abrasion, it is preferentially concentrated, as the rocks containing it disintegrate in weathering. Since it is also a very heavy mineral it is further concentrated by the winnowing action of streams. Consequently placer deposits are the main source of the mineral. It is dredged by large floating machines with buckets digging far below the sufrace. Initial separations are made on the basis of size (screening), and about 90% of the material can ordinarily be wasted immediately. The finer material is treated by gravity separation methods, magnetic minerals are removed with magnets, and some silicates in the concentrate are removed by electrostatic separators or flotation. Pure cassiterite (75% tin) is smelted in reverberatory furnaces with carbon as a reducing agent. It is further refined by oxidizing and skimming contaminants or by electrolysis. Because problems of lifting and supporting bucket lines on dredges are serious, the depth to which this kind of equipment can operate is limited to 30–40 m. New dredges are being built with bucket wheel dredge heads and airlift of the gravel to the boat. These machines are much larger and more expensive than old dredges, but the operating efficiency permits development of deposits averaging 100 grams per cubic meter (3.5 ounces).

Traditionally in Malaysia and Thailand much of the tin has been recovered by "gravel pump" operations of smaller scale. Deposits amenable to this method of operation are being depleted and declining in importance. Concentration methods are the same for the cassiterite.

In Bolivia the tin is largely produced from veins and requires conventional mining techniques. Sulphides constitute an important part of the ore. These are removed by flotation. Recovery of the cassiterite is as low as 50%. In grinding the tin, ore becomes too fine to recover by gravity methods and flotation of cassiterite has not been very successful. In Indonesia lode tin zones occur on Bangka and Belitung Islands and in the mountains of the Malaya Peninsula (Malaysia, Thailand, and Burma). These deposits will become more important as the placer deposits approach exhaustion.

Outlook: Tin is a no-growth metal that will require appreciably higher prices (presently 50 cents per ounce) to justify the capital development to maintain the present level of output. Increased price will continue to shrink the market for the product. About 50% of the market is subject to substitution and once lost, will never be regained. The U.S. Bureau of Mines projected a growth range of −0.7% to over +1.4% annually for the United States over the next 20 years. Because of the price increases that can be foreseen and vulnerability to substitution, a net decrease in consumption, both for the United States and for the world, is thought to be the more probable prognosis. Production in China is reported to be about 20,000 tons per year which places it in fifth place.

TITANIUM (Ti)

Properties and Characteristics

Atomic number	22
Atomic weight	47.90
Isotopes	46, 47, 48, 49, 50
Melting point	1670°C
Specific gravity	4.51
Average in rocks	4400 ppm; mafic 9000 ppm; soils 4600 ppm
Major minerals	Rutile TiO_2(60%); ilmenite $FeTiO_3$(31.6%); titanite $CaTiSiO_5$(24%)

History: The element was discovered in 1790 by William Gregor who called it menaccanite after the Cornish town near the place where he discovered it. Five years later a German, M. H. Klaproth, discovered the same metal and named it titanium after the children of the Greek gods of heaven and earth, the Titans (giants) that first populated the earth. He later discovered it was the same element as that of Gregor, but Klaproth's name was accepted. It was not until 1910 that the metal was isolated. It was used in alloy steel commencing in 1906 and titanium dioxide pigments were introduced in the United States in 1918. The metal remained a curiosity until the discovery by Wilhelm Kroll of a process to produce the metal commercially. Commercial quantities became available in 1948 and very rapid strides were made as it became important in supersonic jet planes.

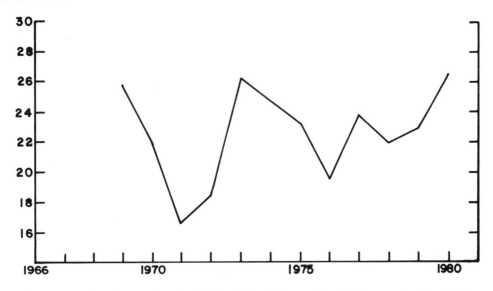

Figure 23 Titanium production in the United States, given in thousands of metric tons.

Uses: There are two distinct classes of use of titanium. By far the largest is pigment, TiO_2. World capacity is estimated at 2.6 Mmt, with production in 1979 of 2.2 Mmt, probably dropping to about 2 Mmt in 1980. Half of this is used in paints with paper taking 22%, plastics 12%, and miscellaneous 15%.

Titanium metal, lower in tonnage by a factor of 20 than the oxide, is enjoying boom times. It is particularly useful where resistance to corrosion from such causes as salt water is required. It has a higher strength-to-weight ratio than steel or aluminum, so it is particularly useful in applications where weight reduction is desirable, such as in aircraft. Much of the metal goes into military hardware—submarines, missiles, supersonic planes, and now into the space shuttle and space stations. Automobiles and other modes of transport are rapidly increasing usages.

Occurence: Titanium is the ninth most abundant element in the earth's crust, fourth of the structural metals. Its percentage in the crust is 0.4%. There are two important minerals, ilmenite and rutile. The former is much more abundant, while the latter is nearly pure TiO_2, and thus a more desirable ore.

Ilmenite contains a maximum of 53% TiO_2. It occurs to some extent in nearly all rocks, but in mineable occurrences it is associated with magnetite or other iron ores. Large deposits are found at Allard Lake, Quebec (the largest known), Tahawus, New York, and near Laramie, Wyoming. There are submarginal deposits, or protoresources, in California, Colorado, Minnesota, Montana, New York, and Rhode Island. It is abundant in the ferruginous bauxites of Oregon. Ilmenite is very resistant to weathering and attrition, so it concentrates in placer deposits. At present these constitute the major source of the element. Concentrations are particularly common as beach placers, modern beaches plus uplifted or abandoned beaches. Drowned beaches, deposits formed at glacial periods when oceans were 100–150 m lower than today, can be dredged and constitute a major protoresource. Beach sands are mined in New Jersey and Florida. The largest placer deposits are in the beach and marine sands of eastern and western Australia, Norway, Sri Lanka, India, and in stream placers in Malaysia. There are some rock deposits containing ilmenite or ilmenite plus rutile that are rich enough to be mined. There are examples of this in Piney River and Roseland, Virginia.

Rutile occurs in granitic rocks and when weathered, it concentrates in placers, frequently with ilmenite. About 86% of the world rutile production comes from the beach sands of Australia, 9% from Africa, 7% coming from Russia, and minor amounts from Sri Lanka, India, and Sierra Leone.

Economics: Titanium ore, or ilmenite, sells for about 6 cents per pound of contained metal, but the metal is quoted (March 1982) at $7.65 per pound. The incremental price is, to a large degree, the result of the very high energy requirement in processing. It requires 1.25 pounds of magnesium at $1.25 per pound and 5 pounds of chlorine to produce a pound of titanium, and magnesium itself is an energy-intensive metal. Plants are capital intensive requiring high temperatures and atmospheres of inert gas.

If the price of ilmenite were increased 100%, it would add less than 1% to the price of the metal but would probably expand reserves by more than 100%. Thus resources are very large. Rutile is the preferred ore of titanium and the price per pound of contained metal is 23 cents. This requires one less processing step, roughly reflecting the price increment. Reserves of rutile are much smaller than those of ilmenite, but again doubling the price of rutile would probably make drowned beach placers commercial and increase reserves in Australia, India and Sri Lanka. This would add 3% to the price.

The strategic stockpile contained 31,377 tons of titanium in 1964, with none of it surplus. The objective was increased to 37,500 tons in 1966 plus 200,000 tons of rutile. This was lowered to 33,500 tons of metal and 100,000 t of rutile in 1969. In May 1973 the objectives were reduced to zero. This was subsequently increased in 1978 to 130,000 st, then 195,000 st of metal, but the quantity remains at 31,000 st. Russia has ceased exporting titanium and has produced a submarine reportedly displacing 30,000 st (a monster) containing 10,000 st of titanium. Japan has been a major exporter but has had to cut back to supply her own industries, meanwhile expanding capacity as rapidly as possible.

Demand has increased more rapidly than production and consumption has increased more than 10% in each of the last two years. Consequently producer price increased from $3.28 to $5.50 in 1980 with free market sales at $15.00. The posted price on sponge in May 1982 was $5.55 per pound. This pressure occurred without the government purchasing any titanium to fill the 160,000-ton gap in the stockpile (1.6 year's world production) or the effects of President Reagan's massive armament program.

Production: Titanium ores are mined primarily by dredging of beach sands, concentrating the minerals by gravity and magnetic methods. The limited hard-rock mining is by open pit, crushing and grinding and the same methods of concentration.

The first step in processing the concentrate is to chlorinate the rutile at about 900°C, producing very reactive liquid titanium tetrachloride ($TiCl_4$). Water and air must be excluded.

The kroll process for production of titanium involves reducing the $TiCl_4$ with magnesium (U.S.) or sodium (Britain) at about 850°C. This is a batch process requiring 6–15 kwh, the higher figure if the magnesium is regenerated. The product is "sponge," which is crushed and leached to remove NaCl and other entrapped compounds. It is then melted in an inert atmosphere or vacuum and cast into ingots and remelted using the ingot as the electrode. Molten titanium reacts with all refractories, so it has to be melted in a copper crucible which is water cooled.

Titanium is used as an alloy, the most common containing 6% Al and 4% V. It can then be fabricated. Welding has to be done in an inert atmosphere.

Outlook: The oxide is a non-metallic substance with paint being subject to the demands of the building cycles. It can be replaced by other pigments. Consumption is likely to be rather static.

In spite of its high price, the superior properties of titanium have brought it from being a curiosity 30 years ago to thirteenth place among the metals, just behind molybdenum. With its rapid growth it is sure to challenge tin for eleventh place with a few years.

There is no real scarcity, just economic considerations that determine the mineral to be used. The price of the ore could be doubled with little effect on price of the metal, but reserves would be greatly increased by the higher price. The United States is now dependent on foreign sources for much of its ilmenite and nearly all of its rutile.

Extensive research is under way to develop a less costly method of producing the metal. A direct electrolytic process has been discovered and used in the laboratory but has not been applied commercially. If the price could be dropped back to the early 1979 level (less than half of the current price), demand would go up even more rapidly. Titanium is certain to be one of the star performers of the 1980s.

TUNGSTEN (W)

Properties and Characteristics

Atomic number	74
Atomic weight	183.85
Stable isotopes	180, 182, 183, 184, 186
Artificial	176, 177, 178, 179, 181, 185, 187, 188
Melting point	3410°C (highest of metals)
Specific gravity	19.3
Specific heat (cal/g)	0.032
Average rock content	2 ppm, very low in soils
Major minerals	Scheelite, $CaWO_4$ (W = 63.9%); Wolframite (Fe, Mn) WO_4 [combination of Ferberite (Fe) and hubnerite (Mn)]

History: Because of its weight, scheelite was called "heavy stone," which in Swedish is *tung sten.* Mr. Scheele discovered that it contained lime and an acid and the material was later named in his honor. In the same year (1781) the metal was prepared. The chemical symbol, W, is derived from the name for the element used in Europe, wolfram.

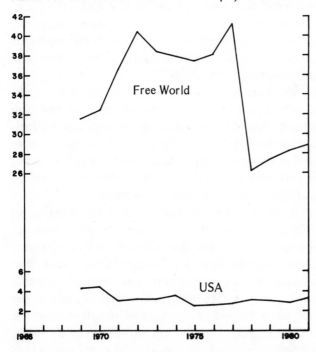

Figure 24 Tungsten production in the United States and the free world, given in thousands of metric tons.

The first tungsten alloy steel was patented in 1857 and tungsten filaments in electric light bulbs were successfully prepared in 1911. Sintered tungsten carbide was prepared in 1923 and became commercial in 1929.

Tungsten is a war metal, with demand shooting up during war time and dropping back during peace.

Uses: The properties which make tungsten useful are its high melting point and tensile strength. It can be alloyed with iron to produce high-quality specialty steels for tools, armor plate, and gun barrels. It was the unavailability of tungsten during World War I that resulted in the development of molybdenum as a substitute. About 50% is used in the manufacture of tungsten carbide, very useful because of its extreme hardness (but much softer than diamond). This material is used in cutting edges for machine tools as well as inserts in rock drills or the lip of buckets and blades or earth-moving machinery. It is also used in tire studs for snow tires and ball-point pen tips. Tungsten has the highest melting point of all metals, 3410°C (6170°F) and is used in gas turbines and rocket nozzles. Because of high shock resistance it is used in punches and chisels. The outstanding use of tungsten alloy steel is for high-speed tools, with as much as 22% tungsten. It retains strength and wear resistance at high temperature. It is the only metal used in incandescent light bulbs (10 million filaments can be made from a ton of tungsten). It has many uses in electrical equipment for contact points subject to wear, either alone or alloyed with copper and silver to increase conductivity.

As inorganic chemicals its compounds are used in textile dyes, ink, paint, and enamel, where the bright yellow color of WO_3 is desired. Some pigments are luminescent and the compounds are used in x-ray screens, television picture tubes, solid lubricants, lasers, and catalysts.

Occurrence: The two important minerals are scheelite and wolframite. The former occurs where a tungsten-bearing granitic rock intrudes and is in contact with limestone. It also occurs in quartz veins and sometimes in schist. Scheelite is a nondescript grayish-white mineral which is noticeably heavy but commonly low-grade and associated with minerals from which it is not readily distinguished. In the light of an ultra-violet lamp it fluoresces brilliant white and even tiny specks of the mineral are easily recognized.

Wolframite is the more common mineral (particularly in China), also occurring in quartz vines. It is an inconspicuous brownish black mineral, but very heavy. By far the most important deposits are in China, where possibly half of the world reserves are located. The United States is second in reserves and about 35% self-sufficient in production. The main occurrences are in California in quartz veins and contact replacement deposits and in the brines of Searles Lake. Colorado is second, with most of the element in the huge molybdenum mine at Climax. Much of the known resources are in the tailings from this operation. **Scheelite** has been reported as extensive in low-grade form in the schist near Idaho Springs. Nevada and North Carolina have important deposits. Thailand, South Korea, Australia, Austria, Bolivia, and Portugal are important producers. Reserves in Canada are quite large and production has rapidly increased to rank it in first place. Brazil, Burma, India, Peru, Japan, and Russia also have tungsten deposits.

Economics: Because of its dominant position in tungsten production, China is in a position to control the price of the commodity. With the new market orientation of that nation, it is not likely to attempt to flood the market and disrupt the price. Actual production is not known, but exports of 25 million pounds were announced in 1979. Only about 30% of this reached the western market, however.

In the last few years (1975-1979) there has been an average deficit in production of 7 million pounds per year. This has been made up in part by releases from the U.S. government stockpile and in part by other sources. As the result price has gyrated from a low of about $30 per short ton unit (1 stu = 20 pounds) in early 1973, to $165 per stu in 1977, and back to about $120 in late 1979 and $121 in May 1982. This is the price for the element in the concentrate before refinement. Tungsten is commonly quoted in a semi-refined form of ammonium paratungstate (abbreviated APT), which may run about $40 per stu ($2 per pound) higher than in the concentrate form.

While the period 1974-1983 has been one of depressed economic conditions, demand for tungsten has increased steadily at 3.4% per year. Since new production has not kept pace, price has averaged 21% per year increase. Whenever the price of a commodity rises spectacularly, attention is attracted to it, and many groups decide to try to enter the business. In minerals, exploration teams spread out to look for new sources. Known deposits of lower grade become economic, and mines are opened (Devon, England 2.5 million pounds, 1985). Existing operations are expanded (Cantung, from 5.7 to 8 million pounds in 1980). New discoveries are programmed to production (Mount Pleasant in New Brunswick, Canada, 3.1 million pounds for 1982; Springer, Nevada, 1.6 million pounds for 1982; plus Strawberry in the U.S., Mac Tung and Log Tung in Canada, and others). The usual result is a period of oversupply, depressing the price, slowing new developments and again, with lagging production, causing a price spurt, and finally to repeat the cycle. Tungsten is late in the current cycle, with supply exceeding demand.

While the inflated price of tungsten has increased nearly five-fold since 1973, it has approximately doubled in real terms. One must keep this in perspective, however. Consumption in the free world is only about 30,000 tons, roughly equal to the output of one modest copper mine, which in turn is small compared to an iron mine. If the mine recovers 0.5% tungsten, the annual increase in consumption (2 million pounds) would be supplied by one rather small mine producing 550 tons of ore per day. If this is recovered from narrow quartz veins, the value of the ore per ton (recovered basis) is about $75 per ton, which is equivalent to gold at 4.7 grams (0.15 ounce). It would be considered a marginal mine in the U.S., Canada, Australia, or Europe. In other words, what looks like a project of good profit potential may not be nearly as attractive when examined in detail. Considering that mining costs have been increasing at about 30% per year for several years, one might be caught in a squeeze unless ore grades are considerably above average, something rare today. It has been reported that some of the mines in China have grades of ore as low as 0.11%–0.13% tungsten. The only way this can operate is by subsidy. The mine is subsidized either by cheap labor or by direct supplement of operating funds or both.

Production: Many tungsten mines operate on fairly narrow veins with a quartz gangue. Thus in underground mines, open stopes, cut and fill, shrinkage or timbered stopes are used, depending on strength of the walls and the availability of timber. In the United States much of the tungsten is a co-product with molybdenum mining; hence large-scale block caving operations are the source of the ore. It is reported that in China part of the tungsten is produced by hand labor in open pits. Major production in the West is highly mechanized, as at the Climax mine in Colorado.

Since most of the ores are complex, a combination of gravity and flotation is used in beneficiation to produce a mineral concentrate, commonly containing 50%–70% WO_3. The two major minerals require different processes to produce the intermediate products, with scheelite being the premium concentrate for treatment. Some scheelite is used directly in steel making. Some ores are reduced in an electric furnace to ferrotungsten, containing over 70% W. This too is used directly in steel making. APT is produced by hydrometallurgy; this product is reduced to metallic powder by carbon or hydrogen. Tungsten carbide (WC) is made from hydrogen-reduced powder, carbon, a cobalt binder—all sintered. Most of the metal products are produced by powder metallurgy.

Since many people are enamoured with large numbers, the minor metals are generally reported in pounds or kilograms. With even smaller quantities, it is in ounces or grams. World production of tungsten in 1981 was approximately 49,000 tons, with 25,000 tons produced in the Western nations. Western consumption was 29,500 tons. The U.S. government stockpile disposed of 450 tons. There were imports from China and some changes in producers reserves. In 1982 Canada reached the number one position in mine production in the free world. The Khao Soon mine in western Thailand, one of the largest deposits in the world, has declined in production because of serious political problems in the area.

Outlook: An effort is being made by the major producing nations to develop an international agreement on tungsten production and pricing patterened somewhat after the Tin Council. The major consuming nations, all importers, have resisted this move. The U.S. stockpile is a factor in the future. In 1964 this stood at 203,710,000 pounds, of which 158,900,000 pounds were declared surplus. This was nearly three year's supply. By the end of 1980 there were still 81.2 million pounds in the stockpile with 30.5 million of this in the surplus category. This large surplus has dampened efforts to develop new production, contributing to the rapid price escalation in 1976–1977. Releases during this period prevented an acute shortage, however, as the "new economics" of the post-petroholic era emerged.

Demand for tungsten products should continue to grow at a rate exceeding the world population growth rate with the industrial nations consuming a disproportionate share. There is no serious competitor for tungsten carbide, and the high temperature strength of tungsten alloys is superior to any substitute. In the United States, with abundant molybdenum, almost all the substitutions that are possible have been made. The problem of one mine of economic size being so large in proportion to increasing consumption will probably continue to disrupt the price with surplus and shortage. The early 1980s are likely to be a period of surplus even with steady growth in consumption.

URANIUM (U)

Properties and Characteristics

Atomic number	92
Atomic weight	238.03
Isotopes	238 (99.3%); 235 (0.7%); and 234 (0.006%); 11 other isotopes do not occur naturally.
Melting point	1132°C
Specific gravity	19.04
Average in rocks	4 ppm
Major minerals	Uraninite/pitchblende, UO_2; carnotite, $K_2O.2UO_3.$ $VO_5.nH_2O$; autunite, $CaO.2UO_3.P_2O_5.nH_2O$

History: This element was discovered in pitchblende in 1789 by Martin Klaproth, a leading German chemist. Since the planet Uranus had recently been discovered, the metal was named uranium. Klaproth thought he had prepared the pure element, but it was actually prepared for the first time in 1841. In 1896 Becquerel discovered that uranium produced radioactive rays

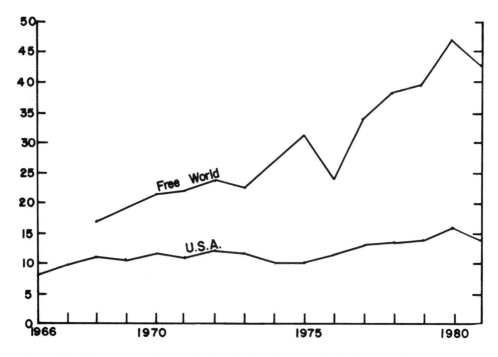

Figure 25 Uranium production in the United States and the free world, given in thousands of metric tons.

that could expose photographic film. In 1898 Madame Curie discovered that uranium ores contained another element, which was named radium. From that time until 1939 production of radium for medical purposes was the only use for uranium ores. Fission was discovered in Germany in 1938 by Hahn and Strassmarin.

In 1939 a group of scientists persuaded Albert Einstein to write a letter to President Roosevelt informing him that uranium might have the potential of being used in a weapon of tremendous power, and warning that Germany was thought to be working on such a development. As a result a super-secret experiment code-named Manhattan Project was initiated. Enrico Fermi and a group of scientists initiated the first self-sustaining chain reaction in a laboratory under the old stadium of the University of Chicago on 2 December 1942. Production of a nuclear device was programmed, and the first weapon was exploded in the New Mexico desert on 16 July 1945. Less than a month later, on 6 August, an atom bomb was dropped on Hiroshima, Japan. Intelligence observers, of whom the author was one, were aghast at the destruction on examining the strike photographs in Manila the next morning. Three days later a second bomb was dropped on Nagasaki and the war came to a speedy end.

President Eisenhower initiated Atoms for Peace, and a program to develop nuclear power resulted. By 1980 there were 405,768 megawatts of nuclear generating capacity in the free world.

In 1979 an accident occurred at the plant on Three Mile Island at Harrisburg, Pennsylaniva. While there were no injuries, a series of "impossible" incidents did cause the release of some radioactivity and severe damage to the plant itself. The reaction to the accident was very strong; there were exaggeration and over-reaction of the press and government. This gave the professional anti-nuclear group ammunition which resulted in seriously delaying the energy independence of the United States.

Uses: There is only one significant use of the element uranium, which is for fission. It has been used as a weapon and stockpiles of nuclear warheads are adequate to kill every human several times. It is used in nuclear power plants and can be a boon in an energy-starved world.

Occurrence: Uranium is a minor constituent in granitic rocks. Sometimes the uranium is sufficiently concentrated in the granite to form veins high enough in grade and of sufficient tonnage to be mined. As these rocks are weathered, the uranium is oxidized to the U^{+6} valence. It is highly soluble in this form. It moves in solution into aquifers along a mountain front in "granite wash," where it is reduced and precipitated. It may accumulate in gravel zones along with placer gold as it has done in South Africa in Precambrian time, somewhat similar in time and character in Canada and Australia.

Sometimes granitic rocks explode to the surface as rhyolitic volcanoes in the caldera stage. Geochemically uranium accumulates in the upper magma zone and when pumiceous materials are blown out in massive eruptions, sometimes 200 km^3 in a single blast, the ash accumulates to great thickness in nearby basins. As the ash weathers, uranium migrates with ground water and enters aquifers. As it migrates it may encounter organic matter—bones, tree trunks, or just disseminated carbon, which reduces it and causes it to precipitate as uraninite or other minerals. Sometimes this type of deposit is remobilized, migrates and is reconcentrated in what is known as a *"roll front"* which may be appreciably higher in grade than the sandstone blanket. This type of deposit, if exposed on the surface, will be oxidized to carnotite or other bright yellow uranium mineral. These sandstone deposits are the type found in the western United States from Wyoming to Colorado, and New Mexico, Arizona, Nevada, Washington, and California.

Still a fourth type of occurrence is with the marine phosphorites where grades are very low. As a co-product, however, it can be economic. Seven fertilizer plants in Florida recover uranium.

There is a finite amount of uranium in sea water, 3 parts per billion. Theoretically, this could eventually become a fuel source, particularly if the water is being distilled for human consumption and other salts are produced from the residue. Massive desalination would be necessary to make this significant, for example enough water to supply Los Angeles. A billion tons of water contains three tons of the element.

Economics: When uranium was first required for the nuclear weapons program, the United States was thought to have very limited resources. Therefore a fixed price was established after the war for purchase of "yellow cake," the concentrated uranium oxide. The result was the "uranium boom" of 1948–1955, and the government found itself swamped with far more uranium than it believed possible. It began reducing the price from $13 per pound to $8, then $6, and still the yellow cake came rolling in. Finally it had to phase out purchases entirely.

The nuclear program was a grand success at the scientific level, but many inventions had to be made to engineer and produce a plant that could burn the new fuel. Thus the gap between filling the military need and the utility requirements building up to production level was longer than anticipated. This was the first "boom and bust" cycle in uranium.

A solid expansion in nuclear power plants was well underway in the late 1960s, with concern being voiced about possible fuel shortages. Uranium exploration expanded again from 15.5 million feet of drilling in 1971 to 34.2 million in 1976, to 45.6 million in 1977. Meanwhile the price had shot up to $44.50 per pound, and manufacturers who had guaranteed to supply plant fuel faced bankruptcy. After the Three Mile Island accident, the rug was pulled out. New orders failed to materialize, standing orders were cancelled, construction was delayed by legal harassment and government changes in regulation. This situation was further complicated by the high interest rates which greatly increased plant costs, changed economics, and made holding stocks of uranium economically impossible. Therefore utilities entered the market selling their stocks. The price dropped to $27 and exploration cut back in 1980 to 27 million feet. Mines were cut back, some closed and the cycle repeated. This is a classic cycle of boom and bust, with which mining has had to cope throughout its history.

Unless the United States opts for a low-growth economic scenario, there will be another boom cycle around 1990. Meanwhile, uranium consumption in the United States will increase at 9% per year on confirmed plants, only slightly behind the rate of the free world as a whole, 9.24% through 1990.

Production: Uranium mines in the United States are generally rather small and in a sandstone, which is mechanically rather strong. Therefore much of the underground mining is in open stopes or rooms, supported where necessary. The larger mines have been able to mechanize. In Wyoming, several of the ore bodies are close enough to the surface and the overburden is too unconsolidated to permit underground mining, so open pits have been used, with rather high stripping ratios. One problem with uranium mines is that radon, a heavy gas and daughter product of spontaneous decay, accumulates in low places in the mine. It is radioactive and poisonous, necessitating careful ventilation of underground workings.

On the coast of West Texas several solution mines have been opened, injecting solvent into the uraniferous horizon and pumping the solute to the surface and to the processing plant. The method is not new, but the conditions for application are more favorable than in many other regions.

In most installations ores are leached by dilute sulphuric acid in the mill then uranium is recovered from the liquor by solvent extraction or ion exchange. In ores too high in carbonates to make acid extraction feasible, an alkaline carbonate solution is used. Solvent extraction is so efficient that it pays to pass mine water with as little as 2 ppm through the plant.

Yellow cake (U_3O_8) is precipitated from solution, dried and shipped to a refinery. The oxide is converted to the gas uranium hexafluoride and goes through the gaseous diffusion process to upgrade the ^{235}U, the fissionable isotope of the element, either to fuel grade or weapons grade. Unofficial estimates are that it requires a minimum of 3 kg of weapons-grade material to initiate a chain reaction that will explode.

For the light water reactors used in the United States, the uranium is converted to UO_2 and pelletized, then charged into alloy tubes to be clustered into a fuel assembly.

Outlook: Nuclear fuels such as uranium and thorium, which can be produced economically contain at least 20 times as much energy as all the fossil fuels combined. Now that society demands more sustained energy production than fossil fuels can provide, and since science has unlocked the secret of utilizing nuclear fuels, their use has become a necessity.

In the developing nation, the United States is regarded as more responsible for the "oil shock" than OPEC. The U.S. has alternate energy sources, but instead of using them it deliberately enters the world market and buys all the oil it wants regardless of price, forcing the price out of economic reach of other nations. Just as the United States sends its seven-foot tall basketball players to compete against the five-foot eight-inch teams in Southeast Asia, the developing nations cannot compete against the economic stature of the United States. With abundant energy resources, the United States has no right to enter the world market and force up the price of oil for nations without alternative supplies.

The halt in orders for new nuclear power plants in 1980 and cancellation of a dozen or more plants previously ordered means that programmed reduction in fossil fuel needs are going to be upset from 1987 onward. It may mean rationing of electricity and turning out street lights at night. Nuclear power *has* to be utilized and it is senseless to debate for a few years, creating unnecessary hardship both in the United States and abroad. The extent of the problems resulting from the Three Mile Island accident was largely the result of human failure. It is reasonable to think the hazard of accidents in nuclear plants has been reduced to one-tenth what it was before TMI. It is important to insist on eternal vigilance, to maintain competence of personnel and safety in operations, but it is also time to set emotional judgments aside and recognize how much damage is being done to the economic environment by the deliberate delaying tactics of a vociferous minority riding on their ability to stir emotions in order to obtain funds for a handsome living.

There are many political problems to be solved in the area of nuclear proliferation and potential terrorist access to explosive grade materials. This includes the irresponsibility of industrial nations supplying weapons-grade material to developing nations and nations conducting sneak bombing attacks on installations of their neighbors. Despite two years of inflation, the price of uranium declined from about $44.50 per pound of U_3O_8 early in 1979, to $27.00 at the end of 1980. Exploration drilling in the U.S. reduced from 47 million feet in 1978 to 27 million feet in 1980. Stockpiles of U_3O_8 available to power generation exceed five years consumption and will continue to grow as past exploration capital is consumed and not replaced. The world will live off its bank account rather than its labors. Eventually the day of reckoning will come, when with shortage, the price will shoot up.

Thus the TMI problem and the strident anti-nuclear group have set back development only in the United States by possibly as much as 10 years. Nuclear energy will grow rapidly in France, Japan, Russia, and other nations that realize there is no viable alternative. Eventually the United States must recognize that it, too, must utilize the energy sources available to it.

VANADIUM (V)

Properties and Characteristics

Atomic number	23
Atomic weight	50.94
Isotopes	50 (0.2%), 51 (99.8%)
Artificial	47, 48, 49, and 52
Melting point	1950°C
Specific gravity	6.0
Average in rocks	90 ppm; Mafic 200 ppm; Felsic 40 ppm; black shale 50–2000 ppm; soils 100 ppm; range 20–500 ppm

Major minerals   Carnotite $K_2O.2U_2O_3.V_2O_5.3H_2O$ (uranium mineral),
with magnetite and ilmenite; roscoelite, K_2 (Mg, Fe)
$(Al, V)_4$ $Si_{12}O_{32}.4H_2O$

History: Vanadium was discovered in 1801 by a Mexican, Andres del Rio, who named it erythronium. He later concluded he had erred, and withdrew the name. It was rediscovered in Sweden in 1830 by Mr. Sefstrom, and named after *Vanadis*, the goddess of beauty in that country. This name was selected because of the beautiful colors of its compounds in solution.

The first use of vanadium was in salts for making ink and as a coloring agent in dyes and in glass. By the end of the nineteenth century its alloys were used in armorplate and in tools. It gained importance in the United States by 1905, when it was used by the automobile industry in steel alloys.

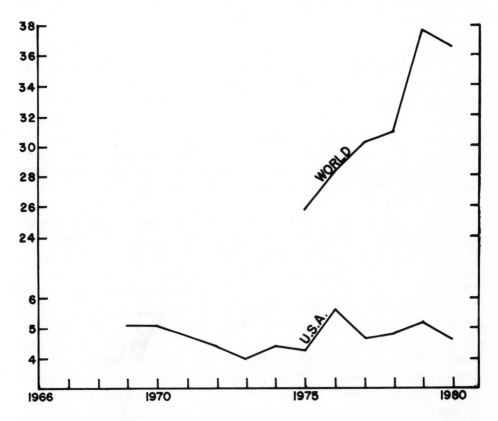

Figure 26 Vanadium production in the United States and the world, given in thousands of metric tons.

Vanadium is an important alloying metal, mainly used with iron but the total world consumption is estimated at 46,000 tons in 1980, about equal to one medium-sized copper mine.

Uses: The most important use of vanadium is an alloying agent, in specialty steel products and titanium alloys. It is particularly important in oil and gas pipe lines. The largest consumption is in construction materials such as "rebar," reinforcing steel. The alloys are becoming more important in machinery, tools, and transportation. Vanadium imparts toughness and shock resistance to steel. It is added almost entirely in the form of "carvan," or vanadium carbide, and "ferrovan," a vanadium-iron alloy. In the United States, about 3% is used as chemical compounds to add luster to glass, as the catalyst in contact sulphuric acid plants, in paints, varnishes and glazes, and in processing colored film. The metal itself has few uses, but appears promising as a structural metal in fast breeder reactors, swelling less than most metals under neutron bombardment.

The United States is the largest consumer and third largest producer of vanadium. Its consumption dropped 18% in 1980, the result of the recession.

Occurrence: One of the most important occurrences is in the uranium fields in the United States. It is an important constituent of some titaniferous magnetites. Many oil and coal deposits contain appreciable vanadium which can sometimes be recovered from the residues. It is present in the phosphate deposits of western United States and is recovered from them. Roscoelite, a vanadium-bearing mica, is also a source. One of the few mines with vanadium as the principle product is a vanadium-bearing clay deposit near Wilson Springs, Arkansas. Two projects in Western Australia are being developed, which will move Australia into fourth position among producers.

South Africa, with two-thirds of the world's reserves as titaniferous magnetite, is by far the largest producer. Russia ranks second, the United States third, and Chile fourth. Over half of U.S. imports come from South Africa. A major new source, capable of producing one-fourth of world requirements is being developed in Poland from vanadium-bearing iron ore.

Vanadium is one of the more abundant metals, constituting about 0.025% in the earth's crust. This exceeds the amount of copper, lead, or zinc. Deposits with a substantial amount of the metal are quite rare, however. The deposit in Arkansas was one of the largest in which vanadium was the primary metal, the grade being 0.56% V. The total tonnage of contained vanadium was 30,000 st. Vanadium is highly dispersed rather than selectively concentrated as are most other alloying metals. Thus deposits of ore grade are uncommon.

Economics: Most of the vanadium is a by-product of other mineral production, namely uranium, iron, titanium, coal, and oil. Thus the supply is rather inflexible. The price per pound of vanadium contained in ferro-vanadium increased from about $3.00 in 1969 to $7.75 in 1981. Thus it has increased much less than petroleum and somewhat less than commodities in general.

With U.S. consumption exceeding production and vanadium's importance in steel alloys, it is classed as a strategic metal. In 1964 the stockpile consisted of 15,730,000 pounds; 12,000,000 pounds were classed as surplus in 1965. By the end of 1968, the stockpile contained 11,218,000 pounds with a total objective of 3,000,000 pounds. In 1973 the stockpile objective was reduced to zero. In October 1976 the objective was raised to 20,190,000 pounds. By early 1981 there were 1,080,000 pounds of vanadium in the stockpile and the objective was 17,400,000 pounds, even larger than the big reserve that had been sold. This is the kind of flip-flop that makes planners look foolish and is very unsettling to the commodity market.

Production: Most of the world's vanadium is recovered from smelting titaniferous magnetite, the vanadium reporting in the slag. It is usually recovered by roasting it with salt (NaCl) and leaching out the soluble vanadium chloride or by direct reduction of the slag to produce ferro-vanadium, the form added to steel furnaces. A similar salt roast process is used on ores and residues, sometimes with solvent extraction or ion exchange for recovery.

Ferrovanadium is produced in an electric furnace. Production of the metal itself in pure form is difficult because of affinity for oxygen. The metal now costs from $33 to $2000 per pound, depending on purity required. Most of this is in the processing, hence it is a limiting factor in its consumption.

Outlook: The United States has large vanadium resources in the Colorado Plateau and the western phosphate fields as well as in titaniferous magnetite deposits. The process for recovery is energy intensive and costly, restricting use of the metal. For many applications columbium (now cheaper) and molybdenum (more expensive) are interchangeable. However, any major switch to columbium would rapidly drive up the price of that metal, since its consumption is much smaller than vanadium.

World supplies appear to be more than adequate at today's prices with major new production coming in Poland and Australia and expansion possible in South Africa. The United States could become self-sufficient at a higher price level or if a breakthrough in processing were to develop. Tonnages of phosphatic shale containing about 0.1% vanadium are apparently very large. They also contain significant zinc and silver. The highest phosphate contents coincide with highest uranium, but not with vanadium, zinc, and silver.

With economic adjustments, supplies of vanadium would easily be adequate for forseeable needs.

ZINC (Zn)

Properties and Characteristics

Atomic number	30
Atomic weight	65.37
Isotopes	64(50.9%), 66(27.3%), 67(3.9%), 68(17.4%), 70(0.5%)
Melting point	419.5°C
Specific gravity	7.13
Average content in rocks	Felsic 60 ppm; mafic 130 ppm; black shale 100–1000 ppm; soil 50 ppm; range 10–300 ppm
Major mineral occurrence	Sphalerite, ZnS (*67%* Zn), smithsonite Zn CO_3 (*52%* Zn)

History: Zinc was used by the Romans to produce brass as early as 200 B.C. but they never produced the free metal. Metallic zinc was apparently prepared in India about A.D. 1000 and in China about the same time. Paracelsus described the physical properties of zinc early in the sixteenth century. Zinc was imported into Europe prior to the eighteenth century to meet the limited needs of industry. The first production in Europe was in the 1730s with William Champion obtaining a patent for production of zinc by distillation in 1738. Efforts to produce it were hampered by the nature of the ore. At the temperature where zinc is reduced by carbon, it is above the boiling point, so the metal was lost. The method used by Champion was to collect the vapor in an external condenser as the liquid. In Europe the commercial form of the metal was called "spelter" which was derived from the Dutch word "spiauter," used for both zinc and pewter at that time. During the early period the mineral smithsonite, zinc carbonate, was the ore of the metal because sphalerite could not be separated from the associated sulphides. Since quantities of sphalerite far exceeded the carbonate, this became the principle mineral of industry when treatment methods were developed.

The first zinc furnace in the United States was built by the government at the Arsenal in Washington, D.C., in 1834. The zinc was produced to alloy with copper as brass for the production of standard weights and measures and soon thereafter for shell casings. The ore came from the very complex occurrence at Franklin Furnace, New Jersey. In 1860, with the start of the Civil War and the breech loading rifles, demand for brass increased greatly and plants were built at La Salle, Illinois and South Bethlehem, PA, using ore from the deposits in Wisconsin. After natural gas was developed in 1895, several more smelters were built in the southwest.

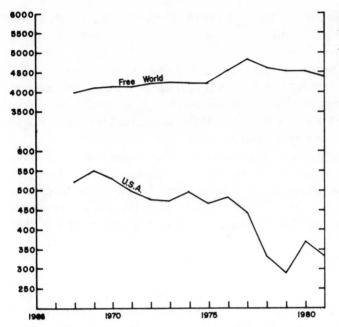

Figure 27 Zinc production in the United States and the free world, given in thousands of metric tons.

Uses: One of the properties of zinc is its high position in the *electromotive series.* It does not corrode easily, so it is extensively used in *galvanizing* iron to protect the iron from rusting, one product being the ubiquitous "G.I. sheets." This accounts for the 40% of all zinc consumption (in the U.S., 45%).

The second major use of zinc is in die castings, accounting for 32% of the metal consumed in the U.S. In 1974–1975 about 50 pounds of zinc went into each automobile, but with the "oil shock" and the impetus to improve gasoline mileage, light-weight materials and smaller size have cut the zinc per car ratio in half. Further modest attrition can be expected.

Third in importance in zinc consumption is brass, the first historical use of the metal, now consuming 14% in the United States, used in plumbing fixtures and decorations. Minor uses include rolled zinc, and as compounds such as zinc oxide in rubber, paints, and medicine.

A new market is developing in nickel-zinc batteries. If these are used as motive power, it could create a major market. Zinc is a "work-horse," ranking sixth among metals in tonnage, 16th among all mineral commodities.

Occurrence: By far the most abundant mineral of zinc is sphalerite, known to the miners as "black jack" or "rosin jack," depending on the color. There are extensive deposits in Tennessee and New York with sphalerite as the principal ore mineral. In the tri-state district (northwest Missouri, southeast Kansas, northeast Oklahoma) the ores are mixed with galena (lead sulphide), and in the west ores are complex and variable in mineral composition. Other elements produced exclusively from zinc ores in the smelter are cadmium, germanium, thallium, indium, and gallium. Other elements largely removed by mineral dressing are copper, fluorspar, gold, lead, manganese, and silver.

Canada, the largest producer, has extensive deposits. The United States ranks third behind the USSR. Australia, with probably the greatest reserves, ranks fourth in production. Other major producing countries are Peru, Mexico, Japan, Poland, Italy, North Korea, West Germany, China, and Yugoslavia. Nearly 50 nations produce some zinc.

There are three major types of zinc occurrence. By far the most important is in bedded deposits in sedimentary rocks. Volcanogenic or "kuroko" deposits are particularly important in Canada and Japan. It also occurs in veins and replacement deposits. These occurrences, with lead in some proportion, have been described more fully above under the discussion of that metal.

Economics: The price history of zinc shows a range between World Wars I and II of around 6–7 cents per pound. After World War II it fluctuated around a level exactly twice as high, 12–14 cents. After the "oil shock" of late 1973, the price more than doubled, reaching nearly 40 cents before dropping back to 30 cents per pound in 1978. It reached 49 cents in 1981 and dropped back to 36 cents in May 1982. With the price increase amounting to about 180% compared to 1000% on oil, zinc is one of the basic metals which had to absorb the deflation of inflated energy price. This has put pressure on the producers, making primary zinc production not very profitable. Growth over the decade 1968–1978 was only 8%. While the United States has abundant reserves and resources, it mines less than half of the metal it consumes.

In a poor financial position as the result of a relatively deflated price, U.S. industry was buffeted by demands that it meet stringent environmental standards. One of the largest smelters closed at the end of 1979. Metal purchases abroad increased, and the value added by refining accrues to other nations, adding to the balance of payments problem and exportation of environmental damage.

Because the price is relatively low, transportation charges of the concentrate to a smelter can be a significant cost item. Deposits in the United States are quite scattered, with the largest mine in New York and others in Tennessee, Kansas, Wisconsin, Colorado, Idaho, Utah, and some other western states.

Zinc was a critical metal during World War II. By 1947 there was an inventory of 275,000 st and stockpiling reached 1.58 million st by the end of 1963. In 1964 the entire stockpile was declared surplus. Fortunately it was not all sold and on 3 December 1969 a strategic reserve was set at 560,000 st. In 1981 the inventory was 376,000 st, and the goal was 1,425,000 st, a level nearly back to the inventory in 1963.

Production: In the sedimentary deposits, room and pillar mining methods are used, leaving minimal pillars and selecting lower grade sections to leave for support of the roof as far as possible. Rubber tired vehicles are quite widely used for haulage, and the rooms are quite large and open. Most of the zinc is mined in this manner.

In the vein mines, appropriate stoping methods to mine at minimum cost are used. On narrow veins this may be shrinkage or cut-and-fill stopes. Where the ore masses are larger, sub-level stoping or even top slicing can be used, although the timber requirement is quite high in this method. Virtually all the zinc is mined by underground methods.

U.S. mine production in 1978 was 333,000 tons, dropping to 330,000 tons in 1981 with consumption in those years at 1,156,000 tons and 910,000 tons, respectively. Since concentrates were imported for smelting, slab production was 485,000 tons and 371,000 tons, the closure of the smelter at Monaca, PA, in 1980 accounting for the decrease.

In the eastern mineral districts the zinc or lead-zinc ores are commonly first crushed and treated by gravity methods to make a preliminary rough concentrate. Heavy media separation in which the medium consists of finely-ground ferrosilicon suspended in water is used in many operations. The density of the fluid is maintained at a level between that of the ore and waste. The ore minerals sink and the gangue is floated off, washed to recover the ferrosilicon, and thrown away. Froth flotation of the slimes is usually required, and if both lead and zinc are present, grinding and flotation of the concentrate. Instead of heavy media, some plants use jigs and tables or a combination of all three methods. The zinc mines recover about 95% of the sphalerite with a concentrate grade of about 61% (cf. pure mineral, 67%) zinc. The lead-zinc mines average about 89% recovery of the zinc as a concentrate containing 58.5% zinc.

In the western complex, fine-grained ores with heavy gangue minerals, the practice is to fine grind and use selective froth flotation to make a series of concentrates of the constituents. About 87% of the zinc is recovered in the zinc concentrate of 54% grade. About 6% of the zinc reports in the lead concentrate, from which a portion is eventually recovered.

Smelting and refining require that the ore first be roasted to oxide, with the sulphur going out with the gases and recovered. The oxide is then dissolved by sulphuric acid and electroplated on aluminum cathodes. This is the high grade product. The alternate route is by reduction with carbon in a furnace, distilling the zinc vapor, condensing it in the molten form, and pouring slab. The product is commercial grade. It can be re-distilled to high purity. The smelting and refining processes are energy intensive.

Outlook: Zinc is one of the cheapest metals; therefore substitution by other metals involves greater cost per pound and can only be justified on the basis of superior properties. There is no effective substitute for zinc as a protective coating for iron and steel. Thus an important segment of the market is dependent upon steel consumption. As greater attention is paid to protecting iron products, thicker galvanizing coatings may be used and more products are likely to be galvanized. This could result in a small increase in consumption. Use of zinc in transportation has been drastically reduced in the last two years as all emphasis in auto manufacture has been to reduce size and weight to increase mileage. Further substitutions by plastic and ceramic materials can be expected, but the biggest drop has already occurred.

With a declining growth rate in the population, demand is likely to decrease in electrical, plumbing and heating installations. As the population levels off, replacement will be the major factor, which suggests a low level of consumption. Titanium pigment has been replacing ZnO in paints. The oxide market is subject to other substitutions. The brightest spot in the outlook for zinc is the possibility of development of electric automobiles using zinc batteries. There are other strong contenders for this market, however.

In 1968 the U.S. Bureau of Mines forecast a growth rate of 1.1%–3.1% per year to the end of the century. In the following decade, however, it achieved only 0.77% growth. Since there appears to be considerable vulnerability in the uses of zinc and with the grade of deposits declining (and hence production costs increasing at a greater rate than the inflator), it would appear that the low range forecast by the Bureau of Mines is likely to be the maximum growth rate. The minimum estimate would be no growth in the United States. This will stretch reserves into the next century. The outlook for growth in other nations is probably a little brighter. The nations with a population growth rate over 1% are going to have such a difficult time paying for their energy needs that growth in consumption will be slowed. This includes all the developing nations that are not self-sufficient in fuel, or those representing about half the world's population.

ZIRCONIUM (Zr)

Properties and Characteristics

Atomic number	40
Atomic weight	91.22
Isotopes	90(51.5%), 91(11.2%), 92(17.1%), 94(17.4%), 96(2.8%)
Melting point	1830°C
Specific gravity	6.5
Average in rocks	140–170 ppm; seyenites 500 ppm
Major minerals	Zircon, $ZrSiO_4$ (50%), Baddeleyite ZrO_2 (74%)

History: The element was identified in 1789 by a German scientist, M. H. Klaproth, and the metal was produced in 1824 by J. J. Berzelius. Metal pure enough to be ductile was produced in 1925, beginning its usefulness in this form. The major mineral is zircon, from which the metal gets its name. The mineral was known as a gemstone which was called *zargun* in Arabic, also called *jargon* in Sri Lanka, meaning worthless (compared to diamond), which is probably the ultimate source of the name.

High purity zirconium was produced in 1944 by the U.S. Bureau of Mines under the direction of W. J. Kroll; the commercial process bears his name. It is the same process used for production of titanium.

Uses: Zirconium is used principally to form the zirconium-uranium "sandwich" used in nuclear power plants, with a small amount going into corrosion resistant applications. Free world consumption was about 400 tons in 1980.

The major proportion of this mineral is used as zircon sand or flour, with about 700,000 tons going into foundry sand, refractories, ceramics, and abrasives.

Occurrence: Over 70% of the free world production of zircon comes from the sand deposits in Australia. The United States is second and South Africa third in production of zircon. Australia has the capacity to produce more but has restricted marketing to avoid forcing the price down to uneconomic levels. Zircon is a common constituent of granitic rocks. It is durable, so it is concentrated in streams during weathering and erosion of the primary host rock. It concentrates with the other heavy minerals, magnetite, rutile and ilmenite.

Economics: Early in the 1970s when it looked as if nuclear power was moving ahead strongly, the demand for zirconium for fuel elements was strong. At that time environmental considerations closed some of the mines in eastern Australia and others were depleted, so there was an acute shortage of zircon. The price shot up to over $400 per ton. New mines were programmed in Western Australia, and brought into production, creating an excess, and the price dropped sharply to $62–$69 (Australia). A minor factor, since tonnages are very small, was the cut-back in the U.S. nuclear power program during the Carter administration (1976–1980). There is no stockpiling program for zirconium.

As a non-metallic mineral it has to compete with quartz, garnet, refractory chromite, and others, but is well placed in its market. The metal has very low *nuclear cross-section*, which makes it very useful in fuel elements. It always contains about 2% hafnium, which has very high cross-section and must be carefully removed in order for the zirconium to be useable in preparing the fuel elements.

Production: Zircon is a co-product of mineral sands poduction, primarily associated with rutile and ilmenite but also accompanying magnetite, gold, monazite, and others. Sands are dredged and separated into constituents by gravity differences, magnetic characteristics, and electrostatic methods. Zircon is used as a non-metallic mineral or ground to "flour" for some applications. To recover the metal, it is fused with coke in an electric arc furnace to produce zirconium carbonitride (85% Zr). The next step is chlorination to $Zr\, Cl_4$, which is reduced in an inert atmosphere to zirconium with magnesium metal (the Kroll process). To produce reactor-grade zirconium (hafnium-free), the chlorinated product is dissolved with acid and separated by solvent extraction, removing the hafnium for further use. The zirconium is precipitated and calcined to ZrO_2, which is rechlorinated and put through the Kroll process.

Outlook: Zircon must compete in the rough world of non-metallics but should hold its own, its price fluctuating with the general economy. Production has been lower for the last three years, following the trend of steel and construction. The metal zirconium is dependent on uclear power plant construction and nuclear power is proceeding rapidly in France, Japan, and Russia. In the United States there have been 40 cancellations of power plants, and no new orders. Zirconium in the United States will stagnate until the need for nuclear power is recognized.

CHAPTER 10

NON-METALS

AGGREGATE

Weights and Types

Ordinary	Sand, gravel
Light	Scoria, pumice, cinders
Expanded (heated)	Perlite, vermiculite, shale
Heavy	Magnetite, barite (for nuclear shielding)

History: The earliest mineral products used in construction were soft brick and, after metallic tools were invented, blocks of stone. Building city walls, temples, palaces, or pyramids was a difficult job requiring many slaves. While the Romans developed cement, they did not use mass concrete. It was not until the 19th century that concrete construction became important, and not until about World War II that concrete design became a science.

Concrete is composed of three ingredients: (1) portland cement as the binder, (2) aggregate as the bulk product which must be cemented together, and (3) water to react with the cement to form new chemical compounds that have structural strength when the reactions are completed. Frequently a fourth material is added. Reinforcing steel is most commonly used for this purpose, but asbestos, fiberglass, and some other fibrous or metallic substances are sometimes used.

Aggregate is used in quantities exceeding the tonnage of all other mineral commodities combined. Almost any strong, durable, and preferably chemically inert rock can be used as aggregate. Most commonly sand and gravel deposited by streams or worked by waves are used. When sand and gravel are not available, a durable, strong stone is quarried and crushed to specification. While sand, gravel, and crushed stone make up over 95% of aggregate used, some natural volcanic lightweight materials, pumice and scoria, and some expanded rocks, vermiculite, perlite, and shale, have special applications.

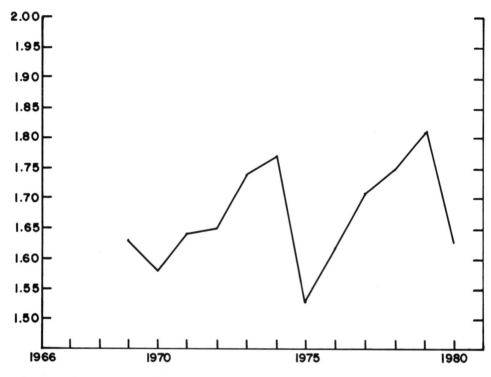

Figure 28   Aggregate production in the United States, given in billions of metric tons.

Uses: Aggregate is used to supply the bulk and much of the strength of concrete. It is used in paving streets and airfields. For paving to be durable, however, the subgrade underlying it must be properly prepared, compacted, and drained. Then an aggregate "base course" must be laid before the concrete is poured. Aggregate is used in concrete made with both portland cement and asphalt. Although the former has higher initial cost, it more than pays for itself in much longer service life. Some country roads are surfaced with gravel only.

Concrete is heavy, and much of the weight of steel required to give a building strength is to support the weight of the concrete itself. Pumice and scoria, lightweight substitutes for sand and gravel, are also used. There are serious problems in quality control with these materials. Vermiculite, a mica that swells several times when heated, has good insulation properties, but little strength. Likewise perlite, a volcanic glass that will expand about 20 times when heated, will make concrete so light it will float, but it has little strength. A third material has been found to expand to about 40% of the weight of sand and gravel. This is a clay or shale composed largely of the clay mineral illite. However, even a little lime in the rock makes it turn to slag instead of swelling to a glassy mass filled with small bubbles. Concrete made with expanded shale lightweight aggregate may weigh 50%–60% as much as ordinary concrete, yet have equal strength to the latter. While more expensive, lightweight concrete may more than pay for itself in the reduced amount of reinforcing steel required and reduced labor cost in structural concrete. It also offers better thermal and acoustic insulation.

During World War I some of the Liberty ships were made of concrete; three of these were made of light weight concrete from shale found near San Francisco. They were named the *Faith*, *Hope*, and *Charity*. Thirty years later they were still afloat, anchored as a breakwater in British Columbia.

Heavy aggregate of magnetite and barite is used in nuclear power plants to provide shielding from the bombardment of radiation.

Concrete blocks are extensively used in construction and they may be made of either light or ordinary aggregate. Large panels are sometimes used, and some pre-fabricated structures are made entirely of concrete.

Occurrence: Sand and gravel are the products of weathering of rocks in hills or mountains. The farther a deposit is from the source, the smaller the maximum size and the fewer the particles of softer stone. Deposits occur in river beds and on flood plains and sometimes in deltas or even beneath the sea. Many times the stream valleys are choice agricultural land or on sites favorable for construction of homes, so there are competing demands for land use.

Where sand and gravel are not available, "hard rock" sources are quarried and the rock is crushed to meet the specifications for the concrete or base course. Since the product is quite heavy, haulage costs are high, so a nearby source is desired. When suburbs are extended to the vicinity of a gravel pit or quarry, the residents object to the shock of blasting or the noise of crushing. There is also the conflict in land use.

Pumice, perlite, and scoria originate in volcanic areas. Pumice may float for a long distance to the site of deposition. Clay and shale occur in many areas, but only a few deposits meet the specifications and most argillaceous materials having the proper chemical composition and uniformity (clayey) are not acceptable to be used in the manufacture of lightweight aggregate.

Economics: Because aggregate sources are fairly common, competition is strong and the price is very low, generally in the range of $6–$10 per ton, or 0.3–0.5 cents per pound. Thus while the ingredients of concrete are inexpensive, the labor, forming, reinforcing steel, and equipment make architectural concrete expensive. Since aggregate is by far the cheapest building material, it is not subject to substitution except by more expensive materials with specially desirable properties. Transportation to the point of use is always a significant cost, and may equal or exceed the price of the product. This cost is accepted because it is still a small part of the cost of the finished product.

Sand, gravel, and crushed stone constitute by far the largest tonnage of mineral consumed by the public. The total value is one of the highest in the mineral industries.

Production Methods: Sand and gravel are excavated with scrapers, shovels and drag lines, or dredges. Large, oversized rocks are discarded or crushed and sized by screening. In use, desired proportions of the various sizes are recombined to give maximum desired properties. That is, a large dam may be able to use cobbles up to 8 or 10 inches, but a sidewalk may require a maximum size of 2 inches.

Crushed stone is quarried by drilling and blasting, then crushing and sizing of the product. This adds an extra cost, which may give a price handicap equal to about 15 kilometers of haulage (by truck). The angularity of crushed stone gives a "harsh" product, which is more difficult to handle, place, and finish than rounded stream gravel.

Expanded clay aggregate is treated in different kinds of kilns and the characteristics of the product vary widely. It may be "harsh" or the individual particles may be rounded and have a dense coating. The latter is the superior and more expensive product.

Outlook: Much of the reputation that the mining industry has had for environmental damage is the result of contact with gravel pits and rock quarries. The operations are deemed to be "unsightly" by people who hate to see holes in the ground. Aggregate sources have to be quite close to the market, hence are accessible to those who worship "nature" and who ignore, the economic facts of life. To build a large building requires that holes of about the same size as the building be dug elsewhere, in someone else's environment. The materials must also be transported to the construction site. During the construction, the building is not esthetically attractive, but the end product is essential to advancement of a community. Likewise, the gravel source is essential to community development. Eventually the deposit will be depleted and the site reclaimed, frequently as a park with trees and a pretty lake; or it may be put to other use. To drive the aggregate producers away is to handicap one's own community and export the "visual pollution" and economic benefits to someone else's neighborhood.

The market for aggregate is entirely dependent on construction, which is a cyclic industry. In the countries with mature, industrial economies, population growth rate has declined materially and will probably continue to drop. Under these conditions, demand for new construction will drop. Thus demand for aggregate in these nations will be moderate and fluctuate quite widely. In the less developed nations, those with adequate indigenous energy sources will probably show strong growth in construction and demand for aggregate.The less developed countries that import a major share of their energy and generally have population growth far in excess of industrial nations are sure to have great difficulty in meeting the minimal demands of their populace, and construction cannot be expected to be vigorous.

ASBESTOS (CHRYSOTILE)

Properties and Characteristics

Composition	Variable depending on form; magnesium silicate
Specific gravity	2.219
Hardness	Ca. 4
Color	Silky luster, greenish white to green in chrysotile, blue in crocidolite
Variety of serpentine	Mountain leather is matted chrysotile fibers, flexible in sheets and mountain cork is thicker masses; both varieties float

History: Asbestos is a popular name for several fibrous minerals which are silken in luster and flexible in small groups. Since 95% of the commercial product is chrysotile, this is the mineral emphasized here. The mineral was known to the Greeks and Romans and the first recorded use was as lamp wicks that did not burn up. Those of the vestal virgins of Rome were made of this material. The fibers could be spun into yarn and since the cloth woven from it was not destroyed by fire, it was used as shrouds for the cremation of nobles. Pliny referred to the cloth as *linum vivum*, the funeral dress of kings.

The modern asbestos industry was initiated in 1860 in Italy. Today the total tonnage of asbestos produced ranks seventeenth, just behind fluorite and considerably ahead of lead.

There are three of six asbestiform minerals with commercial uses. Besides chrysotile they are amosite and crocidolite.

Asbestos has received an inordinate amount of adverse publicity in the past few years. This is a part of the campaign among certain preservationist groups to "paint mining black." It has some properties that can cause health problems, particularly to workers in the asbestos industry who were exposed to large amounts of it in the air and who smoke cigarettes. When the bad effects of asbestos were recognized and understood, corrective measures were implemented. The conditions that are trumpeted by the preservationists and played up in the media are largely those of 30 years ago. The health hazard to the general public from use of asbestos products is minute and possibly less than from some of the substitutes. As long as cigarette

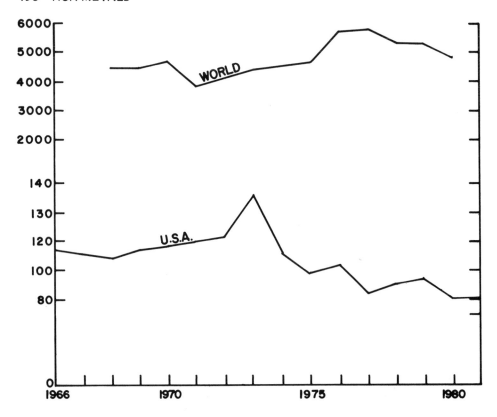

Figure 29 Asbestos production in the United States and the world, given in thousands of metric tons.

smoking, the worst hazard to the health of the public, is not only tolerated but even subsidized by the government, there is little basis for the extremist regulations being imposed on mineral products.

The Quebec Asbestos Mining Association established a grading of asbestos fibers that is quite widely used. It is based on the weights of fibers on various sizes of screens. There are seven major grades (1–7) and for grades 3–7 there are intermediate grades with letter designations. For example 4D is predominately retained on 4-mesh screen, but 4R is largely retained on the 10-mesh screen. The lower the number the better the grade, and because the longer fibers are scarce, the lower numbers have the highest prices.

Asbestos is valuable because it can be woven into fire-proof cloth (it is incombustible). It is also an excellent thermal and electrical insulator; it has high tensile strength.

Uses: By far the largest consumption of asbestos (70%) is in concrete products. It imparts tensile strength to concrete and cement adheres to the fibers. Asbestos-cement pipes are longlasting and relatively inexpensive. Roofing and siding panels are durable, have low maintenance cost, and are fire-proof. Medium length fibers are used for this purpose (grades 4s and 5s). About 10% is used in floor tiles. These are "shorts," or grade 7 fibers. Asbestos paper products account for 7% and for different paper products different lengths of fiber are used, from 3 to 7. Friction products rank fourth in consumption, primarily brake linings, clutch facings, and gaskets, This accounts for 3% and uses fiber grades 3-6. Grades 1-3 are spinning fibers, used primarily in textiles. Other uses include shorts in paints, plastics, sprays, caulking compounds, and insulation.

Occurrence: The mineral chrysotile is the alteration product of peridotite, an ultrabasic rock, under conditions of high pressure and excess water at moderate temperature. It is composed of 80-84% magnesium and silicon oxides in about equal proportions, and 13-14% water, with the balance being largely iron and alumina plus other minor impurities. Generally in large deposits there is evidence of a late stage intrusive which reheated the peridotite or dunite, causing the alteration and hydration.

The most important asbestos deposits in North America are found in southeastern Quebec, Canada. This district produces about 20% of the world's supply. The deposits are massive and can be mined by large-scale methods. The grade of the ore is 3%-4% asbestos. There are other deposits in Ontario, British Columbia, and Newfoundland; altogether Canada produces one-fourth of the world's asbestos.

First in production, with about 2.5 million tons per year, is Russia from deposits in the Urals. South Africa is third, and has the distinction of producing important amounts of all three varieties of asbestos. China, Swaziland, Zimbabwe, New South Wales in Australia, Brazil, Cyprus, and Italy are other producers. In the United States there is a limited amount of production from Vermont, Arizona, and California, but these deposits are rather low grade and deficient in the long fibers. Some of the deposits are quite large but are faced with environmental problems for operating.

Economics: Asbestos is used largely in new construction, so demand is cyclic. The Canadian industry has had much labor trouble, with strikes cutting production. There has been reluctance to invest in new mines in Quebec because the province has been planning to nationalize the industry and has told one company to sell to the provincial government or face expropriation. The government has offered less than half what the company thinks the interest is worth. Even a threat of expropriation immediately frightens off investors. Would anyone deposit his money in a bank that announced it might only let him have half of it back? Corporations are entrusted with the funds of labor unions, pension funds, and banks who get their money from thousands of depositors. They have the responsibility to invest the funds where they will earn interest for the investors and return the money to the investors on demand. Expropriation without adequate compensation is a form of theft.

The United States is largely dependent on Canadian resources to supply its needs. It is particularly deficient in the premium grades. World shortages have been frequent in the past few years. The price ranges from about $100 per ton to over $2000 per ton, depending on the grade of the product.

Several of the asbestos operations are open pit and low cost, but also quite low grade, yielding less than 2% recoverable fiber. The Canadian mines generally average 3%–4% fiber, although some of the rich sections carry as much as 30% fiber.

Production: World production of all grades of fiber in 1979 was 5.3 million tons, with Russia the largest producer. Canada, however, is not far behind. South Africa, China, and Zimbabwe are closely grouped, and Brazil and Italy are significant producers. Mining methods are generally large-scale open pit or underground block caving. Milling methods are distinctly different from other minerals. After crushing, the successive stages of screening, air floating, cyclone collecting, and hammer milling break down the rock and separate first the longest and then successively shorter fibers. Formerly this was a very dusty process, but with cyclone dust collectors, the air quality has been greatly improved and the health hazard materially reduced. The different fiber grades are bagged and sold to product manufacturers. In some cases, there is complete vertical integration.

Outlook: Over 80% of the asbestos is consumed in construction, so demand follows the construction cycle. The United States is about 85% dependent on foreign sources for chrysotile, which is largely imported from Canada. All of the amosite and crocidolite are imported. Domestic increases will be modest but demand is growing much more rapidly in developing nations. In some uses plastics, fiberglass, or natural fibers such as abaca can be substituted, but for uses where an inert or fire-proof or nonconductive material is required, asbestos will continue to dominate.

Reserves of low-grade, short-fiber asbestos are huge but this is not the quality in greatest demand. Reserves in the major producing countries are adequate at expected demand until well into the next century.

BARITE (SOURCE OF BARIUM)

Properties and Characteristics

Composition $\quad$ $BaSO_4 - BaO$ (65.7%); SO_3 (34.3%)
Molecular weight $\quad$ 233.34

Isotopes	135, 136, 137, 138
Crystal form	Orthorhombic complex tabular twins, "roses"
Specific gravity	4.3–4.6
Hardness	2.5–3.5
Characteristics	Highly insoluble; white when pure

History: Barite is a minor industrial mineral that did not have any commercial importance until the latter half of the nineteenth century. The reddish barite "roses" found in Oklahoma and elsewhere were merely a curiosity and a mineral collector's item. The name comes from the Greek word *barys,* meaning heavy. The mineral was studied in Italy in 1602, but barium metal was first separated in 1808. Barite mining in the United States commenced in Virginia in 1845.

Uses: The most important use of barite is as a weighting material in drilling mud in oil wells. Many times fluids encountered in drill holes are under high pressure, and when the confining formation is breached the fluids may blow out, forming a "gusher." Today this is a sign of poor management. By adding a significant amount of barite the pressure can be kept reasonably close to the formational pressure. Special "blow out preventers" are used to contain the difference. About 90% of barite is used for this purpose. Small amounts are used in glass, paint, rubber, pharmaceuticals (the "barium cocktail" used in diagnostic x-ray examinations), and other minor uses in chemical compounds. It is sometimes used as a shielding material in the nuclear industry. The metal barium has no commercial use.

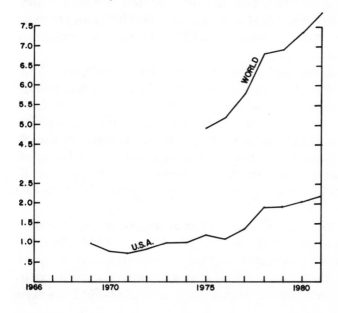

Figure 30 Barite production in the United States and the world, given in millions of metric tons.

Occurrence: Barite is a common mineral of widespread occurrence. It is formed in low temperature hydrothermal deposits, sometimes as veins or as bedded replacement deposits. It is one phase of mineral deposition in the *kuroko,* or deposits of volcanic origin formed on the sea floor.

Major production in the United States comes from Arkansas, Alaska, Nevada, Missouri, and California. Canada, Cuba, Germany, Italy, Great Britain, Mexico, and Russia are important producers. Ireland in Europe, India in South Asia and Thailand in Southeast Asia are the major regional producers.

Economics: Since the market is small and occurrences quite common, the price has been quite low. Consumption is dictated by the migratory nature of oil and gas exploration.

Worldwide consumption exceeds 7,600,000 tons. The price per ton has shot up in some localities to over $100 per ton. Producer prices in the United States are much lower, about $25 per ton for crude, and about $60 for ground barite.

Production: Most barite is mined by open pit methods from quite extensive deposits. Vein and bedded deposits are mined by methods customary for metal mines of similar occurrence. In most instances no beneficiation is necessary. If barite is pure enough to use, it is ground to 95%, –325 mesh. Specifications require a specific gravity of 4.2 for commerce. Since barite is soft and brittle, it can be ground easily. When used as a filler, barite is sometimes treated with sulphuric acid to remove traces of heavy metals and calcium carbonate, then dried and bagged.

Barite is a by-product of the production of fluorite in some localities. The United States is by far the largest producer at 2,000,000 tons per year; in addition, this country imports about 1,400,000 tons per year, consuming about 56% of world production.

Outlook: Barite consumption is directly tied to the oil and gas exploration industry. Since the United States has been intensely explored, consumption had plateaued at about 1 Mmt per year. By the standards of 1970 (petroleum prices), little exploration in the United States could be justified on shore. When the price of petroleum shot upward as the result of the oil crisis, a new oil drilling boom resulted and barite consumption increased 150%. Prospects that had no commercial possibilities with the price of oil at $2 per barrel were quite attractive when the price jumped to $15–$30 per barrel.

With both the industrial nations and the less developed countries reeling under the impact of the price escalations of 1973–1974 and 1979–1980, the consumption of oil dropped moderately and the oil exporting nations found they could not sell all they could produce at any price they wanted to charge. What is a severe recession in many countries in 1981–1982 is a deep depression in others. There are some who consider the resulting incapacity to purchase oil as an "oil glut." The surplus was easily controlled, however, when the cartel cut production modestly.

The slight reduction of oil prices in 1981–1982 by a few nations is almost certain to be short-lived. Thus the oil exploration business will probably continue to be quite active for several years, and the barite industry will have a few more good years. However, the energy input in exploration is rapidly approaching the energy discovered by drilling. Thus regardless of price, drilling in the United States dropped by 20% in the first half of 1982, and will taper off rather sharply by about the end of the 1980s. Barite should not be considered a long-term investment.

BORATES AND BORON (B)

Properties and Characteristics

Atomic number	5
Atomic weight	10.81
Isotopes	Stable—10 (19%), 11 (81%), radioactive 8, 9, and 12
Melting point	Above 2200°C
Specific gravity	2.31
Average in rocks	13 ppm; marine shale 130 ppm; soils 10 ppm; average in crust 3 ppm
Major minerals	Borax, $Na_2B_4O_7.10H_2O$(6.7%); colemanite, $Ca_2B_6O_{11}.5H_2O$(9.4%); ulexite, $NaCaB_5O9.8H_2O$(7.9%); Kernite, $Na_2O.2B_2O_3.4H_2O$(15.8% B)

History: The mineral borax was known and used as a flux in the Far East before the thirteenth century, when it was introduced to Europe. The element was discovered in 1808 almost simultaneously by two French chemists, Gay-Lussac and Thenard, and an Englishman, Davey. Boric acid was produced in Italy in the eighteenth century, but mining of borax started in Chile in 1852. This country dominated world production. Borax was developed in northern California during the Civil War (1864), but the discovery of borax at Searles Lake, California and in Nevada shifted production in the 1880s with major production in Death Valley in 1883–1889. These were the days when large mule teams were used to haul the borax wagons out of desert, with "20-Mule Team" becoming a brand name. Next came the Calico Mountains colemanite deposits, then Furnace Creek, and by 1927 the deposits at Kramer were developed and have since dominated world production.

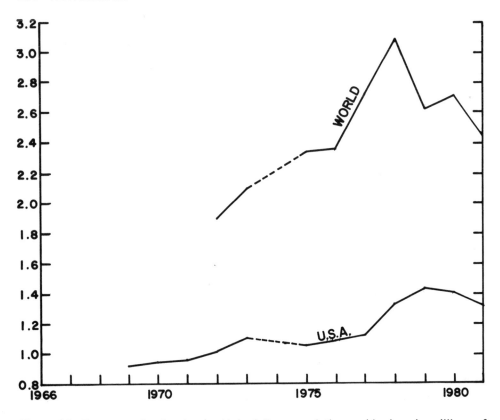

Figure 31 Borate production in the United States and the world, given in millions of metric tons.

The mineral borax was called *buraq* (an Arabic name for a mythical beast) and *burah* in the Middle East; Sir Humphrey Davey coined the name for the element.

Uses: About half the tonnage of boron compounds is used in glasses, particularly fiberglass, to which it adds strength. Colemanite contains calcium as well as boron in the right proportion for glass and is thus preferred for this use. It is a constituent of enamel on metals and glazes on sanitary ware. It is both essential to plant life (hence to animals) and a herbicide. Fertilizer is a major market for borax. It is used in soaps, detergents, water softening, toothpaste, eyewash, as a flux, and as an alloy in hardening steel. The carbide, and titanium, and tungsten borides are among the hardest materials known. As the nitride it is a thermal insulator. When this compound is heated above 1600°C at 70 kilobars of pressure, it converts into a material approaching the hardness of diamond. The hydrides are intensely energetic and can be used as rocket or jet fuel. It is also used in control rods in nuclear reactors.

Occurrence: The salts of boron are all quite soluble and are concentrated in evaporites in the deserts. Only the deserts which contain or are bordered by volcanoes of intermediate to acid character, where thermal springs have brought traces of boron to the surface, have concentrations of commercial size. The best known of these are in the eastern deserts of California at Searles Lake, Death Valley, Boron, and Owens Lake. The main mineral in the producing mines is borax with ulexite and colemanite also being produced. At Boron (or Kramer), the beds of borax and kernite reach a thickness of 60 m, are overlaid by 45–300 m of desert alluvium and are interbedded with black shale, which has protected the borates from solution.

At Searles Lake the brines are interspersed with coarsely crystalline salt and are pumped to the surface for differential crystallization. Trona is the most abundant valuable constituent. California produces about 70% of the world supply of boron compounds.

There are numerous enclosed basins where floodwaters evaporate to dryness called *salares* in the high deserts of the western volcanic belt of South America. Some of these contain deposits of boron minerals that are bedded and are reported to be large. Evaluation is incomplete because of unfavorable economic conditions—high altitude, lack of water or transportation, and remote locations from the coast.

Turkey has long been a producer of borates from rather small deposits. The government has partially evaluated a huge deposit of colemanite, reportedly containing over 500 million tons. This would undoubtedly make it the largest deposit in the world. It is interbedded with marl, tuff, and clay.

Russia is self-sufficient in borax from an area north of the Caspian Sea, where a giant salt dome occurs. Solution of the surface of the salt has resulted in formation of gypsum "cap-rock" and clay beds are also present. The borax deposits are found along fracture zones on the north and south margins of the dome, at the contact between the salt and cap rock.

Economics: With the bulk of world production coming from the eastern California desert, the product is remote from world markets. Thus transportation becomes a major cost item. If the huge Turkish deposits are fully developed they will probably dominate the European market. Because it is particularly suitable in glass production and accessible to the large market of the American east coast, Turkish colemanite may encroach on the U.S. market as well.

Technical grade borax was quoted at $97.50 per ton in 1968, and $201 in March 1982. Thus this mineral has abosrbed much of the inflation induced by the oil shock. Much of the increase has been since 1979. Since the United States is a major exporter of borates, there is no government stockpile program for this mineral.

Production: The original mines at Boron, California, were underground, served by shafts. The district was converted to open pit mining in 1957. Ore is crushed and blended before being dissolved to eliminate insoluble waste. The solutions are thickened at temperatures slightly below that of boiling water. The settled mud is washed and the liquor is evaporated in a vacuum to borax crystals, which are dried in a rotary drier, fused to anhydrous borax, and ground to customer specifications. Brines from Searles Lake are evaporated and crystallized. Potassium chloride for fertilizer is a co-product.

World production of boron compounds amounted to 2.96 Mmt in 1979. Thus it ranked 22nd among mineral commodities by weight produced.

Outlook: Borax has been setting new production records, and sales have been limited by productive capacity. With the very high strength-to-weight ratio of fiberglass and the strong move to reduce the weight of automobiles and other transport vehicles, use of fiberglass will probably continue to increase rapidly. Fiberglass insulation is in great demand for improving the heating characteristics of older homes, and new construction is also using greater quantities. If boron hydrides become important as fuel, this usage could grow spectacularly. If the very hard boron carbide or the borides are developed into cutting tools, this could encroach on the tungsten carbide market. Only the soap and detergent market is vulnerable. Thus borax and other boron compounds should be among the most profitable mineral investments of the 1980s.

It is reported that single filament fibers of pure boron are the strongest and most rigid material known. Reportedly one could be impaled on a fiber so fine it could scarcely be seen. If this material can be developed commercially, it would have many applications.

One environmental problem has risen in geothermal areas where waste water is not reinjected. The effluent may be high in boron salts. While boron is used as a fertilizer, above a rather limited quantity, it is toxic. Streams contaminated with boron from the Tongonan geothermal plant on Leyte, Philippines, were found to inhibit growth of rice when the water was used for irrigation. Reinjection of waste water had to be initiated. Water used for irrigation at the famous International Rise Research Institute at Los Baños, Philippines, was recently found to have a high boron content. Since this water was used for many years, the strains of rice developed by IRRI are boron-resistant.

CLAY

Properties and Characteristics

Kaolinite $2H_2O.Al_2O_3.2SiO_2$

Illite	$K (Al, Fe, Mg)_4 (Si, Al)_8 O_{20} (OH)_4$
Montmorillonite (bentonite)	$(OH)_4 Si_8 Al_4 O_{20}.nH_2 O$
Halloysite	$NH_2O.Al_2O_3.2SiO_2$
Specific Gravity	2.0–2.5
Characteristics	Very soft; white when pure; lumps disintegrate in water

History: Clay is a term applied to a family of minerals that are fine-grained, most of which are plastic and sticky when wet, composed of hydrous aluminum silicates. There is no satisfactory definition of the term "clay," but everyone knows what it is, and commonly thinks of it as "mud." In fact "mud engineering" is a highly specialized field of great importance in drilling for oil.

Clay was one of the earliest mineral products used by man. Certain earthy materials were found to have the characteristic of being easily shaped when wet, but became hard and durable when fired in a simple kiln. A great variety of cooking pots and storage jars was developed. Construction materials were also made from it. City walls were built of soft brick before tools were developed to cut stone.

In its many forms, clay is one of the most important industrial minerals. In tonnage it ranks fourth, surpassed by only one metal, iron ore. Because of widespread occurrence, supply abundance has kept the prices low.

The fine porcelains made by the Chinese as early as the eleventh and twelfth centuries were based on "china" clays plus feldspar and silica. Marco Polo brought some of these wares to Europe, where the technology was less advanced.

Uses: The most important use of clay is in structural materials. In building, clay products such as brick, roofing tile, drain pipe, floor and wall tile, are interchangeable with wood or metal for certain applications. Bathroom fixtures, known as "sanitary ware," are made of high quality white clay, called "china" clay or ball clay, plus feldspar and silica.

The second largest usage of clay is to provide the siliceous component of portland cement, of which it constitutes about 25% of the raw material. Part of this component is usually present in the limestone and is credited to that commodity.

To the manufacturer of brick, the clay that expands in his kiln is "poison." However, another industry has grown to substantial size to take advantage of the property of *intumescence* of some clays. It would rank about twelfth in tonnage if segregated from other clay products. It is called expanded clay aggregate or lightweight aggregate. The clay that exhibits this property is illite when it contains ferrous iron. If the clay contains more

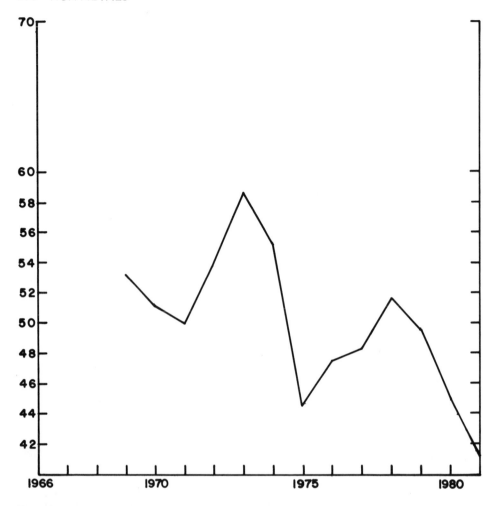

Figure 32 Clay production in the United States, given in millions of metric tons.

than traces of lime, it melts as soon as it softens, so it is unsatisfactory. While the expanded clay aggregate is considerably more expensive than heavy aggregate, in structural concrete the steel requirement is reduced by a large enough factor that it offsets the cost difference. The economics are enhanced by the much lower thermal conductivity of lightweight concrete, cutting energy costs. Standard concrete blocks (8" X 8" X 16") of lightweight aggregate and cement are light enough that one man can easily lay them, reducing labor costs.

Some clays, particularly kaolinite, withstand high temperature without softening or cracking. These are refractory clays, used in kiln and furnace linings to protect the shell or wall from heat in pyro-processing. These are called "fire clays."

Another variety of clay, montmorillonite, has the property of swelling when placed in water. The best source of this clay is in Wyoming, where it is called "bentonite." This particular variety is formed by alteration of pumicite in the sea and contains soda in its lattice. It will increase in volume 20-fold when wet. This property is utilized in mud engineering in drilling oil and geothermal wells. It contributes to preventing loss of drilling fluids into the porous rock formations and helps remove cuttings from the drill bits, thus reducing drilling costs. Because of its adhesiveness, this type of clay makes an excellent binder and is used in making iron pellets for blast furnace feed.

Other important uses of clay are in high-quality paper, in pottery, in glass, and in foundry molds (binding the silica sand). A possible use of clay is as a source of aluminum. There are very extensive shale deposits (lithified clay) in the western United States that contain about 28% Al_2O_3. The United States is almost totally dependent on foreign sources for bauxite and could become totally independent by developing the shale. The problem is that processing the clay is more energy intensive than the bauxite route. Since energy costs have skyrocketed, the economic prospects appear poor. There is a report, however, that Japanese scientists have discovered a method of treating clay to recover alumina which is less energy intensive.

Occurrence: Clays and their lithified equivalents (shale, phyllites, slates) make up a major portion of the Earth's surface. They constitute an important class of sedimentary rocks. The minerals are formed by hydrothermal activity, by weathering of siliceous rocks or by diagenesis, a process of alteration that takes place in buried sediments. Most of the clays of commerce are mined from sediments. Some products, particularly the high-grade kaolinite and halloysite are mined in subvolcanic deposits. Kaolinite also occurs in sediments, where it is called "fire clay" and in residual weathering zones, particularly in Georgia.

Clays are so widely distributed that sources suitable for most uses are generally available locally. Thus these heavy products do not require extensive shipping costs. Some of the scarce varieties such as Wyoming bentonite and Georgia kaolinite are shipped all over the world. In these cases the freight cost may be as much as the price at the mine.

Economics: Brick and tile can be made from a wide variety of clayey materials and processing is unnecessary. For cement, the alumina and silica contained in the clay are used as chemical constituents; imbalances can be corrrected in the plant as long as the proportions are close to the requirements. There are restrictions on magnesia, which is normally within limits, and alkalies (soda and potash) that may require rejecting some deposits. Companies using clay for these purposes ordinarily base their plants near a source of supply, and control and produce the clay themselves. The mines are open pit and no drilling or blasting is required, so operating costs are minimal. No "value" is placed on the constituent, the cost being charged to raw materials. The direct costs may range from 10–12 cents upward to a few dollars per ton.

Special clays such as fire clay (pure kaolinite) may occur in narrow beds that are mined underground, and costs range up to $20–$40 per ton. Processing for special clays (for paper coatings and rubber and paint fillers) that involve removal of some constituents (silica sand) and brightening to make it very white are quite expensive. An "average price" is virtually meaningless, since allocated cost may reflect a percentage of sale price of the manufactured product and there is a very wide spread between the high and low ranges.

Production: The ultimate in simplicity in mining clay consists of a dragline with one operator and one helper digging clay from below water and loading it directly to a barge for hauling by tug to a cement plant. One operator can load 300–400 tons per day. Depending on local conditions, clay may be mined by scrapers or rippers, or may be loaded by small shovels into trucks from open pits. If beds of clay extend underground, they may be mined by coal mining methods, or, if steeply dipping, by stoping methods. If deposits are underground, drilling and blasting may be required. Most operations are quite small, producing a few hundred tons per day, with large mines producing a thousand tons. Productivity per man day ranges from 2–200 tons, depending on the complexity of the mining.

Outlook: Clay and clay products are among the cheapest of all commodities. Therefore there is little chance of substitution by less expensive products. Because they are heavy and raw materials are widespread in occurrence, they do not move far from their point of origin. Special items like Georgia kaolinite and Wyoming bentonite may be utilized anywhere in the world. About 90% of the clay is used in building and construction, including the siliceous portion of portland cement and lightweight aggregate. The building industry is strongly cyclic and in mature economies such as the United States, growth will be modest. In the developing nations consumption should increase more rapidly.

While requiring fuel in processing, clay industries are not energy intensive. With worldwide depletion of forests, more building will be done with ceramic and concrete products, so there will be gains from substitution. Of the special, high-quality clays depletion is more serious, and shortages have occasionally arisen. Processing of some calcium bentonites to produce soda bentonite for drilling mud has filled some of the shortages for this use. High-quality kaolinite is becoming depleted in some areas, and new sources will have to be discovered.

DIAMOND (GEMSTONES AND INDUSTRIAL)

Properties and Characteristics

Composition   Pure carbon
Atomic weight   12.01
Crystal form   Isometric, commonly octahedral
Specific gravity   3.516–3.525
Hardness   10 (on scale of mineral hardness but twice the next
                   mineral on the scale, i.e., corundum = 9)
Characteristics   High index of refraction gives diamond unusual brilliance
                   and high dispersivity gives the play of colors or "fire"

History: Diamonds have been found in India since prehistoric times, probably first recovered about 800 B.C. A river of diamond was mentioned by Ptolemy (A.D. 200). The site he described is thought to be either the Mahanadi River or its tributary, the Ebe River, about 75 km upstream from the town of Sambalpur in the eastern part of the Central Provinces of India. Some of the largest and finest diamonds came from this area. Eastern India from 14° to 25°N was virtually the only source of diamonds until they were discovered in Brazil in about 1725 in Minas Geraes near the town of Tejuco, which was renamed Diamantina.

In 1867 a man by the name of O'Reilly identified diamond in South Africa not far from Hopetown, just south of the Orange River. The story goes that he found a child playing with a 21 carat stone and exhibited it that year in the Paris Exposition, starting a diamond rush. In December 1870, diamonds were discovered at Du Toit's Pan, and shortly later the adjacent pipe called Bultfontein was discovered. Soon a third mine was found by a Boer named de Beer. He started mining what was to be known as the de Beer's Pipe. On 21 July 1871 there was a new discovery, which was called Old de Beer's New Rush. This proved to be the richest of the four pipes clustered in the vicinity. It was later called the Kimberley Mine. The town of the same name developed out on the barren plain to house the miners. This was the beginning of the production of diamonds in Africa, now the source of 75% of the natural stones.

In 1955 General Electric announced the production of synthetic diamond. This process has become the major source of small industrial diamonds used in cutting tools and polishing. A crystal weighing 1.2 carats of gem quality was announced in 1982 by Japan. Synthetics now account for 80% of the industrial diamonds by weight.

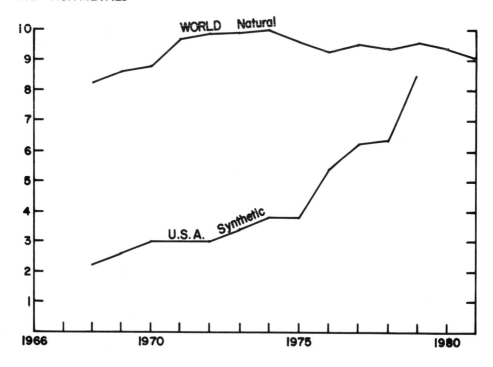

Figure 33 Synthetic diamond production in the United States and natural diamond production in the world, given in metric tons.

Formerly gem diamonds were graded as to quality according to first, second, and third "water," the first being highest. Today one may still hear the term "of the first water" to indicate a superior stone.

Almost all gem diamonds are sold through a tight cartel called the Central Selling Organization. Wholesalers buy at periodic showings called "sights." It is not unusual for rather shabby-looking men to leave a "sight" carrying several million dollars worth of gems.

The largest gem quality stone ever found was the Cullinan diamond, which weighed 3106 carats or 0.621 kg (1.37 pounds). In cutting, about half of the weight is usually lost. Thus it takes a two-carat stone to make a one-carat gem. Several gems may be cut from a large crystal, including *mélée*, the smallest cut stones used to accent larger diamonds or other gems.

Uses: It was not until 1862 that diamond had any use other than as a gemstone. In that year the first diamond drill was built, designed to take cores of rock. Previously all of the diamonds that were not suitable for gems were discarded. Industrial uses developed rapidly, and the price of industrial stones has risen steadily with increasing demand. The total weight of synthetic stones now exceeds natural stones. Of course the major share of natural stones are of industrial quality. In addition to diamond drills, indispensable in mineral exploration, *boart* (the name applied to industrial diamonds) is set in saw blades for cutting stone, and as grit in cutting and polishing. Diamonds are used in glass cutters and in dies for high-speed drawing of fine wire.

Occurrence: Diamond is the highly pressurized form of carbon. It will burn in air or oxygen, and at high temperature and low pressure it will revert to another form of carbon (graphite). The only place where diamond can form is at depths greater than 150 km, thus well within the earth's mantle. The problem is how they get from the high temperature and pressure stability field to low temperature stability without reverting to graphite, a process that takes only a few hours.

Diamonds are found in "pipes," which are literally tubes of access to the earth's mantle. These formations narrow, and many become dikes in depth. Fractures are formed through the crust; they must penetrate deep into the earth, where they encounter pods or concentrations of fluids under extremely high pressure. The fracture or fault provides a channel of escape for a combination of fluids. Liquid carbon dioxide and methane are probably the two main fluids. The fluids, together with rock fragments, are forced up the channel by the pressure, gathering speed as they surge up the channel. They blast out to the surface possibly at supersonic velocity (Mach 1 or greater). The transit time for each surge of fluids from mantle to surface is probably no more than one hour. Thus a mantle mass would blast out at the surface with a gigantic roar. The lifting power of the blast is adequate to excavate a crater sometimes a kilometer in diameter at the surface, tapering downward to the channel-way itself. Once the channel is open, there are likely to be repeated explosions at short intervals, enlarging the pipe and bringing to the surface and into the crater and pipe a mass of material from possibly 200 km depths. This mass is ultrabasic in composition and contains minerals formed and stable at high temperature and pressure. Diamond is one of these minerals; others from the same depth interval are pyrope garnet and magnesian ilmenite, the latter two being in much greater volume than diamond. They are "indicator minerals" used by prospectors.

It should be mentioned that not all geologists agree with this concept of the origin of kimberlite pipes. All do agree that the source has to be from deep in the Earth's mantle. Some kimberlite dikes or pipes do not reach the surface, but these are unlikely to be diamantiferous.

The diamonds occur in a peculiar *blue earth* in the Kimberley mine; this rock is now called "Kimberlite." Kimberlite pipes may originate from a rather broad depth range, but diamonds have to have formed below 150 km. There are many pipes that do not contain diamond. Even pipes from the proper depth zone may not contain a uniform diamond content or a uniform percentage of gemstones.

The diamonds in the upper portion of the forming pipe are exposed to greatly expanded carbon dioxide, which becomes very cold, possibly even forming dry ice. Thus the fluid chills the diamonds, permitting them to survive the transit to near-surface conditions.

After formation of a pipe it may be subjected to erosion for millions of years. The diamonds may be carried away in streams and concentrated in stream or beach placers. Today stream, beach, and marine placers are important sources of diamonds.

One of the bits of evidence that the continents were formerly united in what geologists call "Gondwanaland" is the way the diamond areas of Brazil match those of Africa and those of eastern India match those of northwestern Australia. There are even occurrences in Thailand, suggesting that it too was once attached to India.

Today nearly all of the diamonds are produced by the African nations and Russia, with Venezuela and Brazil producing minor amounts. Diamonds have been found in the glacial material of northern United States, and recently diamond pipes have been found on Somerset Island in Canada. At several points in the United States kimberlite pipes have been found and there has been some production from one pipe at Murfreesboro, Arkansas. There are numerous pipes in Montana that are not diamond bearing. A recent discovery of diamond-bearing pipes in southern Wyoming and northern Colorado is being evaluated. There has been some production from southern Borneo. Recent finds in northwestern Australia are apparently large. No significant production now comes from the famous Indian mines, apparently all of the alluvial class. Known pipes in India were all low grade.

Economics: Just as in other mining operations, the grade of ore that can be mined is determined by the market price of the product. If the price goes up faster than the cost of mining or if new methods reduce cost, the cut-off and average grades can be dropped. This means that what was waste becomes ore in some cases. The average grade in Namibia dropped from 13.43 carats per 100 tons in 1977, to 12.54 in 1979, and 10.3 in 1980. That would represent 0.02 grams per ton or, for perspective, a block the size of a 1×2 m^2 door would contain 0.12 grams of diamond. Today that is an economic deposit. The pipes under test in West Australia appear to be 20 times as rich (194 ct/100 tons) but economics have not been determined. During the first 20 years of operation at the Kimberley mine, the average grade was 0.3 grams per ton; at De Beer's, 0.21 grams per ton; at Bultfontein, 0.07 grams per ton; and at DuToit's Pan, 0.05 grams/per ton. It is very difficult to put a value on the average production at the mine, but if $20 per carat is used, the gross value of world natural diamond production is approximately one billion dollars, or $100 million per ton.

Production: Diamond is always measured by the carat, which has a weight of 0.2 grams. A stone of one carat in the octahedron form would be about one-half centimeter on the axis. Most of the natural stones are much smaller than this. The percentage of gemstones varies widely, from 2% to 95%, the latter being from some placer deposits. World production of natural diamonds was 47.3 million carats (9460 kg) in 1978 and 48.0 million carats (9600 kg) in 1979. Zaire is the world's largest producer at 15.547 million carats in 1979, but only 2% are gemstones; in Ghana 15% are of gem quality. In 1981 Zaire's officially reported diamond production dropped to 5.7 million ct. There has apparently been a tremendous surge in smuggling through Brazzaville, with less than half of the production being reported. Russian production is estimated at 12 million carats, and the amount of synthetic diamond is unknown. South Africa is in third place, behind Russia.

World consumption of industrial diamond now exceeds 150 million carats, including synthetics. Consumption has been rising rapidly, with diamond being one of the fastest growing industrial minerals.

Natural diamonds are mined either from placer deposits or from the pipes. Much of the placer mining is done by hand methods by sinking small shafts to the diamantiferous layer and excavating as much ground as the miners think safe, then abandoning the working and sinking a new shaft. Inevitably, some workers are caught in cave-ins. The gravel and clay are washed and screened to throw away material coarser than about 1.6 cm and everything finer than 0.16 cm. The balance is hand sorted and treated in jigs.

Companies use mechanized equipment, dredges, bucket wheel excavators, and draglines to accomplish the same objectives. One refinement is collection of diamonds on specially prepared grease tables. Diamonds are not wetted by water, so they stick to the grease, which is then scraped off and boiled to release the diamonds. Larger and more modern operations irradiate the concentrate with x-rays as it passes along a conveyor belt. This causes the diamonds to luminesce. The luminescence is detected by a sensor and photomultiplier, which activates an air ejector, blowing the diamonds off the conveyor into a collecting dish.

From the pipes the "blue earth" is removed by open pit methods as far as possible, then by underground mining in a sort of "glory hole" method, block caving the successive levels. The rock is hoisted and crushed by gyratory and roll crushers in stages. Preliminary concentration is done by gravity, using jigs or heavy media separation, followed by grease tables or by Sortex (irradiation and air blower).

Synthetic diamonds are produced in high-temperature, high-pressure hydraulic presses with graphite being dissolved in molten metal (iron) with a catalyst. When super saturation is reached the crystals begin to form. When the mass is cooled, the iron is dissolved by acid, leaving tiny (–20 mesh) diamond crystals. Japanese researchers report they have now produced perfect diamonds up to 1.2 carats in size.

Outlook: With rapid growth in demand for industrial diamonds, the outlook for diamonds is good. Improvement in manufacturing of synthetics with increased size will absorb most of the increase in demand and reduce the inroads of competing materials. Since the grade in a pipe required to be commercial has reduced by one half to two thirds, some of the old dumps are being reworked and old mines reopened to extract low grade material left behind. Some of the other pipes formerly not commercial are being re-evaluated. At the present rate of production, reserves will last about 20 years, showing that either diamonds will become scarcer or more deposits will have to be developed.

Boron nitride is the second hardest synthetic material made, and it is nearly as hard as diamond. It will make inroads on the industrial applications of diamond.

The Ashton Joint Venture in West Australia is reported to control very large diamond reserves in a newly discovered pipe, plus alluvial gravels derived from it. Reportedly it is capable of increasing world production by 100%. There are other diamantiferous pipes in the same district being evaluated. Another major new source is the Jwaneng Mine in southern Botswana, which came into production in 1982. De Beers Consolidated Mines is the operator and stated, "Jwaneng is probably the most important kimberlite pipe discovered anywhere in the world since the original discoveries at Kimberley more than a century ago."

Eighty percent of the world industrial diamond is now manufactured. There have been announcements of major progress in producing larger stones, up to 1.2 ct.

Natural stones of near-gem quality are now being irradiated and treated by lasers to move them into the gem class. Methods of producing color in diamonds have now been developed so the special colors are no longer rarities. However, some of these colors tend to fade, so they must be identified as irradiated stones.

The impact of the development of a major new mining district in Australia will be somewhat lessened because of the price control of the diamond cartel. Nevertheless countries like Lesotho, Zaire, and Namibia with low-grade deposits will be seriously affected. A number of other deposits that are nearly depleted and facing escalating costs will be forced to close.

Diamonds as gemstones have exhibited the classic "boom and bust" cycle during the "oil shock" years. The market indicator, "1 carat D-flawless brilliant" rose to about $65,000, completely out of proportion to supply and cost of production. Then, like silver, it came crashing back down again, quoted at about $19,000 in mid-1982. In April 1982 De Beers stated, "prices currently quoted...are low compared to rough." The frantic efforts to find something that would retain relative value were frustrated everywhere—gold, silver, platinum, diamonds—except in oil, where the oil cartel has orchestrated the huge price increase.

A cartel is designed to control selling prices and quantities of material on the market. It is thus designed to modify the law of supply and demand. It can only succeed when the cartel has control of the product. The CSO has been quite effective in this regard until the recent boom and bust cycle of 1979-1982. When speculators were bidding up the price, the CSO released additional diamonds, trying to prevent the wild upward swing, and was only partially successful. When the price came plunging back down, the CSO "withheld" diamonds. This means they bought them, but did not sell.

Price controls rarely work for long. This effort in diamonds is handicapped by (1) huge new discoveries, with the potential for greatly increasing supply of gems; (2) fall in demand, and a related fall in prices of gems; (3) an apparent ability to produce gemstones synthetically; and (4) very high interest rates, which have to be paid on all the money tied up in diamonds in vaults.

How long the CSO will be able to sustain the price of diamonds is problematical. The myth of "store of value" has been badly shaken. It will not be surprising if this attempt to repeal the law of supply and demand ends in failure.

FLUORSPAR OR FLUORITE

Properties and Characteristics

Composition	CaF_2 (calcium 51.1%, fluorine 48.9%)
Molecular weight	78.08
Crystal form	Isometric, commonly cubic, octahedral
Specific gravity	3.01-3.25
Hardness	4 (on the hardness scale)

History: The name derives from the Latin *fluere*, to flow, which describes its fluxing characteristic. The word "fluorescence" came from this mineral because of its property of emitting light in the visual spectrum when exposed to ultraviolet light. It was carved into ornaments by Greeks and Romans. Agricola (A.D. 1546) mentioned its use as a flux. Substantial production commenced late in the 19th century, with development of the basic open hearth steel process. This is also the source of flourine gas.

Figure 34 Fluorite production in the United States and the world, given in millions of metric tons.

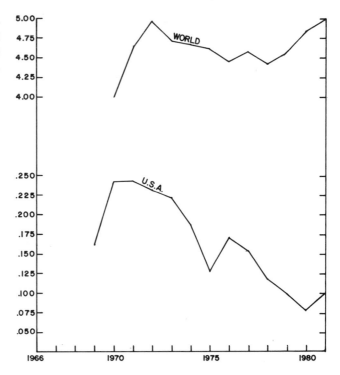

Uses: Fluorite is the major source of fluorine gas and its chemical compounds. About 35% of it goes into this use, which includes aerosols, refrigerants, plastics, and solvents. Second in importance is its use as a flux in steel making, accounting for one third of the production. It is used in making artificial cryolite, the molten bath in which aluminum is produced from the oxide. About 10% is used in various fluxes and ceramics and to prepare uranium hexafluoride for uranium isotope separation. The compound sodium fluoride is used in dental preparations to prevent tooth decay. Teflon is a fluorine product. The aerosols have the property of destroying ozone (O_3) in the stratosphere, and have been banned in the United States.

Occurrence: Fluorite is a common non-metallic mineral of widespread occurrence. Commercial deposits are in fissure veins and in bedded deposits replacing limestone. It is generally believed to be of hydrothermal origin, rather low temperature facies with such minerals as calcite, barite, galena, and sphalerite. It is also found with other veins as a gaugue mineral and is pervasive in low concentration in some plutons. In general, the bedded deposits are the largest and much of the U.S. consumption comes from the deposits of this type in northern Mexico in Coahuila State.

Fluorine is present in phosphate fertilizer raw material and is recovered in processing. This provides about 10% of U.S. consumption.

Economics: Because of the wide variety of occurrences and mining methods, it is hard to generalize on the economics of fluorspar production. Ore zones are generally quite high grade, but almost always contain so much deleterious material that beneficiation is required. There are three grades: (1)acid, containing not less than 97% CaF_2 and not more than 1.5% silica; (2) ceramic, 93–95% CaF_2, not more than 2.5% silica, and not more than 0.12% Fe_2O_3; (3) metallurgical, minimum "effective" CaF_2 of 60% (silica % times 2.5 is subtracted from CaF_2%). Acid grade is about $180 per ton, with metspar about $70 lower. While U.S. resources are substantial, foreign costs are so much lower that 90% of the U.S. requirement is imported.

Production: In the United States large-scale methods such as open pit or top slicing on veins and room and pillar mining of beds are used. The ore is then processed by flotation or heavy media separation. Production has been declining because of unfavorable costs compared with those of foreign competitors. In Mexico much of the production is by hand labor from narrow beds. About half of U.S. consumption is of acid grade. Much of the metspar is now pelletized.

Outlook: Fluorine chemistry is still in the developmental stage. Use of fluorine in aerosols is prohibited by the U.S. government; use in refrigerants may also be curtailed. The problem is the destruction of the ozone layer in the stratosphere. Other countries have not matched the limitations placed by the United States, and in some places leaky air conditioners are considered a lucrative, steady service business. This usage is likely to decline as other countries begin to develop a greater sense of responsibility for protecting the world environment.

While aluminum production has increased greatly in recent years (now the second largest metal in tonnage used), the consumption of artificial cryolite per ton has declined. Research on alternate fluxes that would permit reduction of the energy cost in production of aluminum is underway.

Consumption of fluorite in the United States has been declining gradually since 1970 as the open hearth steel process has declined and usage of aerosols has decreased. If the new chloride process of making aluminum develops (reportedly less energy intensive), further declines in this consumption can be expected. World consumption has increased slightly during the same period. No dramatic changes in consumption are likely during the rest of the century. China has started selling fluorite at prices considerably below prevailing free world prices. This may be disruptive to traditional suppliers. Fluorite reserves appear to be adequate to meet demand. U.S. stockpile goals call for purchase of about 2 Mmt.

GRAPHITE

Properties and Characteristics

Composition	Carbon, when pure.
Atomic weight	12.01 (12 = 98.9%; 13 = 1.1%); 14, radioactive
Crystal form	Rhombohedral (hexagonal)
Specific gravity	2.09–2.23
Hardness	1–2
Characteristics	Very refractory and chemically inert; characterized by extreme softness, greasy feel, and infusibility; excellent conductor of electricity

History: Graphite has been known for hundreds of years. In the Middle Ages it was thought to be a mineral of lead, or at least that it contained lead, so it was called *plumbago*, from Latin. Thus graphite pencils got the misnomer "lead pencils." It was recognized as the element carbon in 1789, and was named in 1879 after the Greek word *graphein*, meaning "to write."

The first graphite mining in the United States was in Massachusetts about 1650, but the operation was not a commercial success. Mining was resumed in 1738, with minor production.

Uses: Graphite is a minor non-metallic product with world consumption only about 600,000 tons per year. The largest market in the United States is in foundry work to prevent metal from sticking to the mold. This form is known as foundry facings. Second consumption in tonnage is in refractories. This includes crucibles for melting metals such as gold. Formerly "crucible steel" was a major consumer, but the electric furnace largely replaced this market. Graphite is soluble in molten iron, and is a key ingredient in high carbon steel. Because graphite is very soft and unctuous it serves as a lubricant, particularly in high temperature conditions. Ranking fifth is use in "lead" pencils, followed by batteries, brake linings, and other miscellaneous uses. While the amount consumed is small, the Sri Lankan graphite is very important for "brushes" in motors. It is used in nuclear piles in power plants as a moderator, slowing neutrons for capture by uranium. This requires very pure material.

Occurrence: The mineral graphite is widely distributed, and is found in nearly every country. Veins are narrow and discontinuous, however, and commercial deposits are rather uncommon. Some of those in production could only be mined in areas of low-cost labor. This particularly applies to Sri Lanka, famous for the production of high quality graphite. Russia and China are the world's largest producers, followed by South Korea, Mexico, Malagasay Republc (Madagascar Island), Sri Lanka, and Norway. While there are numerous occurrences of amorphous and flake graphite in the United States, the grade of the deposits is generally considerably lower than deposits elsewhere, so nearly all U.S. consumption is imported.

There are three forms of occurrence. The most abundant and poorest quality is called "amorphous." It is soft, black, earthy, and frequently impure. It is formed by metamorphism of coal beds. Mexican deposits are of this type, as are those in Korea and part of those in Malagasay Republic and Russia.

The category commonly called "flake" is disseminated in metamorphosed sediments. The graphite probably formed from contained carbon during the process of metamorphism. This type is extensive in the Malagasay Republic and in the USSR. It also occurs in Alabama, where there has been considerable production, and in New York and Pennsylvania. Texas graphite can be either flake or amorphous. This form must be concentrated for commercial use.

The third category is "lump," the crystalline variety, massive in form and occurring in veins. The most important occurrence is in Sri Lanka. The veins occur in very ancient rocks (Archean) that have been deeply buried and folded. One hypothesis is that they originated in hydrothermal solutions; or they may have come from the reduction of carbon dioxide escaping from the Earth's mantle.

Economics: The prices of graphite vary widely. The common amorphous variety is sold at about $85 per ton. Price ranges for flake are $300–$900, depending on specifications. The premium Sri Lankan lump graphite sells at about $2000 per ton, and is in short supply. While labor costs are very low in Sri Lanka, the hand methods of mining are still costly. There is no way that the narrow veins can be mined by mechanized methods. The total world market is so small that one substantial new mine would seriously upset the price. Therefore there is no chance to gain economy of scale.

Production: In Sri Lanka, the graphite is chipped out by hand from veinlets as narrow as 10 cm (4 inches). It is then hand sorted on the surface, both men and women breaking up lumps containing *gangue* (waste) with hammers, sending the lower grade to milling. The milling consists of grinding to liberate the waste and air floating to separate the ore from the waste. A mine producing 3000 tons per year is a large mine in that country. The mines are a government monopoly, nationalized by a former socialist government. Pressure from consumers for expansion of the production has resulted in a program to explore for other substantial deposits and development of them if warranted. The present level of production is about 12,000 tons per year.

Conventional mining methods for undergound operations are used in Mexico, Korea, and elsewhere. In the Malagasay Republic, where the deposits outcrop over extensive areas and deep weathering has released the graphite from the gangue, open pit mining is conducted. Reserves are reportedly large, but at some future time drilling and blasting will have to be undertaken to maintain production. While graphite from this source has set the standard for high quality flake, the size gradation has decreased recently and the Malagasay Republic has had trouble meeting the demand.

Outlook: Since deposits in the United States average about 3%–5% graphite, and the average elsewhere is 25%–98%, domestic deposits can only compete when there is a shortage, such as in wartime. Manufactured graphite can be prepared from petroleum coke or anthracite coal, and it is suitable for many purposes. The specifications vary with the market, and quality varies with sources. Amorphous graphite is in abundant supply, but flake and crystalline have been under pressure. Sri Lankan material, in particular, has been in short supply and no other source can fulfill all of the specifications. Some of the buying appears to be for stockpiling. Just what would happen to demand if supply were increased by 50% (only 6000 tons, or 20 tons per day) is uncertain. Graphite demand will increase if nuclear power plants are constructed. One major new source of high-quality material would upset the market.

GYPSUM AND ANHYDRITE

Properties and Characteristics

Composition	$CaSO_4.2H_2O$; CaO, 32.5%; H_2O, 20.9%; (or without water) SO_3, 46.6%
Molecular weight	172.14
Crystal form	Monoclinic (var. selenite); massive in sediments
Dehydration temperature	212°F (100°C)
Specific gravity	2.32
Characteristics	Upon heating to 320°F (160°C) gives off 75% of the water and in this form will "set" when water is added to plaster (plaster of Paris); one of the softest minerals (2 on hardness scale)

History: Gypsum was used by the Egyptians in the construction of the pyramids. Later the Romans also used it in construction. Because pure crystals are clear and transparent, it was used in windows. The transmitted light looked like moonlight, so it was named selenite after the moon (*selene*, Latin for "new"). Some of the dense white to pink or green varieties

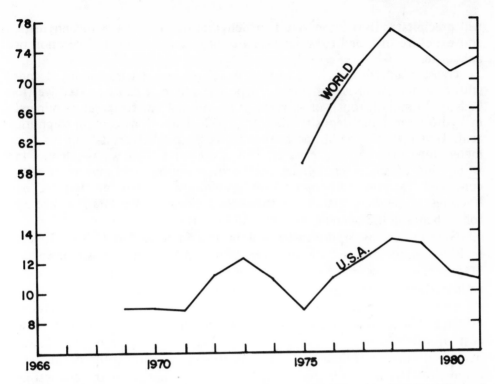

Figure 35 Gypsum production in the United States and the world, given in millions of metric tons.

were used for sculpture since it is very soft. This variety is called "alabaster."

In the eighteenth century gypsum was used as fertilizer, and is still used for this purpose. The process of calcining gypsum to make plaster developed about 1835, but it was 50 years later when a method of retarding the set developed so it could be placed in construction.

Occurrence: Gypsum (containing water of hydration) and anhydrite are two common minerals formed in the marine environment by evaporation of sea water. This requires an arid climate and a bay with a limited but steady inflow of normal sea water. The Kara-Boghaz-Gol in the eastern Caspian Sea is an example of modern deposition. Near the mouth of the gulf the least soluble mineral, limestone, precipitates first. Deeper within the bay, the concentration is sufficient for $CaSO_4.2H_2O$ to precipitate. When the salt has been concentrated to 4.8 times normal by evaporation and the temperature is about 34°C, anhydrite is stable. Further evaporation results in precipitation of ordinary salt (NaCl). Most deposits are a few meters to a few 10s of meters thick, but they can reach thicknesses of hundreds of meters. The depositional basin may be hundreds of square kilometers in extent. The temperature and concentration determines whether gypsum or anhydrite will precipitate. Burial can result in dehydration of gypsum to anhydrite, and exposure of a bed to water near the surface can result in hydration of anhydrite.

Gypsum/anhydrite is also formed in subvolcanic environments. It constitutes a normal phase of *kuroko* deposits, where it can be extensive (to beds of 30 million tons), or as veins. It is a normal low-temperature mineral in hydrothermal ore deposits when the residual solutions contain sulphuric acid. Under these conditions sometimes large, perfect crystals up to two meters long may form in cavities. This is the variety known as selenite. In weathering of shales containing pyrite, the resulting acid may react with contained calcium carbonate forming gypsum, which precipitates on fractures or bedding planes. In this case a single thin crystal, warped to follow bends in the opening, may extend for 10s of meters.

Gypsum is a by-product when sulphuric acid is reacted with phosphate rock to produce phosphate fertilizer. It is also formed in the removal of SO_2 from stack gases for environmental protection. This later may become an important source of gypsum, since it is necessary to dispose of it.

Uses: The largest use of gypsum is in the manufacture of plaster products. Plaster was once applied to walls in buildings by hand, but as the cost of labor increased, prefabricated plaster board or "sheet rock" was developed. In the United States this is almost exclusively the product of commerce. The second important use is as a retardant to control the setting time of portland cement. Its third use is as a soil conditioner in alkaline soils and as a plant nutrient. Where limestone is scarce and gypsum abundant, it can be used to manufacture portland cement, with a co-product of SO_3 gas for use in manufacture of sulphuric acid.

Economics: While gypsum and anhydrite are closely related in origin and composition, gypsum is the article of commerce and anhydrite is a waste product sometimes contaminating gypsum. While anhydrite will hydrate to gypsum, the reaction is very slow and for practical purposes anhydrite must be considered inert as far as the applications for which gypsum is used.

Much of the production of gypsum is by companies that process it for portland cement or plaster products. Thus there is little commerce in gypsum. The value of raw gypsum at the mine is low. The most recent quotes available (1980) are all under $10 per ton. Transportation costs become about equal to product cost if it has to be shipped for any distance. In captive mines, the cost is handled as a part of product cost with no effort to place an intermediate value on it.

Production Methods: Most of the gypsum is still mined by open pit methods, but in regions with no outcrops and buried horizons that can readily be reached from the surface, room and pillar mining methods are used. Average grade of commercial deposits is about 90% gypsum, and no beneficiation is required. World production declined 10% to 67 million tons in 1980, with 70% being manufactured into plaster products, 22% used as cement retarder, and the balance in agriculture. While large deposits are common, there are some areas where it is scarce. It is imported to California from San Marcos Island in the Gulf of California, Mexico, to the Pacific Northwest from British Columbia and to the east coast of the United States from Canada, Jamaica, and the Dominican Republic.

In the developing countries, by far the largest consumption is as cement retarder. Second is in the manufacture of ammonium sulphate for fertilizer. Sheet rock or wall board is not extensively used.

Several methods are used for calcining gypsum. The most common method is in kettles about 10 feet in diameter and 12 feet high. This is a batch process. At about 100°C (212°F) most of the water of hydration boils off. Following this, the temperature rapidly rises to 160°C (320°F). It must not be heated much above this temperature or it will be converted to anhydrite; then it is not suitable for plaster. Gypsum is also calcined in rotary kilns, impact grinding-and-calcining mills, autoclaves, and bee-hive ovens. The product is called "stucco" (not the exterior stucco used on buildings, which is made of portalnd cement). The largest use is in gypsum wall board or sheet rock, manufactured by hydrating gypsum and spreading it on special paper, then sandwiching it with another layer of paper, and allowing it to set. It is also used in tile and roof plank.

In cement manufacture, the cooled clinker is ground together with a carefully controlled amount (3%-4%) of crushed gypsum. It is the ground product from the two constituents that constitutes portland cement.

The special product called "phosphogypsum" is the product of the acidulation of rock phosphate. It must be neutralized, since it still contains acid. Then it is pelletized and heated to the dehydration point. It is probably actually a soluble anhydrite, the alpha form, and is suitable for cement retarder but not for plaster products.

Economics: Because gypsum is widespread in occurrence and can be mined in many areas by low-cost open pit methods, the price is very low—about $7 per ton at the mine. Normally it cannot be transported far without the transportation cost exceeding the value of the product. Many of the producers are integrated from ore to wall board, and some cement plants mine their own retarder.

Gas or oil is used for calcining gypsum, so the costs have risen proportionately to increasing fuel prices.

Outlook: Gypsum products are used most extensively in the industrialized nations. With mature economies, little growth can be expected. Building is a cyclic industry, so gypsum will follow the cycle. The same applies to its use as cement retarder. Should the new economics make it possible to produce sulphuric acid from gypsum, this could change the demand but not as much as would be anticipated, because fertilizer plants could recycle their gypsum waste with only a small amount of make-up acid added to account for losses. They would then have a lime by-product which might be saleable for water treatment or cement manufacture.

In the less developed countries there is less need for labor saving methods of construction, so sheet rock is not commonly used. The major use is as a retarder of portland cement. Little growth is anticipated, but when the recession is over, it should regain its former level.

MAGNESITE (MgCO₃)

Properties and Characteristics

Composition	MgO, 47.6% (CO_2, 52.2%; Mg, 28.7%)
Molecular weight	84.31
Crystal form	Hexagonal-rhombohedral, generally massive.
Specific gravity	3.0
Hardness	3.75–4.25 varies according to crystallographic directions
Color	White when pure

History: The mineral magnesite has been known for centuries, but at first was not distinguished from calcite. Magnesite was recognized as a separate mineral in 1755. The minerals containing magnesium were recognized as containing a new metal early in the nineteenth century.

Since non-metallic magnesium minerals exceed the tonnage of metallic magnesium by a factor of about 50, they are treated as two separate commodities in this compilation. World production of magnesite is about 11 million tons; thus it ties with chromium (the fourth metal) for fourteenth place among all mineral commodities.

Uses: The major use of magnesite is as a refractory in lining the open hearth steel furnaces. With the trend toward electric furnace steel, demand for magnesia, the decarbonated form of magnesite which is actually used, has been dropping. The dead burned product is used in rubber as a filler. Magnesium is an essential plant food and magnesite is used in small amounts in fertilizer. Oxychloride (sorrel) cement, used for flooring, is made from it. It is used in the preparation of silicones, as the sulphate in Epsom salts for medicinals, and in paper and textile industries. About 30 pounds of magnesium in compounds are added per ton of steel. This includes dolomite, but the tonnage worldwide exceeds 10 million tons of magnesium. This is about equal to the quantity used in refractories.

Occurrence: Magnesite is formed by the alteration of limestone or dolomite or from the magnesium silicates (especially those in dunite or serpentine). Bodies are usually tabular to lenticular. It is found in Washington, North Carolina, and at Gabbs, Nevada, the largest producing mine in the United States. Large deposits are mined in Russia with production at approximately 4 Mmt per year. Austria ranks next, closely followed by Greece. Turkey, India, and Yugoslavia are other important producers.

Economics: Magnesite is so dependent on the steel industry that it follows the same cycles. The past few years have been a time of reduced demand resulting in over-production and falling prices. There has been a switch in the steel industry away from the open hearth method, resulting in decreasing demand for magnesite refractory. With the availability of precipitated magnesia of high purity, the demand for the natural, impure, product has been declining. The price of dead burned, fob at Luning, Nevada was $229 per short ton early in 1982.

Production: The mining methods range from open pit with selective benches (wasting low grade material), to open stopes with pillars. With low prices, the intensive labor methods cannot compete. Magnesite is crushed and burned in a kiln to decarbonation, or at high temperature to the "dead burned" stage, meaning it is less reactive with water. Much of the magnesia is then made into refractory brick. Magnesia from seawater is pelletized before going into brick.

Outlook: When the slow period in the steel cycle reverses, demand for magnesite will recover, but the long-range adjustment to the change in manufacturing process will not permit return to the demand level of 1975. Eventually some of the magnesite deposits may be utilized as an ore for the production of the metal. This has not been the case in the past, because the price of the commodity was too high for the competitive sources—sea water and dolomite. Special conditions would be essential to go into production of magnesite today.

PHOSPHATE (ROCK PHOSPHATE AND APATITE)

Properties and Characteristics

Composition	$(CaF)Ca_4(PO_4)_3$ (P_2O_5, 42.3%; CaO, 55.5%; F = 3.8%); $(CaCl)Ca_4(PO_4)_3$ (P_2O_5, 41.0%; CaO, 53.8%; Cl, 6.8%)
Molecular weight	Variable; 482.99 for chloroapatite
Crystal form	Hexagonal (as mineral apatite) or pisolitic and earthy
Specific gravity	3.17–3.23
Hardness	5(apatite on scale of mineral hardness)

History: Phosphorus is one of the major elements required in the food supply for all plants and animals. Animals, including man, obtain it directly or indirectly from plants, which in turn, derive it from soil. In essence, plants mine the phosphorous from the soil. If vegetable matter is removed, the soil becomes depleted. When the population of the world was small and virgin lands were readily available, when soils were "worn out" new lands were cultivated. By 200 B.C. the Carthaginians used bird excrement on their fields to improve yields. The Incas of Peru did likewise. By 100 B.C. the Romans understood that crop rotation, lime, and manure improved crop yields. In the seventeenth century Glauber learned that saltpetre (potassium nitrate) greatly improved plant growth. In 1840 it was shown that organic material was not the main source of plant nutrients. There are small amounts of

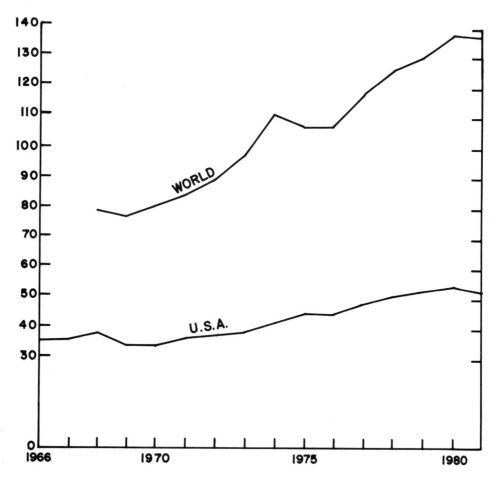

Figure 36 Phosphate rock production in the United States and the world, given in millions of metric tons.

nutrient in compost, and the organic matter improves the soil; but it is totally inadequate for large-scale production of food to feed large populations. About that time it was discovered that acid treatment of bones made them a good plant nutrient source.

Today the fertilizer industry comprises one of the largest segments of the minerals industry, for production of food. A conventional chemical fertilizer contains nitrogen, phosphate and potash and the grade of fertilizer is usually printed on the bag. For example, 10-20-10 represents the percentages of these three ingredients and conventionally they are in the order given above, alphabetically. The chemical abbreviations for the elements are used, so it is called N-P-K.

In 1842 John Lawes, an English farmer, patented the process of treating phosphate nodules with sulphuric acid, and called his product "superphosphate." The same term and essentially the same process is used today.

A term one often encounters with this material is "available" P_2O_5. Ordinary phosphate rock may contain 30–35% P_2O_5, but it is only slightly soluble in soils, so it is not *available* as a plant nutrient. Only that part soluble in water is readily available. However, certain forms are usable under conditions normally found in soil, and the measure of this proportion is solubility in ammonium citrate solution. This is a standard test, called "citrate soluble." This is the measure of the effective or "available" P_2O_5 in fertilizer. Another term frequently used in the fertilizer trade when referring to the raw material, rock phosphate is BPL, which stands for bone phosphate of lime. The content of 72% BPL equals 32% P_2O_5. P_2O_5% multiplied by 2.18 equals BPL.

Uses: About 80% of all phosphorus compounds is used as fertilizer. The second ranking usage is in soaps and detergents, a controversial usage. Third is use of phosphorus compounds in metal plating and polishing. Certain compounds brighten the surface and coat copper and copper alloys to keep them from tarnishing, giving a protective coating that keeps them bright. It is also used for electroplating a nickel-phosphorus alloy on steel, called "nickel plating." While animals obtain part of the phosphorus they need from normal feed, when cattle are being raised for meat, they need additional phosphorus as a feed supplement to accelerate weight gain. This usage ranks fourth in consumption of the element. This requires defluorinated compounds, as the fluorine in natural rock phosphate inhibits animal growth.

There are numerous minor uses, including matches, fire retardant, rat poison, and insecticides, and in soft drinks, tooth paste, and baking powder. It is used in water softeners, dental cement, oil refining, and silk fabrics. During war time it is used in incendiary devices. The element phosphorus spontaneously bursts into flame when exposed to air; thus it has only incendiary use in the elemental state.

Occurrence: Large amounts of phosphorus occur in the depths of the oceans. At some points there are major upwellings of these waters, resulting in prolific production of marine life. A modern example occurs off the coast of Peru. The excreta of living sea animals and the skeletal parts of the dead (such as shark's teeth) accumulate on the sea floor. If there happens to be a sedimentary basin (other than the deep sea) where this phosphatic debris can accumulate, such as a shelf with coastwise currents, appreciable thicknesses of the material can be preserved. When compacted and, millions of years later, uplifted, they are known as phosphate rock deposits. Continents have been rifted asunder, creating new ocean basins; continents have collided, obliterating oceans and uplifting sedimentary basins. Thus phosphate rock deposits can be found today in southern Russia, and in Utah, Wyoming, and Montana, though they were formed near the edge of a continent. Other deposits of similar origin are in Florida, Tennessee, and North Carolina in the United States and in Morocco, Algeria, Tunisia, and in an arc through the Middle East.

When islands are submerged in the tropics, coral reefs form over and around them. Later they may be uplifted and become rookeries for birds. Guano from these birds is high in phosphorus compounds. It seeps into the coral rock, reacts with it, and becomes rock phosphate. Substantial deposits of this origin are mined on Christmas and Nauru Islands.

A third important origin of phosphate is called magmatic. North of the Arctic Circle on the Kola peninsula of Russia, there is a deposit of crystalline apatite in nepheline syenite that can reach 80% apatite. The deposit is two billion tons, and is the main source of Russian production. A different variety of magmatic apatite occurs in carbonatite in the Palabora deposit in South Africa, in Canada, and in Sri Lanka. The latter two have apparently been naturally concentrated by leaching of the limestone that contains them. Still another variation on this type of occurrence is the group of diatremes or explosive breccia pipes in Brazil, where the matrix can exceed 10% apatite. Where phosphate is in short supply and external sources require extensive shipping, this can be commercial. Ordinarily this type of deposit contains sufficient uranium to make it a significant co-product. Sedimentary rock phosphate ordinarily contains 0.2–0.8 pounds of uranium per ton, which is recovered in some operations.

There are several locations in the ocean where marine phosphatic nodules, bones, and coprolites are accumulating. These constitute a marine resource available for future mining. One of the identified locations is off the coast of southern California. Serious evaluation of this large deposit was made several years ago. This area has not been developed because it had been one of the main target ranges for the U.S. Navy. Over the years a large number of "dud," shells that had failed to explode, had accumulated with the phosphorite. The company did not like the prospect of a 16-inch shell exploding as it hit their barge, and abandoned the project.

Economics: Among all mineral commodities phosphate rock ranks fifth in total tonnage, with growth sustained at 6% per year for the past 15 years or more with production of 128 million tons in 1979, estimated at 140 million tons for 1981. This places the gross value of the raw product at about $6.5 billion. However, triple superphosphate with 48% P_2O_5 sells at about $200 per ton. Thus the value of the manufactured product usable for fertilizer would be about three times as high.

One trend has been for the rock phosphate producers to manufacture the finished triple superphosphate, rather than to sell the raw rock, thus keeping the "value added" at home and increasing the cost in foreign exchange to consuming nations. The result, among the poorest nations (those lacking phosphate deposits), is to force a reduction in importation of fertilizer, reducing crop yields and creating food shortages. Since the poorest nations ordinarily have the highest rate of population increase, which reduces real per capita income, this increases the burden on food-exporting nations. With carry-over feed grains at barely marginal levels, when the United States and Canada have a poor crop year with nothing to export, world food supplies will be drastically reduced. Should this coincide with a serious crop failure in South Asia or Europe, the fallacy of the ever-increasing number of mouths at the "banquet of life" (Pope Paul VI) will become obvious to all.

Phosphate fertilizer requires a rather high energy input, largely contributed by the high energy cost of sulphur. The alternative, electric furnace phosphorus, is obviously directly energy intensive. Until the cost of energy is stabilized, there can be no stability in fertilizer costs. Thus food costs will also fluctuate.

Production: The United States produces about 50 million tons of rock phosphate; Russia produces about half that amount. Morocco is the third producer, with 20 million tons. Thus three nations produce more than 75% of the world's phosphate. If the United States were as dependent on imported phosphate as Japan or Europe and the monopoly were as tightly held by three other nations, a cartel far stronger than OPEC would be capable of strangling the world by orchestrating starvation. Only a dozen other countries are self-sufficient in phosphate, none of them industrial nations. The United States exports about 17 million tons per year.

Most of the phosphate deposits are exploited by open pit mining methods. In Florida and North Carolina large draglines remove overburden and excavate the loosely aggregated phosphatic material. It is washed and screened with the coarse product going to the treatment plant. The fine grades that also contain an important amount of phosphate are treated by flotation to recover the valuable portion. The 18 largest nonmetallic mines in the United States are all rock phosphate mines and produce over 10 million tons of ore per year each.

In the western phosphate region, principally Wyoming and Idaho, beds are rather thin (1-3 m), strongly folded, and steeply-dipping. A combination of open pit and underground mining is used. The eastern region of the United States produces the bulk of the ore. In Tennessee the usable material has weathered out of the rock, and the eluvium is excavated. This material is rather low-grade, and probably could not compete, except for a subsidized low price for electricity to produce electric furnace phosphorus.

For the acid process of fertilizer manufacture, the concentrate from mining and milling is finely ground and treated with concentrated sulphuric acid. The products are phosphoric acid and waste gypsum, $CaSO_4.2H_2O$. Potentially the sulphur can be recovered, which would leave lime (CaO) as the by-product. The phosphoric acid is used to treat more rock phosphate, producing triple superphosphate. Alternatively, the acid is neutralized with ammonia, producing ammonium phosphate with two of the essential plant foods, a very concentrated fertilizer.

There is a basic process for production of fertilizer that requires that the phosphate be fused in a rotary kiln with a material such as soda ash (the rock form, trona) or potassium carbonate, which would result in two essential plant foods in one product. It can also be fused with a rock like serpentine to produce fused magnesium phosphate. This process is used in Korea, Japan, and Brazil.

The chloroapatite causes extensive corrosion. If the percentage of this compound is high, it may take special processing to utilize the mineral. Crystalline apatite reacts with sulphuric acid slowly, requiring a longer retention time in processing. For this reason, rock phosphate is generally preferred.

Outlook: There are enough known resources of phosphate to supply demand for two thousand years at present rates of production. The compound growth rate of phosphate consumption of 6% appears to have dropped in the last few years because developing nations have had to reduce their foreign exchange expenditures. If funds were no problem the growth rate would undoubtedly be sustained indefinitely because worldwide soils are becoming more depleted and demands for food are steadily increasing. Just to bring food production up to minimum needs in developing nations would require a big increase in fertilizer. Establishment of a cartel is a real possibility, requiring cooperation of only Morocco and Tunisia, together producing 19% of world supply. These two African nations are in the position of being able to dominate the price structure. The United States is a major exporter (17 million tons in 1980), and thus is in a position to moderate the upsurge in phosphate price if it chooses to do so. But the exports of Morocco and Tunisia are also essential to world food production.

Phosphate mining is an industry seriously impacted by the environmental control craze that has swept through the U.S. bureaucracy. It has added significantly to the cost of production. Every bureau that can think of a way to get into the act is issuing regulations and requiring reports. Among these agencies are the Environmental Protection Agency, Army Corps of Engineers, State of Florida Environmental Regulation Commission, Council on Environmental Quality, Nuclear Regulatory Commission, National Academy of Sciences, Committee on Surface Mining and Reclamation, Rivers and Harbors Commission, Fish and Wildlife Authority, the Bureau of Mines, the Geological Survey, Soil Conservation Service, and other organizations administering the Ports and Waterways Safety Act, Marine Protection, Research and Sanctuaries Act, Noise Control Act, Coastal Zone Management Act, Marine Mammal Protection Act, Endangered Species Act, Wild and Scenic Rivers Act, Soil and Water Resources Conservation Act, Toxic Substances Control Act, Deepwater Port Act and the National Historical Preservation Act. This is a classic example of a sound concept—minimizing environmental damage—going wild when allowed to expand out of control by bureaucracy. If the welfare state must expand to pension this large group of highly paid employees, they should at least be kept out of the way of industries that must earn the money to pay their pensions.

The use of phosphates in soaps and detergents is restricted and may be forbidden unless it can be removed (and possibly recycled) by sewage disposal plants. They reduce the efficiency of sewage plants and, discharged to the waterways are deleterious to aquatic life.

PORTLAND CEMENT

Composition

Clinker $\begin{cases} C_2S & = 2CaO.SiO_2 \\ C_3S & = 3CaO.SiO_2 \\ C_3A & = 3CaO.Al_2O_3 \\ C_4AF = 4CaO.Al_2O_3.Fe_2O_3 \end{cases}$
  Cementitious compounds
    (proportions closely controlled)
  Essential flux
  Reduces heat of hydration

"Clinker" plus 3%–4% gypsum ($CaSO_4 2H_2O$) ground together constitute portland cement; cement plus aggregate plus water yields concrete.

History: The use of cement goes back to the time of the Roman empire. As mentioned in Part I, it was one of the earliest mineral commodities used by man. The discovery was accidental, but some of the Roman concrete has lasted 2000 years.

Figure 37 Portland cement production in the United States and the world, given in millions of metric tons.

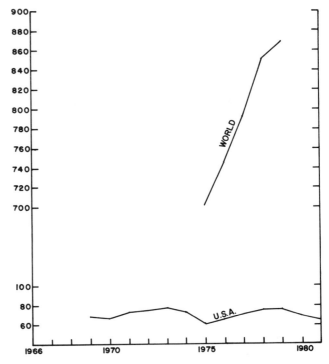

After the sacking of Rome, cement manufacture was forgotten for over 1000 years. Its rediscovery is credited to John Smeaton in 1756. In 1824 Joseph Aspdin advertised that his product was "equal to the finest Portland stone," and the name "portland" now signifies a class of cement meeting exacting chemical and physical specifications. While some manufacturers include "portland" in their company name and others do not, almost all of the cement made today meets the specifications for the product established by the American Society for Testing Materials.

The first cement plant in the United States was built in Pennsylvania in 1872. This was in the Lehigh Valley, where the natural impure limestone occurred with the constituents in the proper proprotions to make a high-quality cement. Suitable materials were soon found in other places, and today 46 of the 50 states and most other countries produce portland cement, about 170 plants in all.

Uses: Modern construction is almost totally dependent on portland cement for the production of high-strength concrete. It is the most durable paving material for highways. It is used in almost all bridges and "fly-overs." No large buildings can be built without it—it is the foundation of even small buildings. Concrete has the unique advantage of being a malleable plastic which will fit any form when fresh. Yet it "sets" in a few hours, and in a few days becomes as strong as or stronger than stone. When reinforced with steel its properties are further improved. It is such an ubiquitous material that it is taken for granted.

Occurrence: The essential ingredients for portland cement are lime, silica, alumina, and iron oxide. The most common sources of these materials are in limestone, which is largely calcium carbonate ($CaCO_3$), with variable amounts of clay or shale, which is a siliceous aluminum oxide. Sometimes ordinary cement (also called regular or Type I) can be made with only two components, if they occur in the right proportions in nature. It is frequently necessary to add silica in the form of sand, sandstone, or other highly siliceous material to bring the silica (SiO_2) up to the required level. This is particularly true if the product is for special applications, such as road paving or dam construction. Under these conditions a higher SiO_2 content is required. These are called Type II or Type V cements. Higher SiO_2 results in a higher proportion of C_2S to C_3S, giving lower heat of hydration (very important in dam construction), greater resistance to freezing and thawing, but slower setting time. Tri-calcium aluminate (C_3A) is the essential bad constituent. Without alumina being present, the cementitious compounds cannot be manufactured. However, in the finished product it contributes no strength (hence is a diluent) and has a very high heat of hydration, which is deleterious in some applications (mass concrete). To correct for this a low percentage of iron oxide (Fe_2O_3) is required. This converts part of the C_3A to C_4AF, reducing the heat of hydration. It also makes the cement darker.

For decorative purposes, white cement is sometimes desired. To produce this the manufacturer goes to great pains to keep iron out. Another special product is high early strength, or Type III cement, commonly called "quick-set." It has a higher proportion of C_3S, hence more limestone.

Certain ingredients are deleterious in portland cement. Magnesia is one of these, and it is common in limestones. The specification limit is 5% MgO and most companies try to hold considerably below this level. Magnesia hydrates slowly and swells as it hydrates. In large quantities it will break up the concrete. Likewise alkalies can be deleterious and the normal limit is 0.6% Na_2O or equivalent. That is, potash (K_2O) expressed as the molecular equivalent of soda (Na_2O) and soda are limited. Active silica particles in the aggregate, such as volcanic glass or opal, are particularly deleterious. Hence it is even more important to limit the alkali content in regions where concrete is subject to freezing and thawing. Phosphate (P_2O_5) is also deleterious, greatly reducing strength if over 0.5%.

The foregoing considerations are all important in selecting the limestone and clay source for raw materials. Commonly the amount of each used is about 76% limestone, 22% clay (or shale) and 2% silica, but if the limestone approaches natural cement rock, the most desirable raw material, a considerably higher percentage of silica may be required.

Gypsum is ground with the finished, burned product (clinker), to control the time of setting. The contractor has to know quite closely how much time he has between mixing water with the cement and the initial set of the concrete. If it sets in his mixer, he has problems.

It should be particularly noted that cement is just one ingredient of the three that goes into concrete. The other essentials are aggregate and water. There are no "cement" walks or roads—they are *always* concrete. In the same way there are no loaves of flour, only loaves of bread, though flour is an essential ingredient.

Economics: Back in the previous economic era before the "oil shock" of 1973, energy was about half the cost of producing cement. This was in the form of fuel and electricity. The cost of both these energy forms has subsequently shot up out of proportion to other costs. Today energy probably exceeds 60% of direct production costs. It varies rather widely between the plant dependent on fuel oil (high) to the plant that has its own coal mine (low) and with the process used in manufacturing. It is highly dependent on the price of fuel. Great emphasis is now placed on reducing energy costs.

Cement is actually a heavy chemical. Since the materials for its manufacture are quite widespread, it cannot be moved far without bumping into the market of a competing plant. With the increase in fuel costs and a resultant increase in transportation costs, cement is even more closely restricted to its own market area. The cost of transportation is the single most significant item in determining the market area. In spite of the high capital cost of the plant and high fuel cost, it still retails for less than 4 cents per pound in most areas. Products that try to compete with it are plastics and aluminum, but they cost 10 to 20 times as much and so can only fill special applications.

Production Methods: Raw materials for cement are ordinarily quarried by open pit methods. Economy of scale usually dictates that a plant will produce a million tons per year or more, so the raw material requirement may be on the order of 8000 tons per day, a substantial mining operation. Large shovels and trucks haul the raw material to a crusher where it is reduced and then ground to fine meal. Historically there have been two processes—wet and dry. The recent trend has been toward the dry process, which involves feeding into a preheater and dust collecting tower. This may require a drying stage if raw materials are wet. Now the process involves pre-calcining or heating the raw material to the point that all the water of crystallization in the clay and carbon dioxide in the carbonates are driven off before the materials go into the rotary kiln. The kiln is a long steel tube 12 feet or more in diameter, lined with fire brick to insulate the steel and conserve heat, and fired with coal, natural gas, or fuel oil. The kiln rotates slowly and the raw material is heated to the temperature where chemical reactions can take place, about 2600°F. The burned material agglomerates to "clinker," normally fist-sized chunks. It then passes to a cooler, where some energy is recovered as the clinker heats the air, which goes into the firing of the kiln. Clinker is then ground to 90% minues 200 mesh (with gypsum) and is ready for sale.

Outlook: Cement consumption is dependent on the construction indùs-try, notoriously cyclic. Its market is "mature" in the United States: that is, it is not likely to develop major new uses. It is also unlikely that a substitute will make significant inroads. In a low-growth economy, cement will be one of the laggard industries.

In the developing nations great emphasis is placed on construction of infrastructure, requiring large amounts of cement. World consumption of cement has been rising quite steeply. Much of the construction has been financed by borrowed money, and most of the nations have borrowed the maximum that they can obtain from all sources. The resulting high demand for money has forced world interest rates to rise to unprecedented levels, and many of the developing nations are on the verge of defaulting on their loans in 1982. It is difficult to see how a rate of construction even close to the recent level can be sustained. Even several of the oil-rich nations have overspent and are curtailing their programs.

POTASH (SYLVITE)

Properties and Characteristics

Composition	KCl
Molecular weight	74.55 (52.4% potassium, 47.6% chlorine)
Specific gravity	1.98
Crystallization	Isometric
Hardness	2
Color	Colorless, white, bluish, or reddish, depending on inclusions; soluble in water; has bitter taste

History: The name potash comes from the technique of collecting wood ashes and leaching them in a large cast iron pot. This technique was imported to the American colonies in 1608. The product was particularly important in making soap. Soda ash began to encroach on the potash market in 1823 after the much cheaper Leblanc process for manufacture was developed.

Potash is potassium oxide, K_2O, which does not occur in nature but is the basis of calculating the content of the active ingredient. Pure sylvite contains the equivalent of 63.2% K_2O. The element potassium does not occur in the free state, and in the metallic form has no significant use. It decomposes

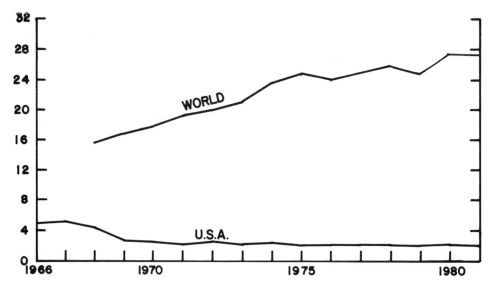

Figure 38 Potash production in the United States and the world, given in millions of metric tons.

water and bursts into flame. There are three natural isotopes of the element (39, 40, and 41) and the atomic weight is 39.10. The abundance of ^{40}K is only 0.012%, but this isotope is of great scientific interest. It is radioactive, with a half life of 1.2 billion years. Part of the ^{40}K decays to ^{40}Ar, giving off one gamma ray per atom of ^{40}K. With a mass spectrometer the amounts of these isotopes can be measured and the apparent age of the rock which contained them can be calculated. This is useful in the range of 200,000 to 200 million years or more, hence it is one of the important methods of determining the age of rocks (geochronology).

The first mineral proved to contain potassium was leucite, in 1797. The vital importance of the element to plant growth was discovered in the nineteenth century by von Liebig, who published his first article on the subject in 1840. Potash was identified in the brines in Stassfurt, Germany, in 1843, and this deposit dominated the market for many years. With depletion of the American forests, it was no longer profitable to burn trees to obtain the ashes to leach the potash after the Civil War.

In 1910, the prelude to World War I, some of the contracts for purchase of potash from the German cartel were cancelled and potash was recognized as a strategic mineral. The U.S. Geological Survey studied the brines in Searles Lake, California, and instigated a testing program in the Permian salt section of west Texas and southern New Mexico.

In 1925 an oil well drilled in Eddy County, New Mexico was found to contain sylvite. This initiated an exploration program in the vicinity, leading to the first mine by the U.S. Potash Co., commencing production in 1931.

A German immigrant, Charles Boettcher, after retiring as a wealthy man, went back to Germany for a visit and observed the developing sugar beet industry. He thought the soils in his home state of Colorado would grow beets, so he smuggled some beet seed into the country and tested them. As a result he started Great Western Sugar Co. Next he found he had to import potash from Germany, since beets require much potash to produce sugar. Potash had been discovered in New Mexico, but the salt content was fairly high, so he financed the research to develop the separation of the two minerals and started the Potash Co. of America. The mine was developed in 1933. (This story continues: he had to import cement from Germany to build his sugar mills, so built his own cement plant near Pueblo, Colorado. Boettcher later lost control of Great Western Sugar but the cement and potash companies were merged in Ideal Basic, now one of the largest producers of both commodities in the United States.)

The world's largest producing potash deposits in south central Saskatchewan were discovered during oil drilling in 1943 and confirmed in 1947. Canada is now the largest producer in the world. A second important basin was recently discovered in New Brunswick, and it is now being developed.

Uses: Potassium in the form of soluble salt is one of the most important elements in plant growth. It is also vital to all animals. Without adequate amounts of potash, plants cannot utilize the energy of the sun to convert carbon dioxide and water into organic compounds through photosynthesis. Thus to have intensive agriculture to feed a populous world, potash fertilizer is essential. It is the K in the standard fertilizer formula N-P-K. This usage accounts for about 95% of the total consumption.

Until 1890, industrial uses accounted for more than half the potash consumed. Today these uses account for only about 5%. Potassium aluminum sulphate is used in dyeing and printing fabrics, purifying water, and in baking powder. Potassium bichromate is an oxidizing agent and is used in dyeing, tanning leather, electroplating, photography, poison, fly-paper, glue, mirrors, and in electric batteries. Potassium cyanide is used to leach gold ores, in heat treatment of steel, and in engraving and lithography.

The explosive action of potassium nitrate was discovered in the fourteenth century, when it was used as the major ingredient in black powder (74.6% potash, plus charcoal and sulphur). This compound is known as nitre or saltpetre. It is found in the desert of Chile; at one time this was the main source of the compound. It also occurs in manure and this was an important early source for black powder. This form, though quite impure, was known as "manure salts."

A large tonnage of potash feldspar (orthoclase) is used in ceramics because of the characteristics that potash contributes to the ceramic body.

This is not included in the production of potash, however.

The use of 7%–8% of potash in glass is essential for the highest quality products. In enhances the luster and results in musical tone. This is the product called "crystal" or cut glass. It gives brilliance to colored glass for use in stained glass church windows.

There are hundreds of other minor uses for potash in industry, medicine, and technology.

Occurrence: There are many potash minerals, and the crust of the earth has an average 3.1% potash (potassium is the seventh most abundant element in the earth's crust). The important deposits are formed by the evaporation of sea water and precipitation of sylvite, KCl (63.2% K_2O); langbeinite, $K_2Mg (SO_4)_2$ (27.7% K_2O); kainite, $MgSO_4.KCl.3H_2O$ (18.9% K_2O); carnallite, $KMgCl_3.6H_2O$ (16.9% K_2O); or polyhalite $2 CaSO_4.K_2SO_4. 2H_2O$ (15.6% K_2O)—depending on temperature and concentration in the saline basin. By far the most important is sylvite.

There is another series of minerals formed mainly by igneous processes. The most common are orthoclase, $KAlSi_3O_8$ (16.9% K_2O) and Muscovite (or sericite) $H_2K Al_3 (SiO_4)_3$, but these are not used for production of potash. Leucite, $KAl(SiO_3)_2$, is a rock-forming mineral containing 21.5% K_2O. It is rarely sufficiently concentrated to be considered a source of K_2O, but some production has been derived during shortages. A deposit in the Leucite Hills of Wyoming is one of the best known occurrences.

Still a third type of occurrence is as alteration products around large bodies of sulphide mineralization. Most common of these is alunite, $K_2Al_6 (OH)_{12} (SO_4)_4$, (11.4% K_2O) and jarosite, $K_2Fe_6 (OH)_{12} (SO_4)_4$ (9.4% K_2O). There is no demand for these minerals since much higher grade and more easily used minerals are available in abundance. If deposits of alunite of several hundred million tons size were found, they could be a source of potash and alumina, which might be commercial.

Origin of the evaporite minerals is discussed at some length in the sections on "Salt" and "Gypsum." Sea water contains 0.05% K_2O. Thus concentration by evaporation and partial crystallization is more than 1000:1 to form a sylvite deposit. It is one of the "mother liquor" compounds after limestone, gypsum, and sodium chloride have crystallized. Magnesium salts are also present and local conditions determine which of the potassium-magnesium minerals will be formed.

Near Carlsbad in New Mexico the sylvite bed is about 3 m thick and occurs within a massive salt (NaCl) formation. A few hundred feet higher in the salt is a langbeinite bed of similar thickness. Both beds are mined.

The second important potash deposit in the United States is in the Paradox Basin of eastern Utah and western Colorado. One mine is operating in this sector. The bed is badly folded and faulted, making mining difficult.

The United States ranks fifth among producing nations, but production is declining.

The huge deposit in Saskatchewan, Canada, containing 40% of known reserves, begins in the United States on the border of North Dakota and Montana, where it is very deeply buried and stretches 800 miles (1300 km) across the province and into Alberta in a belt 200 miles (320 km) wide. The bed is eight feet (2.4 m) thick. Developing this bed at a depth of 3300 feet (1 km) was very difficult because unconsolidated horizons containing much water were encountered. Only by freezing the ground could shafts be sunk through it. A second important potash zone has recently been discovered in New Brunswick, Canada; a mine to produce one million tons per year is being developed. This deposit will have a great advantage from the standpoint of transportation, being nearer the coast than most of the deposits of the world.

Russian deposits are located on the west side of the Urals in Perm Province, in an area of 600 square miles (1550 km^2) and at other points. Russian production has been dropping steadily, from being the number one producer in 1977 with 8.3 Mmt, to 6.6 Mmt in 1980, appreciably below Canada's production.

East and West Germany rank third and fourth, and France is sixth in world production. Israel is seventh, with production by evaporation of Dead Sea brine. Jordan is undertaking a similar program from the same source. Spain is eighth, and deposits are reported to be large in Andalucia.

What appears to be a huge potash deposit, covering 10,000 km^2 and with an average thickness of 37 m has been discovered on the Khorat plateau of eastern Thailand, extending north into Laos. While drilling is not adequate to class any of this as "reserves," the resources may exceed those of the rest of the world. Most of the potash is in the form of carnallite, part as sylvanite. The depth of the potash is about 90-530 m. Plans to fully explore and exploit the deposit are being made. Because it is the only potash deposit in South or East Asia, an area containing 60% of the world's population, it should prove to be a very important resource. The chemical symbol for the element, K, is derived from the Latin name, *Kalium*, which in turn is derived from the Arabic word for alkali.

Economics: Potash is normally sold on the basis of K$_2$O content on a per unit (percent) basis. Prices have been increasing a little ahead of the average of inflation, but far less than the rate of increase of oil prices. Increases to May 1980 over the previous year were about 20% and to May of 1981 an additional 10%-12%. Demand is strong and supplies were rather tight until 1982. Production in Canada is expected to double in the 1980s. In May 1981, the price was around $130 per ton at the ship.

Transportation is a major factor in all the major producing areas. When one notes the total lack of potash production in Asia, the home of over half the world's population, the problem of an adequate supply of fertilizer to produce the food for the underdeveloped nations is obviously immense. The United States now annually consumes 50 pounds of potash per person and if Asia were to use the same amount, this demand alone would be twice the total production of the world. Rice, the staple in the region, requires a minimum of potash, but sugar cane (or beets) demands large amounts to produce sucrose. The potash goes into the molasses and remains in the pulp, the bagasse, where it can sometimes be recovered. This emphasizes the importance of the huge potash deposit being explored in Thailand.

Production: In the largest deposits the beds of potash extend for many miles, so mining follows the methods used in recovering coal. A shaft is sunk to the potash stratum and entries are driven in all directions. Laterals extend out to the property or economic limits and rooms are excavated. The main entries are maintained as haulage ways for many years. The size of the rooms and the percent of material left in pillars depends on the strength of the "back" (roof) and the depth, or weight of overburden. Sometimes it is possible to remove the pillars in a retreating system, increasing the percentage recovered. Longwall mining, where up to 90% of the mineral is extracted, is possible if there are no important surface structures that will be damaged during the settlement stage.

Normally the sylvite (or sylvanite, the mixed K and Na chlorides) has a little iron contaminating it, which gives an attractive red tint to the mineral. Since the floor is salt and dry, when sprinkled with water it becomes hard and dust-free. Haulage ways are literally subterranean superhighways, with large trucks speeding along them in attractive tunnels. When beds are folded or dipping rather steeply, mining becomes more complicated, but conventional methods can be applied.

Generally the minerals are separated by conventional flotation methods. However, the solubility of potash is higher in hot solutions rather than cold, while salt changes little in solubility with temperature. By dealing with saturated solutions, pure KCl can be crystallized on cooling.

Some solution mining is used, particularly for beds that are difficult to mine by conventional methods. Fractional crystallization is used in this case, and also for the brines from Searles Lake, California, where potash is a co-product with borates.

Outlook: With population increases still out of control in many nations and growing aspirations for a better life, adequate food is the first essential. Thus use of fertilizer, the only way to increase food production substantially, is sure to escalate at a rate exceeding that of most commodities. An intensive program to accelerate potash production in Canada may result in over-production in a few years, which will slow the price rises for a time.

Reserves are adequate for thousands of years, but poor distribution makes formation of a restrictive cartel possible. The United States currently imports 70% of its needs, largely from Canada. Production in the United States could be expanded, but the grade and physical problems would require a higher price to be economic.

Israel is planning to increase production from the Dead Sea and to maintain the water level will pump water from the Mediterranean Sea and use the large drop in elevation to generate power. Jordan is planning to produce potash from the same source.

When needed, the oceans are an endless source of potash. Evaporation in desert lands will permit concentration of potash, but will produce 50 times as much salt, which could create problems. If a solvent extraction technique that is selective for potassium could be developed, the sea could become a major source of potash.

SALT (NaCl)

Properties and Characteristics

Composition	39.34% Na, 60.66% Cl
Molecular weight	58.454
Crystal form	Cubic
Specific gravity	2.165 (pure crystal)
Hardness	2.5
Melting point	800.8°C
Solubility	35.7 parts in 100 parts of water at 0°C
Characteristics	Occurs in seawater in the amount of 2.7% by weight; plastic under pressure.

History: Since mammals (including man) evolved from creatures in the sea, they have retained the physiological need for salt. Animals acquired their needs from "salt licks" and primitive man did likewise. A secondary source was from eating the flesh of his prey. Because it is essential to man it has had religious significance, has been used as money, has caused wars and has been a convenient substance to tax. The Latin word is *sal*. Part of the Roman soldier's pay was in salt, hence the word "salary," according to Robert T. MacMillan of the U.S. Bureau of Mines. Today only about 3% of salt is used for human consumption. The chemical symbol for the element, Na, is derived from the Latin name *natrium*.

Uses: About 70% of the salt produced goes into the chemical industries. Of this, 95% is used for production of soda ash or chlorine and caustic soda.

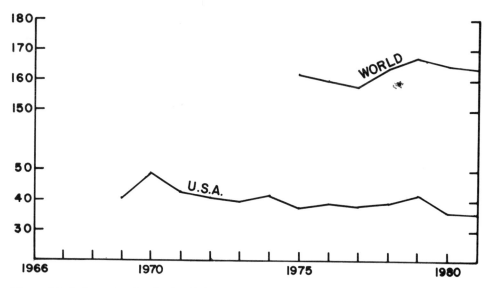

Figure 39 Salt production in the United States and the world, given in millions of metric tons.

With production now at about 185 million tons per year, it is the largest tonnage heavy chemical. The second usage is for melting ice from sidewalks, streets, and highways. The third use is food processing; the fourth is for animal feeds (salt blocks, etc.); the fifth, direct human consumption (table salt); followed by miscellaneous uses, such as water softening, pulp and paper, oil, metals, and rubber. There are literally thousands of individual uses.

Occurrence: The oceans contain 2.7% salt by weight—an endless, readily available supply. Under special natural conditions this is concentrated by evaporation into relatively pure deposits of very large size. Minerals are precipitated during evaporation in accord with their solubility, least soluble first, most soluble last. The sequence of main precipitates is limestone, gypsum, anhydrite, salt, potash, then miscellaneous minor constituents if evaporated to dryness. Each of these may overlap the minerals on either side.

If an arm of the sea or a bay is largely cut off from the main ocean and the climate is dry so that salt concentrates to a brine and precipitates, this is called an evaporite or salt basin. Some of the salt beds formed in this manner reach several hundred meters in thickness. They may intertongue or overlap gypsum on the side nearest the water inlet and underlie or inter-tongue with potash salts in the inner-most zone.

Some of the salt basins are as large as 100,000 square miles (259,000 km²) in the Permian basin of southwestern United States, and 180,000 square miles (466,000 km²) in the Louann Permo-Triassic basin underlying the Gulf Coast. Under the eastern United States (New York, Pennsylvania, Michigan, Ohio, and West Virginia) is another huge salt basin of Silurian age. Five of Canada's provinces have important salt deposits. Japan is the only major industrial nation that is dependent on imported salt for a major amount of its needs (about 35%).

Salt diapirs or domes have been described under sulfur. There are about 300 of these distributed along the Gulf Coast from Alabama to Mexico, with the source the Louann salt bed. Similar features are found in Colombia, Germany, Spain, Rumania, Egypt, Algeria, Morocco, Angola, Iran, and Russia.

There are also large lakes that have concentrated salt such as Great Salt Lake, Utah. The region is a desert, and much of the Wasatch mountain range on the east side of the basin receives heavy snow fall. On melting, it leaches salts out of the rocks and flows into Lake Provo, which acts as a pre-evaporation pond. The resulting brackish water overflows into the Great Salt Lake. Here the brine is concentrated nearly to the point where salt will precipitate. The density of the brine is so high that a swimmer cannot sink in it. Extensive areas west of the lake, formerly under water, are underlain by salt. This area is known as the Bonneville salt flats, where automobile speed records are established. A railroad causeway across the lake with narrow inlets from the south to the northern portion resulted in more extensive concentration in the northern portion, sufficient to make extraction of lithium feasible. Salt is also produced from this lake.

An unusual salt lake is found on the Altiplano in southern Bolivia. This is a remnant of an inland sea originally several hundred kilometers long, which drains Lake Titicaca and the ranges of the Andes to the east and west. It is a desert area, and the southern-most depression of the old sea is called Salar de Uyuni. This depression is 200 km in diameter and the surface is a layer of quite pure halite (salt) three meters thick. Under the salt layer is a brine that is reported to be at least 400 m deep. This is an unusual situation, with salt having a specific gravity of about 2.4, remaining on top of brine with a specific gravity of 1.5. Theoretically the salt should sink to the bottom. However, the load capacity of the salt has been found adequate to support 20 tons. The area of salt is 31,000 km^2, or 94 km^3 of crystalline salt, equal to 228 billion tons, with that of the brine probably 10 times greater. The word *salare* means "salt region." There are several similar basins in the area, as well as dry lakes called *playas*, which contain evaporite minerals. There are many large playas in the Andes along the Pacific coast of South America. They are also common in other desert areas.

Salt evaporation pans are common in areas with a seasonal dry climate. South San Francisco Bay is an example of a climate with five feet of net evaporation per year. Hence it is amenable to salt production.

Economics: Cost of mining rock salt is low and large scale underground methods are used. Large caverns will remain open, and they do not leak. Bulk rock salt sells for about $10 per ton. The great majority is used directly in this form.

Much of the salt is produced by pumping water into the salt horizon, dissolving the salt, and pumping it directly into a plant for chemical processing. There is no sale of salt under these circumstances, and a price is given for accounting purposes only of about $5 per ton. This probably approximates production cost. Solar evaporated salt sells for about $12.50 per ton. These figures show that the energy content is very low.

For human consumption and some chemical purposes, the salt must be more highly purified. Brines from the wells can be carefully evaporated, or rock salt can be dissolved and reprecipitated, evaporating the brine by heat, requiring fossil fuels. This is a more expensive process, and the product sold for an average of $61.64 per ton in 1979, in bulk quantities.

Thus salt is one of the cheapest commodities in the United States, and consumption is high.

Production Methods: There are three major methods of producing salt. The first and simplest is the solar evaporating pond. Commencing with ordinary sea water, the loss must be 13:1 before salt starts to crystallize, so the area of concentrating ponds is much larger than that of crystallizing ponds. The water is pumped through a series of ponds. Iron and gypsum precipitate in the earlier stages. When the salt reaches a saturation of 26.0° Baumé (a means of measuring concentration of solutions) or 35.7%, the salt begins to precipitate. The brine continues concentrating to 29° Bé, but at that point the residual brine, the bittern, is pumped from the pond and either wasted or used for extraction of magnesium. When vacuum dried, the precipitated salt is 99.9% pure NaCl.

About 60% of the salt mined in the United States is by dissolving the salt from the underground rock formation and pumping it to the surface. A nearly saturated brine results. After treatment to remove impurities the brine goes directly to the plant for manufacture of soda ash, or to evaporation.

The balance of the salt is mined by room and pillar methods. The height of the room depends on the thickness of the salt bed. In the salt domes the rooms stand well up to 100 feet (30 m) high. Pillars are calculated to support the "back" (roof) and walls. Salt mines are clean, essentially dust-free, with a uniform, rather mild temperature. With the white walls they are easily lighted, thus among the most pleasant of all mines to work in, contrary to the implication of the saying "back to the salt mines." Rock salt produced in this way is crushed and sized for marketing.

Chlorine is produced by electrolysis of the brine producing caustic soda, with sodium hydroxide as a co-product. If molten salt is electrolyzed, chlorine and metallic sodium are produced. There is presently little demand for the metal. It reacts explosively with water, freeing hydrogen, which may burn. It is lighter than water (specific gravity 0.97), and has a high coefficient of heat transfer. Its melting point is 98°C, and it has a high boiling point. It is likely to be used as the coolant in fast breeder reactors.

Soda ash, other than the natural product, is produced from salt by the Solvay process. This requires salt, ammonia, and limestone. The salt is in brine solution and ammonia is dissolved in it. CO_2, burned out of the limestone in a kiln, is added to the solution, forming ammonium bicarbonate, which reacts with the salt to form ammonium chloride and sodium bicarbonate, which is then calcined, driving off CO_2 to go back into the process. The lime is hydrated and used for recovery of the ammonia.

Outlook: Salt is the raw material for such a broad spectrum of chemical products and so abundant in nature, that its importance will continue to grow at least as fast as the economy. The metal sodium could have an appreciably greater demand if the fast breeder reactor becomes an important method of generating electricity. Sodium is an excellent conductor of electricity. If it can be adapted in installations where it is not exposed to air or moisture, it can be used for this purpose. Should the sodium-sulphur battery for motive power develop, this could increase the demand.

The development of the huge trona deposits (see later section) has almost eliminated the use of salt in the production of soda ash in the United States. It could cut the consumption of salt in other industrial nations in the next few years.

SILICA (QUARTZ)

Properties and Characteristics

Composition	SiO_2 (Si, 46.75%; O, 53.25%)
Molecular weight	60.08
Crystal form	Hexagonal rhombohedral
Specific gravity	2.65–2.66 in crystalline quartz
Hardness	7
Melting point	1723°C

History: Silica, in the form of flint, was the first mineral product man learned to use. Flint is a cryptocrystalline form of silica that has the property of flaking when pressure is applied. With practice, one can shape tools from it quite readily. Today counterfeiting of "Indian" arrowheads is quite common. Flint has the unusual property of sparking when struck. It was used by early man to start fires. Silica is composed of the two most abundant elements in the earth's crust, silicon and oxygen.

Some of the myriad forms of silica are colorful, and very attractive and were used for decorative purposes thousands of years ago. One precious stone, opal, is composed of silica and water. By weight, semiprecious stones composed of silica make up over 80% of the entire gemstone industry. Some of the names are: rock crystal (colorless), smoky quartz (usually called smoky topaz), amethyst (purple), citrine (yellow), rose quartz or Bohemian ruby (rose-red), prase (leek green), sapphire quartz (blue), Venus's hair or hair stone (with fine crystals enclosed), cat's eye (reflects a wave of milky light), tiger eye (yellow to brown wavy luster), wood-stone or petrified wood (various colors), chrysoprase (apple green), jasper (red, brown, yellow, green, blue), avanturine (speckled metallic sheen, usually reddish brown), mocha stone (tree-like dendrites, black or brown), moss agate (green dendrites), carnelian (red chalcedony), sard (brown chalcedony), plasma (green chalcedony), heliotrope (green chalcedony with blood-red flecks or streaks), and agate (sometimes multi-colored).

Silicon is a metal that does not occur in nature in the free state. In the periodic table of elements, silicon is a "cousin" to carbon and has many chemical compounds similar to those of carbon. Its strong affinity for oxygen is probably the reason it did not become a more important element in the evolution of life on the planet. Some plants, such as bamboo utilize it in their structure, and sponges and radiolaria use it in their hard parts. The exoskeleton of diatoms is composed of silica.

The new computer industry is dependent on silicon chips, but by weight, this is an extremely small factor.

Uses: As mentioned above, the best known uses of silica are in gemstones and computers. By far the biggest consumption (possibly 300 million tons) is in Portland cement. However much of this is in the silicate form (clay or shale) and probably only about 10% of the total is in the mineral form of silica, generally as sand. Data on silica are sparse but in the United States, over 10 million tons are used annually for molding and foundry sand (refractories), and a like amount in manufacturing glass, probably 100 million tons on a worldwide basis. It is extensively used as an abrasive for sand blasting, grinding glass and stone cutting. It is used to produce sodium silicate (water glass), silicon carbide (one of the hardest substances known), silicon alloys like ferrosilicon, silico-manganese, silicon-chrome and silicon-titanium. There are other ceramic uses, and the broad field of silicone chemistry is still developing. This includes elastomers (silicone rubber) and oils. It is one of the most utilitarian substances, yet few statistics on its use are compiled. It would probably rank fourth or fifth, in the 200 million ton range, among the giants of the mineral industry, not counting the materials containing silica as a part of their molecular structure.

Occurrence: Silica is nearly as ubiquitous as air and water. The ultimate origin of much of it is in igneous rocks as discrete crystals, crystalline masses, or as veins cutting through all types of rocks. Quartz is one of the most indestructible of minerals, so when other minerals weather and disintegrate, quartz remains, often moving into streams where the grains become rounded, forming sand. Where conditions are favorable, large deposits of nearly pure quartz sand form in the sea. These may be consolidated and uplifted into the continents and later, if grain size and purity are appropriate, may become glass sand deposits. The sands may be metamorphosed into quartzite, common in mountainous regions. Some of the coarse-grained igneous veins or pegmatites contain massive quartz that is nearly pure. These, too, are utilized. Many of the uses do not require high purity, so various sandstones or quartzites can be used. While for special purposes some silica is transported many miles, silica suitable for most purposes is generally available at most localities.

Economics: Silica is an ubiquitous mineral, so prices are generally quite low. Glass sand may be available at $3-$5 per ton, delivered to the factory. Depletion sometimes requires locating a new source, however, and transportation costs rapidly exceed the cost of the raw material. If one goes to the market to purchase silica, prices are more substantial. Two factors influence price: fineness and purity. Grinding cannot be done in a mill with steel liners or balls; rather it must be ground in a mill with ceramic liners and balls. Prices in May 1982 (Elco, Illinois, bagged) ranged from $72 for −200 *mesh* and 96% silica to $95 at −325 mesh and 99.5%; and $196 for −10 microns, 99%. Grinding is power intensive. None of these materials would be suitable for glass sand. The specification on size for glass is normally −20 plus 200 mesh, with iron limited at about 0.05%.

There is another category of silica that has a small market, quartz crystal. This has special electronic applications, and suitable crystals are rare. Depending on size and grade (the larger the more expensive), the price in May 1982 was $2.50-$60 per pound. Smaller crystals for fusing are priced from $440 to $2500 per ton.

Because of its widespread occurrence, the price of silica is low. This even applies to the gemstones. While some varieties are beautiful (amethyst, for example), they are classed as semi-precious and are quite inexpensive.

Production: For many uses high purity is essential. If the silica has to be mined, there is danger of contamination by iron, one of the most deleterious impurities. Most of the machinery is made of iron or steel; as silica is harder than ordinary steel, wear is high. For some applications mills lined with porcelain and porcelain grinding balls are used to minimize contamination. In other cases high intensity magnetic separators are used to remove magnetite, other less-magnetic, iron-bearing minerals, and small steel fragments that enter the circuit.

Commonly glass sands are unconsolidated and need only washing and screening to produce the purity of silica required.

A specification for glass sand might be:

SiO_2	99.0	minimum
Al_2O_3	0.20	maximum
Fe_2O_3	0.05	maximum
CaO	0.05	maximum
MgO	0.05	maximum
Alkali	0.01	maximum

This would probably produce an amber glass, suitable for bottles. For flint glass the specification might be limited to 0.02% Fe_2O_3. Actually there is no need for such rigid specifications for glass sand. The important thing is absolute uniformity. Lime and soda and some feldspar are usually added. The quality can usually be met without increasing price inordinately, and uniformity of product can be assured by uniformity of raw material, so specifications are followed carefully.

For crystalline quartz to be used in electronics, the crystals should be alpha (low temperature) quartz with no twinning, without flaws (feathers), and clear. Slight tint does not seem to be deleterious. Crystals larger than 500 g are preferred, since there is much waste. Synthetic crystals are now common and superior in quality.

Outlook: Most of the silica goes into construction, either directly or indirectly. Thus demand follows the building cycle. Prices are among the lowest of all mineral commodities, so substitution is not a danger. On a worldwide basis, there is no forseeable shortage of silica. In some regions where glass has been manufactured for many years, deposits are being depleted and silica must be imported over increasing distances.

As some of the metals become scarce, glass or ceramic products will be able to encroach on some of the markets. For example, fiberglass has excellent structural strength and durability. The energy component of glass containers is less than that of aluminum and glass bottles are re-usable. Throw-away bottles have caused a littering problem.

SULPHUR (S)

Properties and Characteristics

Atomic number	16
Atomic weight	32.064
Isotopes	32(95%), 33(0.8%), 34(4.2%), 36(0.02%), and three radioactive nuclides 31, 35, and 37

Melting point	Rhombic, 112.8°C; monoclinic, 118.9°C
Specific gravity	2.07
Specific heat	0.175
Average rock content	990 ppm (igneous), 8000 ppm (limestone), 850 ppm (soil)
Major mineral occurrence	Native sulphur, pyrite (FeS_2); anhydrite ($CaSO_4$)
Strength	High compressive strength; greater than concrete.

History: Since sulphur occurs in the elemental state, it was known in prehistoric times. The name comes from Latin, and means "burning stone." Most people in the United States spell the name with an "f," but those working with the element professionally (and in the U.K.) spell it with "ph." Egyptians used it in 2000 B.C. to bleach their linens. It is one of the main ingredients in gun powder, the famous "black powder" discovered by

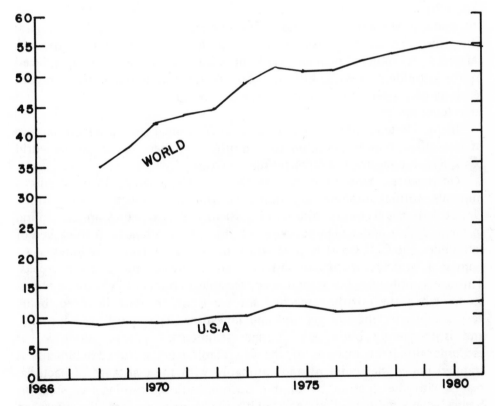

Figure 40 Sulphur production in the United States and the world, given in millions of metric tons.

the Chinese (and others). The ingredients are saltpetre (74.6%), charcoal (13.5%), and sulphur (11.9%). First used in guns early in the fourteenth century, black powder was the only explosive used for 600 years. Its discovery was probably about A.D. 1250.

Sulphuric acid was apparently prepared by Arabian chemists in the eighth century and was used by the medieval alchemists. The lead-chamber process of manufacture was introduced in England in 1746 and to the United States in 1793. The contact process of acid manufacture was developed in the 1890s, permitting production of pure H_2SO_4.

Dr. Herman Frasch discovered a process for mining sulphur from salt domes in 1894 by using superheated steam, reducing the price and making it one of the most important raw materials for the heavy chemical industry.

Uses: By far the largest amount of sulphur is used for the manufacture of sulphuric acid, and the largest percentage of this goes into manufacture of phosphate fertilizer. It requires 0.95 tons of sulphur to manufacture one ton of P_2O_5 plant nutrient. So if world food supplies are to increase, sulphur production must increase in proportion. The second-ranking usage is in pulp and paper. There are two processes. The sulphate process uses sulphuric acid. The other, the sulphite process, uses sulphurous acid (sulphur in the S^{+4} valence state). Mineral pigments rank third, but this process is being replaced by the chloride process. Other important uses are in manufacture of rayon, leaching of copper and uranium ores, explosives, iron and steel pickling, and petroleum refining.

In the United States 63% of all sulphur consumed goes into manufacture of phosphate, ammonium sulphate, and other fertilizers. On the whole world basis, 57% is consumed in fertilizer manufacture.

Occurrence: Sulphur occurs as the free element and in hundreds of minerals, both as sulphides and sulphates. The most important source in the United States is from salt domes in Louisiana and Texas; they are also found in Mexico. Salt under high pressure will flow like toothpaste. A thick bed of salt under the Gulf Coast is covered by thousands of feet of sediments. At points of weakness *diapirs* of salt have risen through the overlying rocks. This salt is not pure, but contains appreciable amounts of gypsum and limestone. When the intrusion reached the sea floor, the salt dissolved, being very soluble, leaving the gypsum and limestone. This is called "caprock," and is frequently buried by younger sediments. Hydrogen sulphide gas escaping along the margins of the salt diapir from intruded sediments is trapped under the sediment and, probably with the assistance of bacteria, reacts with the gypsum by double decomposition, forming free sulphur. Some believe methane first reacts with the gypsum to form the hydrogen sulphide gas. Sulphur collects in the caprock (mainly the limestone), which may be quite porous. The percentage of sulphur in the caprock varies from

0% to as high as 40% in commercial ore zones. About one salt dome in ten on the Gulf Coast contained commercial sulphur concentrations, but about eight of them produced less than 250,000 tons, and hence were marginal. There were ten with reserves over 9 million tons. The two largest were Grand Ecaille, Louisiana, and Boling, Texas, with 41 and 88 million lt, respectively.

Sedimentary sulphur is the form in the huge deposits in Italy, Poland, and Iraq. Other deposits in west Texas and New Mexico contain about half the remaining *Frasch* sulphur of the United States. It is also present in Mexico. The chemistry of origin from gypsum is the same as above but the gypsum is of normal evaporite origin.

Second in importance of production (36%) is sulphur recovered from "sour" gas. The natural gas at some locations has a high content of H_2S which makes it valueless until the hydrogen sulphide is removed. Alberta, Canada, is the largest producer of this type of sulphur, with the United States second. Refining of high-sulphur petroleum results in recovery of substantial amounts, now 16% of world sulphur production.

"Pyrites" are third in importance as a source of sulphur accounting for 19%. This includes three minerals, pyrite and marcasite (both FeS_2) and pyrrhotite ($Fe_n S_{n+1}$). Pyrite is the most important. Some very large massive sulphide deposits are composed largely of pyrite, averaging 90%. These are of volcanogenic origin sometimes formed in the ocean or shallow marine basins. The Rio Tinto deposit in southern Spain is one of the most famous. They are also formed in the subvolcanic environment on land by replacement, in association with elemental volcanic sulphur. Japan is the largest producer of this type of sulphur. Frequently, pyrite is a consituent of other ores, such as copper, lead, zinc, silver, or gold. It can be recovered as a separate by-product. Pyrite and marcasite are normal constituents of sedimentary rocks, including coal, and when coarsely crystalline, can be removed from the coal.

Volcanic sulphur is important in some regions of recent volcanic activity. The sulfataric stage is late in the eruptive cycle. Deposits containing sulphur, pyrite, and marcasite form by replacement of tuffs and flows. Sometimes the sulphur becomes heated, melts, and forms sulphur flows. The Matsuo mine in northern Japan is one of the largest producers. Huge deposits are located in southwestern Bolivia on the Chilean and Argentinian borders, at very high elevations. Significant deposits are located in the Philippines and in California.

Sulphur is an important constituent of smelter gases and is present in stack gases from coal-fired power plants and some cement plants. It is generally too dilute to be collected economically, yet so concentrated that it is environmentally undesirable. It is the source of "acid rain," which has become a problem in some areas.

By far the largest deposits of sulphur are in the huge gypsum/anhydrite evaporites. These are formed after limestone has been precipitated and before salt is sufficiently concentrated to precipitate. These are found in many parts of the world and constitute a sulphur protoresource that may some day become economic.

Economics: Production of sulphur is a matter of energy balance. This is best illustrated in the Frasch method of extraction. Sulphur melts at 119°C and is highly fluid up to a temperature of 159°, but above that the viscosity increases rapidly, so it is essential that the temperature be closely controlled. If the rock represents 80% of the volume and the sulphur 20%, the entire mass must be heated to about 145° by superheated steam. This may require from 1500 to 8000 gallons (5–27 metric tons) of hot water per ton of sulphur recovered. The water may have to be softened before it can be used, a process that is also energy intensive. Few Frasch mines are likely to be opened in the future. Very important in the energy balance is the heat of combustion of sulphur when burned to SO_2 for manufacture of acid (8.9 million BTU per long ton). In larger plants this heat is utilized in processing.

The price of sulphur was generally under $35 per ton in the post-war period except during temporary periods of short supply, such as 1967. At the beginning of 1979, Frasch sulphur at Gulf ports was $60 per metric ton on the spot market. During the year the world price of oil nearly doubled (not the U.S. domestic price). By mid-year the price of sulphur was $90, by October it was $115, and in May, 1982 it was about $140 per ton. This only partially reflected the increase in oil price. The Iranian revolution stopped production of sulphur in that country. Bad weather in both Poland and Canada, the two largest exporting nations, severely curtailed production there. This was followed by labor strikes and damage to two of Poland's molten sulphur ships. Then the war between Iraq and Iran curtailed sulphur production in Iraq, contributing to the price rise.

With Frasch sulphur likely to decline in importance the bulk of production will have to turn to recovered sulphur (sour gas), which requires considerably less energy (and is a by-product) and from pyrite, also using moderate amounts of energy. Gypsum/anhydrite remains in the background as a protoresource and it may become economic at the new price level. The process of recovering it involves using the calcium oxide to produce portland cement and the SO_3 to manufacture acid. It is energy intensive, but may become competitive where there is a market for both products.

Two other possibilities may develop. Phosphate fertilizer may be priced out of the market, curtailing food production in the beleaguered third world, or there may be a shift to electric furnace phosphorus as a step in manufacturing fertilizer (although electric energy costs are rising rapidly also).

Strangely, in some markets sulphuric acid has become virtually a waste product. Environmental restrictions have resulted in collection of sulphur gas which, when converted to acid for disposal, has flooded the market. This has happened in Australia and Japan. Under these circumstances it may be necessary to mine limestone for neutralizing the acid; then disposal of the residual gypsum becomes a problem. This is more expensive than giving the acid away.

When pyrite is used to produce acid, both the iron and the sulphur burn to oxides, so it is an exothermic reaction, producing excess heat. This process will probably become more competitive.

Production Methods: The Frasch process involves drilling a series of wells into the deposit and pumping superheated steam down special tubing, heating a volume of rock above 119° so the sulphur will melt. Then through the same tubing, compressed air is blown to lift the molten sulphur from the formation. It is normally 99% pure and requires no further processing for acid manufacture. Commonly it is maintained in the molten state, so it can be pumped and easily handled. One of the cost factors in many areas is an adequate supply of soft water. Salt water is highly corrosive, and hard water results in precipitation of sediment in the pipes. This is particularly true in southern Louisiana, where the salt domes occur in the coastal marshes or even offshore. The water treatment plant adds on the production cost. Recoveries may be rather low, particularly in low-grade deposits. Natural gas may contain as much as 30% hydrogen sulphide. It is removed by a solution of ethanolamine, leaving a "sweet" gas. The solution is heated to drive off the H_2S, leaving the ethanolamine for reuse. Part of the H_2S is burned to SO_2 and water; then the SO_2 is reacted with the balance of the H_2S to yield very pure sulphur vapor, which is condensed and cooled.

Pyrite is directly converted to SO_2 and then to sulphuric acid. Finely ground pyrite is burned in a fluosolids burner and the SO_2 gas drawn off. The pyrite may be a by-product, hence an inexpensive raw material. If it is mined as an ore itself, it requires crushing and grinding to prepare it for burning.

Volcanic sulphur has been a minor source because it normally occurs with volcanic ash and separation is difficult. In Japan and Bolivia it is recovered by partially burning the sulphur, using the heat evolved to melt an additional portion. Total recovery is quite low and the fume is discharged to the air. More recently, sized ore and superheated steam have been introduced to an autoclave where the sulphur is melted and collected in the bottom, where it can be tapped.

Tremendous quantities of sulphur are discharged to the atmosphere by utilities in their stack gases. This is a very dilute source from the industrial standpoint, but because of the need to remove it from the gas for the sake of environmental protection, this could become an important source of sulphur in the near future. Any sales of acid would help defray the cost of removal. With the great increase in cost of Frasch sulphur, hence elimination of the main low-cost source, recovery of sulphur from gases of combustion may soon be cost effective.

Outlook: Sulphuric acid is one of the most important heavy chemicals. Its consumption has been considered a sensitive barometer of industrial production. With world production of sulphur at about 54 million tons in 1980, all forecasts are for steady but modest growth. On the negative side, if the price of sulphur for the acid process of producing fertilizer exceeds the cost of producing electric furnace phosphorus, there could be a major shift in consumption. On the positive side, the sulphur-sodium battery gives far greater current density per pound of battery than the lead-sulphuric acid system. Should it be adopted for motive power in electric vehicles, it could moderately increase consumption. Another potential new use is as a binder for brick and concrete blocks, replacing masonry cement.

On the other hand, sulphuric acid is being phased out in the *pickling* of steel and the manufacture of pigment. It may lose its position in manufacture of rayon. Should recovery from stack gases become an important source, combined with the great increase in energy cost for production of Frasch sulphur, a major shift in the industry could result.

TRONA (SODIUM SESQUICARBONATE)

Properties and Characteristics

Composition	$Na_2CO_3.NaHCO_3.2H_2O$
Molecular weight	226
Crystal form	Monoclinic
Specific gravity	2.11-2.14
Hardness	2.5-3

History: While the mineral trona has been long known, the huge evaporite deposit near Green River, Wyoming, was discovered in 1938 while a prospector was drilling for oil. Much of it is on lands owned by the Union Pacific Railroad, granted to it at the time of building the railroad across the continent. Deposits of quite similar composition were formed at Searles Lake, California, as brine in deposits also containing salts of lithium, boron, potassium, bromine, and trona. These two deposits are the largest known. Owens Lake is also large, and the first important production of trona

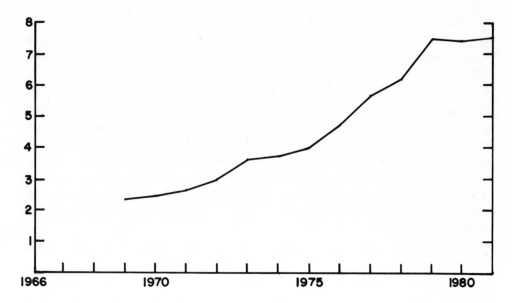

Figure 41 Trona production in the United States, given in millions of metric tons.

came from this source about 1886. Minor production came from Big Lake, Nevada, as early as 1875.

Use: The only important use of trona is for the production of soda ash. This has almost completely replaced the Solvay process of manufacture from salt in the United States.

Occurrence: In the middle Eocene period, in what is now the central Rocky Mountains of Wyoming, Colorado, and Utah, three large lakes formed. They had no outlets to the ocean and the climate was relatively dry, so evaporation about equalled inflow. Salinity built up and precipitating carbonates formed what is today known as the Green River formation. The most significant constituent of this formation is that it contains the largest oil shale deposit in the world, over a trillion barrels of petroleum.

For a short time the lake precipitated trona over a large area of southern Wyoming near the town of Green River. This deposit is 2.5–6 m thick (averaging 3 m), and contains several hundred million tons of the ore in a relatively pure form. The bed is flat, and lies about 450 m below the surface.

In California the series of lakes between Owens Lake and Searles Lake constitute another evaporite sequence of continental saline minerals. Searles Lake is the last in the series, the lowest of the sequence, and captures the overflow from Owens during times of heavier precipitation. Salt precipitated and the remaining liquors still intermixed with it contain an estimated 150 million tons of trona. Owens Lake probably contains a third as much.

There are other saline basins that should contain large amounts, in Egypt, Central Asia, across North Africa, and in the deserts of western South America. The important deposits today are in Wyoming and California.

Economics: Thirty-five years ago a large majority of the soda ash of commerce, one of the most important heavy chemicals, was manufactured from salt by the Solvay process. By 1980, 16 of the synthetic soda ash plants in the U.S. had shut down, and only the Allied Chemical plant in New York was still operating. Stringent environmental regulations and the cost of energy had combined to wipe out an industry. The natural sodium carbonate deposits now produce nearly all the requirement. Efforts are being made to penetrate the European market but in spite of a price advantage, trona has made small inroads.

The price of soda ash averaged about $86 per ton at the mine in the United States, with prices in Europe ranging up to $156/st.

Production: Trona beds in Wyoming are examples of ideal conditions for room and pillar mining. A new effort involving solution mining is being developed that should give a higher percentage of extraction. The process calls for dissolving the trona for refining in any event. It is then precipitated, filtered, dried, and calcined to Na_2O. In California production starts from the brine, which is purified by selective crystallization, and then given the same treatment.

In 1980 about 7.43 Mmt of soda ash were made from trona in the U.S., representing about 18 Mmt of the mineral as mined. Thus trona ranks as the twelfth largest mineral commodity by tonnage, yet few people have even heard of it.

Outlook: Soda ash is the most important basic heavy chemical, comparable to sulphuric acid on the acid side. Chemical industries are sure to grow at a greater rate than the economy as a whole, so domestic demand should increase at a moderate rate. The foreign producers are likely to turn to American production rather than build new, expensive, energy-intensive plants that can only produce at a higher cost.

The potential for finding additional large deposits in other nations is good. The mineral is very soluble, so it does not outcrop. Thus it can be found only by drilling. In most instances, drilling an oil well would pass through a bed of trona and the mineral would dissolve in the cuttings. If the cuttings of trona did reach the surface, the mineral would probably not be recognized. The saline lake deposits in desert regions are places where trona is most likely to be recognized.

The recent discovery of nahcolite in the Green River oil shale zone in eastern Utah may prove to be a significant new source of soda ash. This mineral, $NaHCO_3$, is natural sodium bicarbonate that occurs on bedding planes and fractures in the oil shale, together with dawsonite ($Na_3Al(CO_3)_2 \cdot 2Al(OH)_3$), which is a possible ore of aluminum and may be separated from the oil shale in the process of mining.

GEMSTONES

History: A gem is a stone that has intrinsic value—that is, value attributed by society independent of any utilitarian characteristic. It must possess beauty, durability, hardness, and rarity, and must be large enough to be used for adornment or decoration, usually after being cut and polished. Naturally occurring gems are considered to be more valuable than synthetics, even though the composition is identical and the synthetic may be more perfect and of better color.

While there are differences of opinion as to which minerals can properly be classed as gems, there are 10 minerals out of several thousand which, when meeting the specifications, are always in the precious class: diamond, corundum, chrysoberyl, spinel, beryl, topaz, zircon, tourmaline, garnet, and precious opal. That list may seem to be lacking in some of the most important gems, but they are there, hiding behind their ordinary names. Corundum is ruby and sapphire, chrysoberyl is alexandrite and cat's eye, and beryl is emerald and aquamarine. Feldspar, jade, lazurite, olivine, quartz, and turquoise are often added to the list of precious stones.

Other stones of value are classed as semi-precious. Some very beautiful stones come in this class because they are not rare.

Colored stones were picked up by primitive man and carried as talismans. They were thought to have magical powers. The concept of birthstones evolved from this primitive belief. When stones of particular beauty were found, they were frequently pre-empted by the king or given to him to curry favors. Thus the finest stones became symbols of regal wealth and power. As early as 3700 years ago emeralds were systematically mined in Egypt. These mines continued to produce through the time of Cleopatra. The Spanish found the Indians in Peru worshipping an emerald the size of an ostrich egg. Other gems were vested with religious significance; examples include jade Buddahs in Thailand, jade temples in China, and in Christian countries, the "pearly gates" to Heaven.

The earliest records of gems come from the earliest civilization, Sumer in Asia Minor. Stones dating back nearly 6000 years have been found. The popular style of the early period, lasting through the Roman Empire, was engraved stones, the scarab or beetle, being very common. Generally these were engraved from semi-precious stones, but emerald and ruby were sometimes used. Cameos and intaglios were also popular in the Roman period.

Diamond was known in Rome by A.D. 100, mentioned by Pliny. Julius Caesar was an avid gem collector, and if an emperor learned of a fine stone, it was easy to coerce the owner to contribute it to the crown. For example, the Koh-i-noor diamond was stolen in India and given to Queen Victoria in 1850 for the British crown jewels. Ratnapura, Ceylon (Sri Lanka) was known as the Valley of Gems in the tales of the Arabian Nights, and it is still one of the major sources of sapphires.

Economics: All gemstones are rare forms of common minerals, which themselves have very little value. There are all gradations in quality, with off-color or imperfect stones having value depending on the degree of perfection.

Workmanship has a great deal to do with value. A ruby that is not cut with the table (the flat surface on top) parallel to the base of the crystal (the basal pinacoid) will be pale and of less value. Perfection in faceting is essential to give maximum color, which is linked to value. Of course gemstones must be well polished without scratches on the facets.

Part of the intrisic value of gems is that great wealth can be concentrated in very small packets. People fearing persecution and loss of property may convert their holdings into gems. Likewise, at times of loss of confidence in government when economic systems are being grossly mismanaged and inflation is destroying values, people try to get assets in a form that will retain value. Gems are classic vehicles for these purposes. The surge in buying gems in the 1970s was based on general fear of economic mismanagement by even major governments.

When one thinks of gems as a refuge from inflation, he reads advertisements of jewelers that say "diamonds are forever." If someone rushes to the jewelry store and buys a few carats, then later turns around and tries to sell (or pawn) them, he is in for a rude shock. The retail markup on gems is *very* high. Unless one is willing to take the time to learn a great deal about gems and investigate the wholesale sources, then buy carefully and wisely, he will probably be better off with some other investment. Gold or platinum can be valued much more accurately, but of course a fortune in precious metals cannot be concealed in one's mouth.

CAVEAT EMPTOR

Never was the warning "let the buyer beware" more important than in buying gems. Venality springs eternal. There are more schemes to cheat the unwary in gems than in almost any other field. The greater the profit to be made by cheating, the greater the likelihood that it will take place. Some of the common methods are listed below.

Substitution: A colorless sapphire or quartz may be sold as a diamond, or a garnet or tourmaline for a ruby. These substitutions are quite easy to detect by a gemologist, but a novice may be "conned" by a convincing spiel.

Doublet: Two small precious stones may be cemented together on the *girdle* to simulate a more valuable large stone. This can generally be detected with a good hand lens, but if the stone is set, to do this is more difficult. Never buy a mounted stone without removing it from the setting for examination. Incidentally, just having a hand lens and knowing how to hold it, even if one does not know what he is looking at, will make the vendor's story stick much closer to the truth. Another form the doublet may take is to use a genuine stone for the portion above the girdle and a completely different stone below it. This can be a semi-precious stone or it may be colored glass, in which case detection may be more difficult if the glass is fused to the precious stone. This is called a semi-genuine doublet. If it is just cemented, boiling water will make the two fall apart. A false doublet may be made by using quartz above the girdle and colored glass below. If a cavity between two quartz pieces is filled with colored liquid it is called a hollow doublet.

Imitation: Counterfeiting precious stones from glass has developed into quite an art. A soft lead glass is used and this is called "paste" or "strass." Sometimes owners of fine stones have "paste" copies made and wear them, keeping the genuine stone locked in a vault. By dissolving lead in the glass it can be given the approximate specific gravity of a genuine stone and it also takes on high luster and dispersion of light. The recipe for imitation diamond is SiO_2 (41.2%), potash (8.4%), and litharge or red lead (50.4%). The glass will take a high polish but it can be easily scratched and, if worn, the sharp corners rapidly wear off and the luster disappears. Glass almost always has small bubbles in it.

Synthetic: The U.S. Federal Trade Commission requires use of this term for stones of gem quality fabricated from the same chemical compounds that occur in the natural stones. Many of the precious stones can now be made by combining the ingredients in proper proportions and fusing them, then growing a crystal from the melt. Rubies, sapphires, emeralds, and alexandrites can all be fabricated in this way. They are perfect in color and free of flaws, thus equal to the natural stone. An expert can usually distinguish between the synthetic and natural by the lack of flaws. All physical properties are identical.

PRECIOUS STONES

Brief mention of some of the more important gems will be made. Diamond has already been discussed in some detail in another chapter, since it is a very important industrial mineral.

Ruby (corundum): Crystal system is hexagonal, more commonly known as the prism. Specific gravity is 4.0; hardness, 9; composition of gemstone Al_2O_2 (97.32%), Fe_2O_3 (1.09%), and SiO_2 (1.21%). The color is the result of a small amount of chromium. In synthetics, as much as 4% potassium chromate may be added. The finest color is called "pigeon's blood" red. This has just a tinge of violet. The best rubies come from Burma, near Mandalay. Near the town of Mogok the rubies occur in an impure metamorphosed limestone. As the limestone erodes, the resistant rubies collect in the sands of the rivers draining the area. Limestone forms karst topography with many caverns, and in the alluvium of the caves rubies are also concentrated. Here sapphires and other colors of corundum are rare. Rubies are also found at Chanraburi in southeastern Thailand where they weather out of a basic basalt flow. At this location sapphires are more common and the rubies are not the best quality. Sri Lanka is another source of alluvial rubies that are thought to have eroded out of metamorphosed limestone. They are not common, but some of the finest stones are from this country. Rubies are also found in Afghanistan, Kampuchea, Zimbabwe, and, in the United States in North Carolina and Montana. A few have been found in Australia.

Sapphire (corundum): Physically the same as ruby. Composition is Al_2O_5 (97.51%), Fe_2O_3 (1.89%), and SiO_2 (0.80%). Thus it is higher in iron than ruby. The color is from a small amount of titanium. Some sapphires contain a star pattern showing six rays when well developed, which is apparent when the stone is cut cabachon (rounded) with the flat side perpendicular to the crystal axis. Apparently this phenomenon is caused by minute rods of rutile (titanium oxide) oriented parallel to the crystal axis. One of the most important occurrences is at Chanraburi in southeastern Thailand, where sapphires weather out of a basic basalt. Sri Lanka is particularly famous for sapphires, production going back nearly 2000 years. A series of hydroelectric dams is scheduled in one of the most famous gem valleys, the Mahaweli River, and the digging areas will be flooded. In order to salvage the gems, the government has leased areas to dredgers who plan to try to recover large quantities in a short time. This could mean that the sapphire price will drop in the 1980s; then after the stones are absorbed, will rise owing to lower production. There are many, widespread occurrences of sapphires in Australia. A restricted area in the mountains of Kashmir has produced some fine stones and they are known in the United States from North and South Carolina and Helena, Montana. In Europe they are found in the Iserwiese district of Bohemia, Czechoslovakia.

Chrysoberyl: Crystal system, rhombic; hardness, 8.5 (the third hardest mineral); specific gravity, 3.68–3.78; composition Al_2O_3 (78.92%), BeO (18.02%), Fe_2O_3 (3.48%), Cr_2O_3 (0.36%). There are two gemstones from this mineral. *Cymophane* is better known as cat's eye. The stone can be milky, white, bluish, or greenish white, and rarely golden yellow. It is cut cabachon and across the curved surface is a silvery line or streak of light that appears to move when the stone is turned. This is termed *chatoyance* and is caused by many microscopic cavities on the surface of the stone. It only occurs in the milky or cloudy stones. The most important occurrence is Minas Novas, Brazil, where it weathers out of granite and gneiss, found only in stream gravels. Sri Lanka is another famous locality for cat's eye. It occurs with the sapphires. The second and more valuable gem of chrysoberyl is *Alexandrite.* This gem is very rare and may be more valuable than diamond. It displays a remarkable dichroism or two distinct colors. In sunlight it is a grass green to emerald green, but in artificial light it is columbine-red to violet. Thus it looks like emerald by day and amethyst at night. The stone was named after Czar Alexander II of Russia, where it was first discovered in 1830 in the Ural Mountains. It occurs there with emerald. This was the only known occurrence for many years. It is now found in Sri Lanka, and the stones are finer than those from Russia. They are most highly prized in Russia.

Spinel: Crystal system, isometric, cubic, or octahedron; specific gravity 3.6; hardness 8; composition, Al_2O_3 (70.43%), magnesia (MgO), (26.75%), Cr_2O_3 (1.12%), and FeO (0.73%). The chromium is probably the source of the red color in the gem variety. A transparent stone may be difficult to distinguish by eye from ruby but with a polariscope it is readily differentiated because of the crystal systems. Perfect crystals are more common than rubies. The stone known as the Black Prince Ruby in the British crown jewels is actually a spinel of fine quality.

Beryl: Crystal system, hexagonal; specific gravity, 2.7; hardness, 7.5; composition (emerald) SiO_2 (67.85%), Al_2O_3 (17.95%), BeO (12.4%), MgO (0.9%), Na_2O (0.7%), water (1.66%). The variety of beryl with an intense green color is known as *emerald.* The color, undoubtedly caused by a small amount of chromic oxide, is so well known it is just called "emerald green." It is one of the softest precious stones, yet it is rated as more valuable than diamond. It is relatively brittle and there is a folk-tale that if a woman's emerald fractures or chips it is evidence of infidelity. The finest emeralds come from Colombia near Muzo where the crystals occur in black limestone with calcite crystals. At Muzo distribution appears to be random. Most crystals are cloudy, containing minute fractures, although with good color they are still valuable. The step cut is sometimes known as "emerald cut" since it is often used for this gem. The Indians of Peru had many fine emeralds, but they never disclosed the source to the Spanish and it has never been found. Other famous occurrences are in Upper Egypt near the Red Sea and in the Ural Mountains of Russia, in both localities from schist. Minor occurrences are in the Salzburg Alps, in North Carolina, and at a few points in Australia, usually in schist or pegmatite. Gems of similar appearance are green corundum, green garnet, hiddenite, which is very rare and more valuable than emerald, diopside, alexandrite, green tourmaline, and chrysolite. Much of the green material sold is glass, distinguished by being soft. Some good quality synthetic emerald is now being grown. *Aquamarine* is a much more common gem of beryl composition but light blue to greenish blue in color. A rose-red variety is known as *morganite*, and *golden beryl* is yellow. Aquamarine is a beautiful stone and the only reason why its price is low is because it is not sufficiently rare. It is abundant in Minas Novas, Brazil and in Mursinka, Ural Mountains, Russia. It is found in India, Australia, Europe, and the United States.

Topaz: Crystal system, rhombic; specific gravity, 3.55; hardness, 8; composition, SiO_2 (33.3%), Al_2O_3 (56.5%); fluorine (F) (17.6%). Crystals as large as 137 pounds (63 kg) have been found. It has perfect cleavage, which makes it susceptible to fracture. When colorless it resembles diamond. It is frequently pale blue to blue and close to aquamarine in color. There are many shades of yellow, but a natural red is rare. However, yellow topaz when heated and cooled carefully will become rose-red. Topaz in small crystals is common in granite, gneiss, and crystalline schist formed by fluorine in the magmatic vapors. Famous localities are Saxony, Minas Geraes, Brazil, the Urals of Russia, Sri Lanka, and Australia.

Zircon: Crystal system, tetragonal; specific gravity, 4.61–4.82; hardness, 7.5; composition, SiO_2 (23.77%), ZrO_2 (76.23%). In the reddish-yellow color range (orange) it is known as *hyacinth*, which has brilliance and luster. A garnet has very nearly the same color, called hessonite, but frequently sold as the more precious hyacinth. The color is apparently the result of small amounts of contained iron. Small crystals of zircon are very common in igneous rocks. The only important source of gem quality zircon is Sri Lanka in the gem gravels.

Tourmaline: Crystal system, hexagonal (usually prisms); specific gravity, 3.0–3.2; hardness, 7.25; composition, H_9Al_3 $(B.OH)_2$ Si_4O_{19}. This is a general formula; the H_9 may be replaced by variable amounts of Al, Fe, Mg, Na, or K. A representative analysis of dark blue tourmaline is SiO_2 (36.22%), B_2O (10.65%), Al_2O_3 (33.35%), FeO (11.95%), MnO (1.25%), MgO (0.63%), Na_2O (1.75%), K_2O (0.40%), Li_2O (0.84%), H_2O (2.21%), F (0.82%). Most tourmaline is black (high in iron) and the colored varieties are opaque. Only the transparent varieties are used as a gem and then special names are applied to them. Schorl is colorless and not used as a gem. Red is known as rubellite and it may be as beautiful as ruby. Blue is rare, known as indicolite. Brown tourmaline is known as dravite and can range from greenish-brown to straw yellow. A peculiar form found in Chesterfield, Massachusetts is green on the outside and red on the inside. Known as watermelon tourmaline, it is a curiosity only. Tourmaline is most commonly found in crystalline rock such as granite. The most important gem localities are Brazil, Sri Lanka, and Russia where beautiful red stones occur in the Ural Mountains (Siberian ruby). The same variety is found in Burma and near Paris, Maine, in the United States.

Garnet: Crystal system, isometric, very commonly as the rhombic dodecahedron (24 faces); specific gravity, 3.4–4.3; hardness, 6.5–8. Garnet comprises a whole family of minerals, complex silicates with variable metallic components. Demantoid, SiO_2 (35.50%), Cr_2O_3 (0.70%), Fe_2O_3 (31.51%), CaO (32.9%), MgO (0.21%), Pyrope, SiO_2 (41.35%), Al_2O_3 (22.35%), Cr_2O_3 (4.45%), FeO (9.94%), MnO (2.59%), CaO (5.29%), MgO (15.0%). Garnet is a metamorphic mineral, occurring in schist and gneiss or in contact zones.

(1) Hessonite or "cinnamon stone," rich yellowish red color often mistaken for hyacinth (zircon) or even more difficult to distinguish from rubicelle (spinel). Occurs abundantly in Sri Lanka.

(2) Alamandine, formerly called carbuncle. The color is deep red and is sometimes called precious garnet. It may closely approach ruby in color. Sri Lanka is the most important source of this variety, which is sometimes called Ceylon ruby. It is widespread in India and is found also at Minas Novas, Brazil, Northern Territory of Australia, east Africa, the Alps, and in Spain.

(3) Pyrope or Bohemian garnet is a deep, rich, blood-red color. It is a magnesian garnet and occurs with diamond or in metamorphic rocks. The most famous locality is in Bohemia (Czechoslovakia) where pyrope is sold by the "loth" (equal to 16²/₃ grams). In the United States they are called "Colorado" or "Arizona rubies" after states where they are found. "Cape ruby" comes from the diamond pipes of South Africa.

(4) Demantoid beautiful emerald green to yellowish, occurs in the Urals.

Precious Opal: Amorphous (non-crystalline); specific gravity, 1.9–2.3 (lightest of the precious stones); hardness 5.5–6.5 (soft for a precious stone). Composition, SiO_2 (90%), water 10%, traces of other compounds. Opal is translucent and ordinarily almost colorless. Precious opal is noted for its beautiful play of colors. White (milk opal) does not have the play of colors. The famous localities are Hungary, Australia, Honduras, and, for fire opal, Mexico. Opal generally occurs in quite recent volcanic rocks.

Jade: The name is given to three distinct mineral species that look very much alike and have virtually identical properties. The minerals are nephrite (an amphibole high in lime), jadeite (a pyroxene high in soda), and chloro-melanite (fairly high in both soda and lime). One of the principal characteristics of jade is its extreme toughness. The minerals consist of a felted mass of fibers, interwoven rather than oriented. It is almost impossible to break a rounded pebble with a hammer. Primitive people made it into tools such as the axe and adze, taking advantage of the toughness. It is particularly prized in the Orient where it is called *yu* by the Chinese. Jade is most commonly carved into figures. The most highly prized colors are creamy white (mutton-fat jade) and a deep emerald green, although a wide range of colors occurs — apple green, pink, brown (a weathering color), and nearly black. Hardness ranges from 5.5–6.0 for nephrite and 6.5–7.0 for jadeite. The specific gravity of nephrite is 2.9–3.0, that of jadeite, 3.3. While jade is the favorite stone in China, there is argument as to whether it occurs there or has all been imported. It appears that nephrite does occur but the fine jadeite is brought in from the famous locality in northern Burma near Sanka on the Uru River. Nephrite is abundant on the west side of South Island, New Zealand and the Maoris worked it into tools and ornaments. Huge boulders of nephrite of fine quality have been found in British Columbia. There has been substantial production from Wyoming, and it is found on the California coast. It is found in Central America, from Colombia to Mexico but is rare. Some material of jade composition has been found in the Alps. The occurrence is with the very basic rocks of the type known as alpine ophiolites. Imitation objects of chrysoprase (quartz variety) are common in Australia and they are of equal beauty. Serpentine (very soft) and glass are other imitations.

Quartz: Crystallization, hexagonal; specific gravity, 2.65; hardness, 7.0; composition 100% SiO_2. Quartz is classed as a semiprecious mineral largely because it is common, thus lacking that quality of rareness required by gems. On a weight basis it probably makes up 85% of the gemstone trade. It is sold under many names. Some of the more common are:

(1) Amethyst. Lovely deep violet color which should be without flaws or clouds or off-color zones. Oriental amethyst is the precious stone of the composition of ruby and sapphire. The two most famous sources are Brazil and Sri Lanka, but it occurs in many other places.

(2) Citrine is a yellow quartz. Much of it is prepared by heating amethyst or smoky quartz. It greatly resembles yellow topaz. It occurs in southern Brazil and in Minas Geraes.

(3) Rose quartz, called bohemian ruby, can be a fine pink to rose-red color. It is found in Sri Lanka, Brazil, India, the Urals, and the Black Hills of South Dakota.

(4) Prase is a translucent variety leek-green in color formerly called "mother of emerald." It occurs abundantly and is very low priced.

(5) Sapphire-quartz is a little used blue, crystalline quartz. It is found in veins at Mooseck, Salzburg, Austria.

(6) Venus hair, or flêches d'amour, is a quartz with fibers of asbestos or thin prismatic crystals of rutile inside.

(7) Cat's eye. Some quartz has the property of chatoyance, a wave of milky light when cut cabachon, similar to cymophane (chrysoberyl), caused by enclosed parallel asbestos fibers.

(8) Hawk's-eye is identical to tiger-eye, but the colors are blue. The color is caused by fibers of the blue asbestos mineral, crocidolite. It is the same condition as sapphire quartz only in the latter the fibers are not oriented parallel to each other. When the crocidolite is altered, it breaks down to limonite, hydrated iron oxide, and the fibers become yellow to brown, creating the tiger-eye.

(9) Tiger eye is a quartz with a fine fibrous structure, yellow to brown in color with a sikly luster which reflects on every alternate band. When the stone is shifted slightly, the alternate bands reflect. It is this shifting of light that makes the stone attractive. It comes from South Africa, where it is quite common.

(10) In Petrified wood, wood fibers are replaced by quartz, sometimes in brilliant colors. Wood fossilized in this manner is shaped and polished into attractive ornaments. Petrified Forest National Monument in Arizona is an outstanding occurrence.

(11) Chrysoprase is a very fine grained translucent quartz hornstone with a beautiful apple- to jade-green color. The color is from the nickel silicate present in the hydrated form. One shortcoming is that it tends to lose water of hydration, and hence its color. However, the color can be restored by immersing it for a time, and in fact, some dull chalcedony can be turned into chrysoprase by immersing it in nickel sulphate solution. The result may be superior and more permanent than the natural stone. It is brittle and must not be heated in working or it will lose its color. It occurs in Germany, at Riddle, Oregon, and abundantly in Australia, where it is produced extensively.

(12) Avanturine is usually reddish-brown to yellow. This form of quartz seems to have a metallic sheen that is caused by the enclosure of scales of mica. It is found in the Urals of Russia, India, and China where the green variety is highly prized. Avanturine glass is made by a secret process that consists of adding copper (2½%) to a glass that melts at a temperature below the melting point of copper. The product is beautiful, usually more so than the natural stone.

(13) Jasper is an impure, massive, very fine grained quartz with a dull luster and conchoidal (glass-like) fracture. Iron oxide is one of the main impurities, and shades of red to brown to yellow are most common. It occurs in nearly every country. The forms are opaque.

(14) Chalcedony is a microcrystalline form of quartz that is very common, used by stone-age people for arrow heads, spear points, and axe heads. Usually a dull color, but colored varieties can be very attractive. It is known by many names. "Flint" is the form for tools, and several other forms are listed below. The forms are translucent.

(15) Carnelian is a red chalcedony used as beads by pre-historic people. It takes a nice polish. It is flesh-red, and very common.

(16) Sard is brown carnelian.

(17) Plasma is green chalcedony, common in ancient Rome but the source is unknown. It is found in India and Egypt.

(18) Heliotrope or blood stone is plasma with bright red specks in it. It is common from India, Brazil, and Australia.

(19) Agate is a whole family of similar forms of chalcedony. It is built up in layers that may have different colors. If bands of pronounced different color alternate, it is called *onyx* (named for the prominent color, like carnelian agate). Other names prefixed are ring-, eye-, fortification-, land-scape-, ruin-, cloud-, star-, shell-, coral-, and moss. Agate dyeing and cutting is done on a production line basis, with the methods used in obtaining the colors being closely guarded trade secrets, with much of the work done in Germany. However, there are many small "mom and pop" lapidaries working these stones. Black agate is apparently produced by immersing the stone in a solution of honey and water for a few weeks at a temperature slightly below boiling, adding water as needed. Then it is immersed in hot sulphuric acid. The sugar that has been absorbed is carbonized, turning the stone black. Green agate is very common and attractive, the green coming from nickel sulphate.

Lapis Luzuli: Crystal system, isometric (rhombic dodecahedron), but crystals rare; specific gravity, 2.4; hardness, 5.5, composition, SiO_2 (43.26%), Al_2O_3 (22.22%), Fe_2O_3 (4.20%), CaO (14.73%), Na_2O (8.76%), SO_2 (5.67%), S (3.16%), but highly variable. The stone is opaque and the value is dependent on the beautiful blue color, which should be a dark azure with some black zones and some white spots which are calcite. Normally there are small crystals of pyrite scattered through it. Heat treating pale stones darkens them and enhances the value. The color is the result of the mineral hauynite which predominates, and *ultramarine.* The most famous occurrence is in northeastern Afghanistan, visited about 1271 by Marco Polo. Another locality is Lake Baikal, Siberia. It is abundant in the Andes in Chile and from Mount Vesuvius in Italy.

Turquoise: Never occurs as distinct crystals. Specific gravity, 2.6–2.8; hardness, 6.0; composition, Al_2O_3 (47.45%), Fe_2O_3 (10%), CuO, (2.02%), CaO (1.85%), MnO (0.50%), P_2O_5 (28.90%), water (18.18%). Thus it is a hydrated aluminum phosphate, dependent on copper for its medium blue to green color. The blue color tends to fade on exposure. It is formed during weathering in desert lands and Persia (Iran) was an ancient source of fine stones. It generally occurs in thin veinlets and in mining, a fracture a few millimeters thick will be followed as far as possible. The Sinai peninsula of Egypt is a famous location. In the United States it was found in New Mexico, Arizona, southern Colorado, and in Utah. Its mineral name is calaite, a name that is virtually unknown. Much of what is sold as turquoise today is artificial or imitation. Commonly a turquoise glaze is put on a ceramic base. Large pieces are rarely genuine, but the imitation pieces are sold for high prices.

Other Gemstones: Several other mineral species occasionally occur as fine stones which are used as gems. Only a few warrant mention here. *Amber* is a fossilized resin that may be deep yellow to red in color. It was one of the earliest gems used, being a medium of exchange in Europe in the Neolithic period. It is very soft, but is made into necklaces or carved into figures. Plastic imitations are common. *Peridot* is a form of the very common mineral olivine which is sometimes cut as a deep green gem. Another name for the same stone is chrysolite. It is about the color of bottle glass, hence little value is placed on it. Names one may occasionally hear are feldspar, andalusite, kyanite, axinite, idiocrase, cordierite, dioptase, epidote, sphene, prehnite, chrysocolla, and obsidian. Staurolite occurs as interpenetration twins known as fairy crosses, more of a curiosity, but worn as a pendant. Another curiosity is the tektite, also called moldavite, rizalite or many other place names. These are dark brown to black droplets of glass which have passed through the atmosphere. Apparently the product of impact melting when large meteors strike earth, they were blasted into orbit and melted on re-entry. They have a peculiar pitted surface. They are composed of glass of composition of andesite or normal continental rocks. If cut, they lose their luster rapidly because of their softness. Very small ones are sometimes mounted whole in rings or earrings or worn as pendants.

Source information on gems is readily available, but one outstanding voluminous work on the subject is *Precious Stones*, by Dr. Max Bauer published in German in1896 and translated and published in England in 1906. It has been reprinted by Charles E. Tuttle Company, Rutland, Vermont in 1969. Anyone moderately interested in gems should obtain this volume.

Alchemy: The pre-industrial revolution, sub-scientific efforts at chemical investigations. They generally involved mystical approaches and largely concentrated on transmuting base metals into gold or silver.

Alteration: Any change in the mineralogic composition of a rock brought about by physical or chemical means, especially by action of hydrothermal solutions or weathering.

Amber: Resin of a tree which has been indurated (fossilized) and is prized for its yellowish brown to red color.

Anfo: Ammonium nitrate (fertilizer) plus fuel oil, which is a widely used heavy explosive in mining.

Aqua regia: A mixture of equal parts of hydrochloric and nitric acids. This is one of the few substances which will dissolve the "noble" metals, gold and platinum.

Arbiter process: A hydrometallurgical process for extracting copper from sulphide concentrates by ammonia and oxygen followed by solvent extraction and electrowinning.

Beneficiation: Any process for increasing the grade of an ore mineral. It is a concentration process, such as gravity concentration or flotation.

Blast furnace: A large furnace commonly used in production of pig iron. Ore, coke, and a mineral to facilitate production of fluid slag (limestone or silica depending on the ore) are fed in at the top and air or oxygen blown in to burn the coke, reduce the iron, and melt the iron and slag.

Block caving: A large-scale low-cost, underground mining method involving blocks as large as 60 X 60 X 200 m which are undercut and break up by slumping downward. The method is used when large blocks of ground are quite uniformly mineralized and fractured.

Blue earth: Unoxidized slate-blue to blue-green brecciated rock in the diamond pipes, the Kimberlite below the zone of weathering.

Brass: Alloy of copper and zinc first used in the Roman Empire.

Breast: In flat-lying ore bodies the working face is sometimes called the "breast."

Bronze Age: Bronze, composed of copper and tin, was the first alloy manufactured by man. The metal so dominated early civilization that the name was given to the period. The age continued from about 3200 B.C. to 1200 B.C.

Calcining: A pyrometallurgical process involving heating to the point that a chemical change takes place. It may involve driving off water or hydration of carbon dioxide.

Cartel: A group of producers of a commodity who form an agreement to restrict production and set prices that are not related directly to costs (e.g., OPEC).

Cast iron: Iron that is melted on reduction in a crucible or furnace and can be poured into a mold.

Cathode copper: Copper refined by the electrolytic process. Copper goes into solution from the anode and plates on the cathode.

Cathodic protection: A metal to be protected is connected electrically with a more easily corroded metal such as magnesium. This sets up an electrical circuit which corrodes the sacrificial anode (magnesium), while the metal to be protected (like iron in a pipeline) is unaffected.

Chalcolithic Age: The spreading of the use of the first metal, copper, gave its name to the period 4200–3200 B.C.

Chalk: A soft and frequently impure form of limestone formed from the shells of foraminifera.

Chert: Fine-grained sedimentary rock composed of silica (SiO_2) used by primitive men for tools because of its hardness and characteristic fracture which leaves a sharp edge. In part referred to as "flint."

Concentrate: The product of a process, usually hydrometallurgical, of increasing the grade of an ore by selectively removing the waste portion. It is the product that goes to the refining stage.

Continuous miner: A large mining machine used in rather thin, flat-lying beds of soft ore (coal, salt, potash, trona). It has a rotating head with many cutter teeth which tear out chunks of the ore and transfer them to a belt conveyor for removal from the face or breast. It can mine a large tonnage at low cost. It is used in room and pillar and longwall retreating methods.

Converter: A massive pyrometallurgical device that is used in refining copper matte or pig iron. Air is blown through the molten mass to oxidize and remove unwanted constituents.

Cut-and-fill: A method of mining steeply dipping ore bodies where the ore is removed from the stope after blasting and waste is put back in to fill the void, leaving enough room to drill and blast the next cut from overhead.

Cut-off grade: The minimum mineral content that can be profitably mined. This fluctuates with price of product, taxes, and other costs.

Cyanidation: A hydrometallurgical process for recovering gold and silver from ores involving dissolving the precious metal in a potassium cyanide solution and precipitation by zinc powder or carbon-in-pulp.

CYMET: A hydrometallurgical process for refining copper concentrates by solution developed by Cyprus Mines, in pilot plant stage of development.

Depletion: A mine has a finite quantity of mineral and once it has been produced the mine is forced to close. The extraction of the mineral is said to deplete the deposit.

Diapir: A body of rock which cuts through other rocks as a result of squeezing and plastic flow, intrusion, or explosion.

Dipper: The bucket on a shovel.

Distillation: A process of refining a metal by vaporizing the product and condensing it externally. Mercury and zinc are refined by this method.

Doublet: Two smaller gemstones cemented together on the girdle to give the appearance of a larger and more valuable gem.

Draw points: Openings into an ore zone where the ore is removed for transport out of the mine.

Draw raise: A passage between a transportation level and the ore zone that is used in removing ore from a stope.

Dredging: The method of mining loose materials covered by water. Requires a drag line or machinery mounted on a barge or boat. It usually includes the separatory equipment as well.

Dross: The scum that forms on the top of a molten metal in smelting.

Drift: A passage driven more or less horizontal along a vein to provide access to an ore zone and commonly transportation of ore.

Electromagnetic prospecting: Exploration that involves use of a magnetic field induced by alternating current. The field is induced by a coil and can be used on the ground or from aircraft.

Electrometallurgy: A method of refining metals involving either plating in a liquid bath (copper) or separating in a molten bath (aluminum).

Electromotive series: A table in which the metals (and a few non-metals) are arranged according to the voltage developed relative to hydrogen as 0.0 v. The most reactive with negative potential (lithium) is commonly first and least reactive (gold) last.

Electrostatic concentration: A method of separating minerals that depends on the differences in attraction and repulsion in a strong electrical field.

Eluvium: An accumulation of weathered rock on or at the foot of the slope where it originated.

Evaporite: A sedimentary rock produced by evaporation of a saline brine beyond the point of solubility of a mineral, such as salt, potash, trona. May be formed in a salt lake or an isolated arm of the sea in a desert region.

Flash smelter: A method of pyrometallurgy used in refining copper. It is a special design of reverberatory furnace that increases SO_2 in the gases, improving pollution control.

Flint: Fine-grained sedimentary rock composed largely of silica. Originally the term was restricted to nodules of silica in the Cretaceous limestones of Europe. The term was imported into the U.S. and used for a chalcedony or chert used by the Indians in making tools.

Float: Minerals or rock fragments that have been displaced from their original source after being detached. Transport can be by gravity, glacier, streams, or waves.

Flotation: A hydrometallurgical process for concentrating ore minerals by selectively attaching artificial bubbles to economic minerals, resulting in the bubbles and ore particles floating to the top where they are collected.

Frasch process: The method of recovering elemental sulphur from limestone by injecting superheated steam through a well, melting the sulphur and pumping the molten sulphur to the surface.

Galvanizing: Used here in the common (but incorrect) sense of applying a coating of zinc to iron to protect it from rusting.

Gaseous diffusion: A method of separating isotopes depending on the slightly greater passage of the lighter isotope through a membrane, for example ^{235}U from ^{238}U using the compound uranium hexafloride.

Gasohol: A mixture of gasoline and 10–15% ethyl alcohol which can be burned in automobile engines without modification of the carburetor.

Geochemistry: A study of the chemical properties of earth materials. It is applied to exploration by measuring the different concentrations of elements in alluvium, soil or rock with anomalously high concentrations indicating possible ore deposits.

Geophysics: Application of physical processes to studies of the earth. Where different minerals have sufficiently different physical properties from their host rocks and occur in large enough concentrations to be detected, this can be applied to exploration. Examples are magnetism and resistivity.

Geothermal: Thermal energy contained within rocks. Generally refers to energy that can be recovered and utilized economically.

Girdle: On a faceted gemstone, the widest circumference of the stone, the portion grasped by the mounting. It separates the "crown" from the "pavillion."

Gravity concentration: A method of separating minerals which depends on their differences in specific gravity. Examples are jigs and heavy media separation.

Green pellets: Soft rounded mixtures of a mineral and binder. If the binder is a cement it will harden naturally. If a clay, such as iron pellets, the pellets must be heated to give them cohesion.

Heading: An underground horizontal mine working that is being extended by mining.

Heavy media separation: A means of separating minerals dependent on differences in specific gravity. A finely-ground, heavy material such as ferrosilicon is suspended in liquid (usually water) by agitation and the concentration is closely controlled to fall between the specific gravity of the minerals to be separated. The light minerals overflow and the heavy minerals sink and are drawn off. Also called the "sink-float process."

Holocene: The geological term for the present interglacial dating from about 11,500 B.P. The Neolithic Age of the archeologist commenced at the same time.

Hydrometallurgy: A method of separating minerals and selectively concentrating a valuable constituent in a medium of water. Example flotation.

Ice Age: Period of continental glaciation when sea level dropped as much as 100–150 m as water was heaped on the continents in the form of ice sheets. The last glacial stage ended about 11,500 B.P. There have been more than four in the last 2 million years.

Induced polarization: A geophysical exploration method involving charging the natural battery set up around sulphides and a few other minerals and measuring the response. Useful in discovering concentrations of sulphides.

Interglacial: Stage between times of continental glaciation when sea level was high, as it is today. Such periods last many thousands of years.

Intrinsic: Value attributed by man distinct from utilitarian value, e.g., beauty of a flower, desirability of gold.

Intumescence: The property of swelling. Here the mineral mass is heated to the melting point and gas released at that point (SO_2, CO_2) causes the mass to puff up with formation of bubbles that are retained on cooling.

Isogons: Lines on a map connecting points of equal magnetic declination or deviation of a compass from true north.

Jig: A device for separating fairly coarse minerals according to their difference in specific gravity. It is usually done with water as the medium and involves pulsing the fluid from the bottom, permitting the heavy particles to sink, where they are drawn off.

Jumbo: A machine mounting two or more drills used in drilling large rock faces. Usually the drills are air powered.

Karst topography: Terrain that develops on limestone outcrops as the result of differential weathering and solution. Caverns develop and drain the area and when large enough their roofs collapse. The result when maturely developed is an area of rounded hills with intervening valleys with no streams flowing through.

Kuroko: Japanese for "black ore" which is a volcanogenic massive sulphide ore of copper, zinc, barite, pyrite, and other minor minerals.

Laterization: Characteristic weathering of large masses of intermediate to ultrabasic rocks in the tropics in which silica, calcium, and magnesium oxides are removed and alumina, nickel, cobalt, platinum, gold, titanium, and iron are concentrated in the residue.

Leaching: A hydrometallurgical method of selectively dissolving a mineral constituent from an ore then recovering it from solution. Examples vat, heap and *in situ* leaching.

LIX: Abbreviation for *L*iquid *I*on e*X*change, a system of hydrometallurgical concentration of metals such as copper.

Lode: A miner's term for a mineral deposit, usually a vein, pod, or lens.

Longwall retreating: A method of underground mining of nearly flat lying mineral deposits (coat, salt, potash, trona) commencing at the boundary of the deposit or property and mining back toward the entry, permitting the surface to cave and drop to a new level.

Luddites: Ned Lud, a mentally deficient youth, smashed a stocking weaving machine early in the Industrial Revolution. Workers opposed to the introduction of machines adopted the name Luddites and smashed other machines. Now the term applies to anti-intellectuals and anti-progress groups.

Magnetic anomaly: A magnetic force field of unusual intensity, usually indicating above average magnetite in the rocks.

Magnetic concentration: A method of separating minerals based on their different magnetic susceptibility. The magnetic mineral is attracted to the magnet and removed from the non-magnetic. Usually the magnetic mineral is the valuable one, but in ceramics the reverse is true.

Magnetometer: An instrument used to measure the intensity of the earth's magnetic field. It is used in exploration with anomalous fields sometimes indicating valuable mineral concentrations.

Manda: A hypothetical unit of exchange equal to the energy output of one man in one day, approximately four horse power hours, or 10,188 BTU or 2566.8 Calories.

Marine nodules: Agglomerations of metals formed on the deep ocean floor containing about 25% manganese (hence sometimes called "manganese nodules") plus variable amounts of nickel, copper, molybdenum, cobalt, and other minor constituents. Today they are protoresources which may soon become economic.

Matte smelting: A pyrometallurgical process for converting a concentrate into a melt with controlled sulphur content. It is done in a reverberatory furnace.

Mesh: refers to size of standard sieves used in grading sizes of mineral particles. Unfortunately there are several different standards with slightly different specifications. The main ones are Tyler, ASTM, and metric. For example, 100 mesh means there are 100 holes per linear inch (Tyler).

Mesolithic: Middle Stone Age. Man developed bifacial stone tools. The time range was from 50,000 to 10,000 B.P. *Homo neandertalensis* dominated in Europe during the early portion, *Cro Magnon* man in the latter part.

Middling: In hydrometallurgical concentration a product which does not contain enough of the valuable constituent to go into the concentrate but too much to throw away. It requires further treatment.

Mill: (1) a machine for grinding ore. (2) A building housing the concentration plant. (3) The process of concentrating the ore mineral.

Mineral policy: The sum total of laws, regulations, agreements, and customs that affect the production, utilization, conservation of and commerce in mineral commodities.

Mother liquor: Residual concentrated brine solution after salt (NaCl) has been precipitated by evaporation.

Neolithic Age: New Stone Age dating from about 10,000 B.P. to 6000 B.P. or to the beginning of the use of metals.

Nephrite: One of the jade minerals, commonly green in color. Because it is very tough and fairly hard it was used in Neolithic tools in some regions.

Nuclear cross section: A measure of the frequency of collisions between neutrons and an atomic nucleus. Zirconium is low, hafnium high. The unit of measure is the barn, 10^{-24} cm^2.

Obsidian: A hard, black to brown volcanic glass which fractures conchoidally with a sharp edge, making it a good stone for tools.

Open hearth: A pyrometallurgic furnace for making steel.

Open pit mining: Method for mining deposits of minerals which occur close to the surface involving removal of overburden then the ore. Frequently this is on a very large scale, involving hundreds of thousands of tons per day.

Ophiolite: A distinctive suite of basic to ultrabasic rocks which formed on the ocean floor but is tectonically trapped in continental or island arc crust.

Order of magnitude: Difference in size by a factor of ten. A kilometer is three orders of magnitude longer than a meter.

Paleolithic: The old Stone Age extending from the first use of crude stone tools to about 50,000 B.P.

Photoelectric sorting: A method of concentrating minerals based on a marked difference in reflectivity (white from black). A photoelectric cell "sees" the light particle which actuates a mechanism pushing or blowing the selected particle out of the conveyor stream. Used for coarse diamonds with x-ray energy source.

Pickling steel: A cleaning process that washes the surface of steel with an acid solution.

Pikul: The largest weight one man can carry (133$\frac{1}{3}$ pounds or 60.5 kg), used as a standard in selling tin.

Pisolite: A small generally spherical mineral aggregate that has built up around a core particle. Bauxite and some limestones form in this way.

Placer (short "a"): A concentration by moving water, generally a stream, of valuable minerals which have been liberated from rock including gold, platinum, diamonds, tin, etc.

Playa: A shallow desert lake basin, dry most of the year, usually leaving deposits of soluble salts after evaporation of the water.

Pliocene: On the geological time scale from about 5 M.Y. to 1.8 M.Y.B.P. Period in which man developed from ancestral creatures.

Pluton: A body of intrusive igneous rock.

Porphyry copper: A disseminated deposit of copper minerals formed by thermal solutions permeating through a volume of rock. The solutions are mobilized and probably sourced from an intrusive sequence, at least part of which is rock with a porphyritic texture, i.e., with two distinct sizes of crystal grains, which can be large.

Protoresource: A mineral composite which will probably become an economic resource in the future. Uranium made this jump in 1945. Oil shale and marine nodules are in this class today.

Pyrometallurgy: Fire refining of a metal.

Quartzite: A rock composed of silica (SiO_2) which has been metamorphosed from sand into a compact, dense stone that breaks with conchoidal fracture leaving a sharp edge which led to its use in tools.

Radiocarbon date: Cosmic rays striking earth convert a portion of the nitrogen (^{14}N) to radioactive carbon (^{14}C) which has a half life of 5730 years. Since the flux of cosmic rays is on average constant, the ^{14}C reservoir is constant and the proportion of the isotope can be measured on charcoal, wood, etc. The rate of decay is a measure of time since death. Effective to about 35,000 B.P. Great care must be taken to avoid contamination by older or younger carbon.

Raise: A mine working driven from one level to a higher level to provide access between levels.

Refining: The metallurgical process of producing a product with the specifications required by industry from a concentrate or raw ore. It may be pyrometallurgy, electro-metallurgy, or in some cases hydrometallurgy.

Refractory: In the metallurgical sense (1) an ore that is hard to treat (2) a product used to line a pyrometallurgical furnace which melts at a higher temperature than the process material and does not react with it.

Remote sensing: Any means of measuring physical properties from a distance, most commonly from the air or from a satellite. The meaning used here applies to properties of rocks or minerals.

Reserves: Mineral resources that have been measured to the extent to satisfy the engineer for planning extraction.

Resistivity survey: A geophysical method of exploration involving measuring differences in resistivity of terrain. Low resistivity sometimes indicates sulphide mineralization.

Resources: Quantities of mineral that are technically reasonable to expect after detailed exploration and development have been conducted.

Roasting: A pyrometallurgical method of treating mineral concentrate, commonly to oxidize the ore and drive off sulphur. Frequently a source of pollution.

Roll front: An ore body of uranium or vanadium in sandstone, usually narrow and "c" or "s" shaped in cross section, much longer in the third dimension. It is a location of oxidation and reduction.

Room and pillar mining: A method of underground mining of flat-lying to gently dipping ore zones involving mining out rectangular portions of the ore (rooms) but leaving major portions to support the overlying ground. The width of the rooms should be such that stress will arch and transfer to the pillars. Coal and non-metallics are mined by this method. From 40–60% of the ore is left in the pillars.

Scintillation counter: An instrument used to measure intensity of radiation. It is used in exploration for uranium and thorium. A detector intercepts the radiation and converts it to light (photons) and a photomultiplier tube amplifies the light which is then converted to electricity and measured on a meter.

Scrying: Crystal gazing, used by "fortune tellers."

Schon's law: Almost nothing new works.

Seigniorage: The difference between the market price of a metal and an arbitrary value assigned to it for monetary purposes.

Severance tax: A tax on gross production of a resource independent of profit. Producers dislike this tax because it does not drop if a company loses money. Thus it shrinks the nations mineral reserves, causes "high grading" of a mine.

Shaft: A hole downward, vertically or at an angle, to enter a mineral zone.

Shaking table: A gravity concentrating device for medium fine ore minerals. The table has low rifles along its length and is tilted perpendicular to the length. It is bounced vertically and shaken parallel to the length. Minerals with water are fed at a top corner and light particles jump over the riffles while heavies are transported lengthwise, where they are collected.

Shrinkage stoping: A method of mining steeply dipping veins where the walls are quite strong. After blasting, enough of the ore is removed to permit working in the stope to drill the next overhead block. After the entire stope has been broken and about one-third of the ore removed, the balance is drawn from the bottom as needed. Commonly the stope is refilled with waste after ore is removed.

Sintering: Heating an ore or concentrate to the point of incipient fusion at which point the particles will stick together.

Slag: The waste product from pyrometallurgy.

Solution mining: Dissolving or melting the ore minerals directly from the ground. Uranium and sulphur are mixed by this method.

Solvent extraction: A hydrometallurgical method of extracting valuable metals from dilute solution by using a LIX reagent in kerosene, which can then easily be separated from the water. The metal, commonly copper, can then be separated from the kerosene solution by sulphuric acid and plated out by electrolysis.

Sponge iron: Iron reduced from the oxide to the metallic state without melting. Particles stick together but the mass is porous, like a sponge.

Square set stoping: A method of mining veins where the walls and ore are weak and require timber framework for support. Since it uses much timber and labor, it can only be used for rich ores.

Stainless steel: An alloy principally of iron and chromium (to 13%), with some nickel and other elements for special products.

Steel: Alloy of iron and carbon with other metals (molybdenum, nickel, chromium, tungsten, cobalt, manganese, vanadium, etc.) to give it special properties.

Stockwork: A system of strong but discontinuous and intersecting fractures creating permeability which is frequently the locus of ore deposition.

Stripping: (1) In mining, the removal of waste in an open pit mine. (2) In hydrometallurgy, removing metal from solution in solvent extraction.

Sublevel stoping: A mining method applied to large veins which are not amenable to caving methods. Little timber is required so costs are moderate.

Taconite: A low-grade ore of iron (magnetite) that can be concentrated magnetically and is commonly sintered or pelletized for blast furnace feed.

Telethermal: An ore deposit formed at a fairly low temperature by circulating hot water and at shallow depth with little wall rock alteration.

Tuyères: Openings into a smelter blast furnace where air or oxygen is blown into the firing zone to support combustion.

Ultramarine: Now an artificial azure blue pigment. Formerly a natural mineral comprising a portion of lapis luzuli which was ground and used by artists. It was then very expensive.

Ultramafics: Igneous rock low in silica, composed of very basic minerals, e.g., dunite, peridotite.

Valence: In chemistry, the property of an element that determines the number of other atoms with which an atom of the element can combine.

Vein: A structural break in rocks that have been permeated by hydrothermal solutions, dissolving some of the rock constituents and replacing them with foreign minerals. Sometimes the added minerals are valuable and sufficiently concentrated to mine. They may range in width from a few millimeters to over 100 meters and vertically to over a kilometer and along the length to 10s of kilometers, although most are considerably shorter than this.

Volcanic ash: Finely pulverized rock blown out of a volcano during eruption.

Wire bar: Copper that has been electrolytically refined and melted then cast into a standard size for drawing into wire. It is the common form sold in the market.

M. Bauer, *Precious Stones*. C. E. Tuttle Co., 1969 (republished version of original, 1896; English version 1904, plus new material) 647 pages. Part 1: General Characteristics of precious stones; Part 2: Systematic description of precious stones; Part 3: The determination and distinguishing of precious stones; Appendices, Pearls and Coral, Synthetic Gems. Comprehensive study of gems and their raw materials for the interested amateur and the expert. Well illustrated.

R. W. Boyle, Geochemistry of Gold and its Deposits. *Geological Survey of Canada Bulletin 280*, 1979, p. 584. A comprehensive and well-prepared study of gold deposits. Contains 86 pages of references, averaging 35 references per page for those desiring to delve into geology of gold in some depth.

I. S. E. Carmichael, F. J. Turner, and J. Verhoogen, *Igneous Petrology*. McGraw–Hill Book Co., 1974, 739 pages. For the graduate student specializing in petrology; an excellent theoretical reference.

D. R. Coates, *Environmental Geology*. John Wiley & Sons, 1981, 701 pages. Glossary and Appendices. An excellent study of world environment from the geological point of view by one of the leaders in the field.

A. B. Cummins and I. A. Given, editors. *SME Mining Engineers Handbook*. Society of Mining Engineers AIME, 1973, volumes 1 and 2, 2666 pages. The most comprehensive and up-to-date work on mining methods.

Engineering and Mining Journal. McGraw–Hill, Inc. Monthly publication noted for current statistics. Carries good technical articles and recent developments throughout the world.

P. T. Flawn, *Mineral Resources*. Rand McNally & Co., 1966, 406 pages. Particularly good on U.S. stockpiling programs to 1965.

M. Gary, R. McAfee, Jr., and C. L. Wolf, editors. *Glossary of Geology*. American Geological Institute, 1972, 805 pages plus 52 pages of source information. Recognized as authoritative definitions of the important geologic terms.

J. L. Gilson, editor, *Industrial Minerals and Rocks.* American Institute of Mining, Metallurgical and Petroleum Engineers. Third edition 1960 (plus older and newer editions), 934 pages. Chapters on each of the important industrial minerals by experts in the field.

H. E. Hawkes and J. S. Webb, *Geochemistry in Mineral Exploration.* Harper & Row, 1962, 415 pages. Data on metallic elements amenable to geochemical exploration and exploration methods.

Mineral Facts and Problems. *U.S. Bureau of Mines Bulletin* (671) 1980, p. 1060. This is a comprehensive review of the major mineral commodities, carefully prepared and edited by the USBM, updated every five years. Issues of 1970 and 1975 were also used as source information.

Minerals Yearbook, U.S. Bureau of Mines. Annual series on the mineral industries, largely statistics on U.S. production. Comprehensive and accurate, issued in three volumes.

Mining Annual Review, Mining Journal 1982. 568 pages. This annual publication issued in June covers developments in 63 major commodities and 130 countries plus good summaries of each phase of the minerals industry such as exploration, surface mining. Many of the advertisements are particularly informative about the industry.

Mining Journal, The Mining Journal Ltd. (London). Weekly newspaper airmailed around the world. The best publication on current activities. Always carries editorial review of a commodity, nation, or issue affecting mining. Quarterly review of gold.

P. H. Nixon, editor, *Lesotho Kimberlites.* Lesotho National Development Corp., 1973, 350 pages. Studies by 28 experts in the field of kimberlites, the rock that sometimes contains diamonds.

R. N. Shreve, *Chemical Process Industries.* McGraw–Hill Book Co., 1956, 1004 pages. Basic data on major chemical processes.

A. F. Taggart, *Handbook of Mineral Dressing.* 1945, 1744 pages. Somewhat out of date but the fundamentals are still valid. Excellent data.